W9-BRX-736

NINTH EDITION

OFF THE BEATEN PATH ®
VERMONT

A GUIDE TO UNIQUE PLACES

Revised and Updated by

CINDI D. PIETRZYK

gpp®

travel

Guilford, Connecticut

All the information in this guidebook is subject to change. We recommend that you call ahead to obtain current information before traveling.

To buy books in quantity for corporate use
or incentives, call **(800) 962-0973**
or e-mail **premiums@GlobePequot.com.**

Project Editor: Lauren Szalkiewicz
Layout: Joanna Beyer
Text Design: Linda R. Loiewski
Maps: Equator Graphics © Morris Book Publishing, LLC

ISSN 1533-8037
ISBN 978-0-7627-9209-2

Printed in the United States of America
10 9 8 7 6 5 4 3 2 1

This book is dedicated to the residents of Vermont, past and present.
Thank you for sharing your state with me.

VERMONT

NORTHWEST VERMONT
& THE
CHAMPLAIN VALLEY

NORTHEAST
KINGDOM

■ Burlington

St.
Johnsbury ■

Montpelier ★

CENTRAL
VERMONT

MIDDLE
WEST
VERMONT

■ Rutland

CONNECTICUT
RIVER VALLEY

SOUTHWEST
VERMONT

■ Bennington

Brattleboro ■

Contents

Acknowledgments

First and foremost I wish to acknowledge the original authors of this book, Barbara Radcliffe Rogers and Stillman Rogers. Without them there would be no *Off the Beaten Path Vermont*. Thank you for laying the foundation for the rest of us.

My next thank-you goes to Kevin Sirois, former editor at Globe Pequot Press, who once again threw caution to the wind and hired me to author a book. Thank you, Kevin, and I wish you the best of luck in your endeavors. This leads me to Tracee Williams, Lauren Szalkiewicz, and the incredibly talented staff at Globe. I have enjoyed working with you again and am always amazed by how seamless you make the impossible process of publishing a book.

My sincere thanks also goes to Chad Abramovich for allowing me to reprint text from his blog *Obscure Vermont*. The following text was used in this book with Chad's permission: Ice Beds of White Mountain, St. Albans Bay Schoolhouse, and Curious Centennial Woods. He also contributed to the information on The Bennington Triangle, Bigfoot Rock in Wallingford, the Patch Hollow massacre, and the Boy with the Boot. For more of Chad's urban travel adventures, read his blog *Obscure Vermont* (urbanpostmortem .wordpress.com) and follow *Obscure Vermont* on Facebook. Thank you, Chad!

I appreciate all the suggestions I received from those in the know about Vermont, especially Jana Pietrzyk and Kathy Cunningham.

Thank you to Sue B., my running partner, therapist, and cheerleader. I really don't think I would have survived this one without our miles of talks.

Finally, my biggest thank-you goes to my family—we survived another one. Thank you. I love you all with all my heart.

Introduction

Vermont is as much a state of mind as it is a place. To the rest of the country, the Green Mountain State signifies a back-to-basics attitude that is becoming an all-too-rare commodity today. The people who live in Vermont hold on fiercely to this attitude because they are well aware that it is one of the last bastions of peaceful rural life, of our roots. That's why tourism is a leading industry in the state.

This attitude is at the bottom of one of the hottest debates to embroil the state in years: to zone or not to zone. Those Vermonters who are in favor of limiting development and establishing specific criteria about what residents can and can't do with their land want the pastoral Vermont landscape to stay the same for future generations. Those Vermonters who oppose zoning tend to have great pride in their ancestors, that they were able to create this state from nothing more than rocks, thin soil, and sweat. They say, "My family fought for it, I own it, and it's mine to do with as I wish. Don't you trust me, an eighth-generation Vermonter, to know what's best for the state?"

What these actions have in common is a desire to hold on to the old way of life, but with two very different views of the best way to make it happen.

Many people have wanted a part of the state. Before it became a republic in 1777 and was granted statehood 15 years later, everyone from New Hampshire to Massachusetts to New York fought over the land that even then possessed a special but hard-to-define aura.

Because Vermont relies so heavily on tourism these days, even in some isolated pockets of the state it's difficult to find attractions that are specifically geared toward locals, unless you count feed and grain stores.

It used to be true that you weren't considered a native until your family had lived here for eight generations. Given the great exodus from the state during several periods in its history, those eighth-generationers are not easy to find. Many of Vermont's hill towns lost half their populations during the great westward expansion, but even though some Vermont towns continue to have smaller populations than they did in 1840, the state is making a comeback. In 1850, 154 towns in the state had more than 1,000 people. By 1960 that figure had fallen to 94; but today 158 out of Vermont's more than 250 towns are above that number.

Basic Travel Information

Visitors come to Vermont throughout the year; however, some months and seasons are more beautiful—and thus more crowded—than others. Foliage season—usually the last two weeks of September and the first two weeks of October—is Vermont at its best and most crowded. Rooms at inns and hotels, despite sharply increased "foliage rates," typically fill up six months in advance, so it's best to make reservations early.

The last two weeks of October in Vermont are generally just as gorgeous. And while many places and shops will have closed for the season, there are still lots of attractions to explore. You'll find less traffic; unhurried, friendly service; and some of the maples and oak trees still radiant with their color. Best of all, the weather is perfect: sunny, warm, Indian summer days interspersed with cool, crisp nights accompanied by the smell of wood smoke.

In summer Vermont is lush, green, and fragrant. During the winter, the Presidents' Day holiday usually finds the ski areas throughout the state at their busiest; try visiting a week or two later instead. Some of the roads that are closed in winter and spring are marked on good road maps, and

Reservations at State Parks

Reservations for camping can be made up to 11 months in advance. (A camping site for the entire month of July, for example, can be reserved in August of the previous year.) To make a reservation 14 days or less in advance, call the individual park directly (see listings at vtstateparks.com). For reservations 15 days or more in advance, reserve online or call (888) 409-7579.

Some Vermont parks are open year-round. Others open in late April, still others in late May. Closing dates for those parks vary from mid-September until mid-October, depending on area climates. All parks have minimum reservation periods. Prior to March 1, you'll have to stay four nights at most parks; after March 1, however, that stay can be reduced to two nights. If you bike or paddle to a campground and wish to stay for one night, call the park or reservation center to see if they can accommodate you.

A season-pass car sticker costs $80 and is a good option for frequent park visitors (up to eight people per vehicle). See the Vermont State Parks website listed above for details.

Restful Wi-Fi

All Vermont visitor centers at highway rest stops now offer Wi-Fi access, so anyone with a laptop and wireless capabilities can use the Internet from anywhere on the premises. It's not free, but you can buy in various time periods, even by the year, a plan designed for business travelers. Now you can get a map, ask directions, browse the brochure racks, walk the dog, take the kids to the bathroom, and check your e-mail all in one stop.

others are closed temporarily if they're simply impassable. In spring many tourist-oriented businesses shut down from March through mid-April, during the notorious "mud season" and before the first buds appear on the trees. During the spring thaw, high water can close many of the smaller bridges.

Vermonters are frugal Yankees to the core, and they simply can't see any reason to waste all those condo and hotel rooms, restaurants, shops, and recreation facilities at the foot of their ski slopes after the snow melts. Nearly all ski areas have become year-round recreation resorts, with guests paddling happily during the summer in ponds that provide snowmaking water six months later, or riding the lifts for mountaintop views in August where cross-country skiers glide in January. Everyone wins, especially visitors looking for a base that includes activities for days when they don't feel like touring the countryside. Just as in winter, these resort complexes offer package deals that may include golf, guided hikes, nature programs, meals, day camp, and water sports.

Seasonal attractions in small towns throughout Vermont include sugar-on-snow festivals in spring and Fourth of July celebrations and parades in summer. Winter features ski races and Christmas fairs and bazaars.

Tourist Information

The *Vermont Chamber of Commerce* (PO Box 37, Montpelier, VT 05601; 802-223-3443; vtchamber.com) is a great place to start. Here you can learn all things Vermont. Visit their website and click on "Vermont Vacations" and you will be directed to VisitVT.com, where you can order a free Vermont Vacation Guide or browse several eGuides focused on different seasons. When you click on "Order Your Free Vermont Vacation Guide," you will be directed to vermontvacation.com, "The Official State of Vermont Tourism Site," where you will have access to all sorts of online travel planning tools along with more Vermont information. This site is sponsored by the **Vermont Department of Tourism and Marketing** (1 National Life Dr., Montpelier, VT 05620-0501; 800-VERMONT or 802-828-3237).

Welcome centers are located on I-91 (Massachusetts border), I-89 (Canadian border), I-93 (New Hampshire border), and on Vermont 4-A at the New York border. A complete selection of brochures is available at each welcome center.

In today's world, social media sites are invaluable for up-to-the-minute news on all your favorite places. We strongly suggest you "like," "follow," and "subscribe" to places you plan to visit. This way you'll be alerted to special events, pricing, and changes before you hit the road. If you're unsure where you want to head, visit our Facebook page, "Off the Beaten Path Vermont, 9th edition"; if it's in the book and on Facebook, it's in our list of "likes." Peruse the list to see what strikes your fancy.

If fine arts and creativity is your thing, the **Vermont Crafts Council** (PO Box 938, Montpelier, VT 05601; 802-223-3380; vermontcrafts.com) is the place for you. The website offers listings of crafts shops, events, and "open studio" tours.

Downhill ski enthusiasts will want to check out the **Vermont Ski Areas Association** (26 State St., PO Box 368, Montpelier, VT 05601; 802-223-2439; skivermont.com). Nordic and alpine skiers in Vermont have their own snow conditions website to check: xcountryski-vermont.com.

Best Attractions and Other Attractions Worth Seeing

Within each chapter we have listed five of the best attractions to visit. These are just our personal picks; yours may be different and we look forward to hearing from you. We give you a list of names and you will be able to find the specifics within the text.

Our lists of Other Attractions Worth Seeing in each chapter are places we wanted to mention but thought they were either on the path too much to be listed in depth or maybe they were just getting started and were not quite established yet. We give you the basic information to allow you to find more information on them if you choose, but we have not provided a write-up on them within the chapter.

We've also given you a list of Annual Events within each chapter. This is not an exhaustive list, but some of the best and brightest.

Places to Stay & Places to Eat Price Codes

At the end of each chapter are additional area accommodations and restaurant listings for your convenience.

The rating scale for accommodations is based on double occupancy and is as follows:

Inexpensive: Less than $100 per night
Moderate: $100 to $200 per night
Expensive: More than $200 per night

The rating scale for restaurants is based on the price of an entree without beverages, desserts, tax, or tip, and is as follows:

Inexpensive: Less than $10
Moderate: $10 to $20
Expensive: More than $20

Please remember, these are rough guidelines and should not be considered actual rates. Always call ahead to confirm.

A Final Word

Finally, we ask for your help. One single book about the state of Vermont can never do it justice, but we hope we've made a dent. There are so many places we would have loved to include, but we simply can't fit them all. That's why we keep coming up with new editions. Our research is constant. To that end, we hope to hear from you. Please e-mail, write, visit our Facebook page, whatever you are comfortable doing, and let us know if there is some place you think we should include and we'll put it on our list. Let us know what you liked or didn't like about the book. We take feedback seriously and look forward to hearing from you. We hope you enjoy this ninth edition.

NORTHWEST VERMONT & THE CHAMPLAIN VALLEY →

Proximity to Lake Champlain has had a huge effect on the development of the northwest corner of the Green Mountain State. It all started with the French explorer who named the lake, Samuel de Champlain. Thanks to his colonizing efforts—he founded the city of Quebec in 1608—Champlain was named the "Father of New France." Access to the major thoroughfare and trade route of **Lake Champlain** allowed settlement to occur relatively early in Vermont's history. Burlington, for instance, was chartered in 1763, and **Swanton,** northernmost town on the lake and historic site of the Abenaki Indian village of Missisquoi, was chartered the same year. Settlement of a town by families from Connecticut or Massachusetts would take longer, but towns and villages on Vermont's northwestern shore were populated about the same time as those on the state's southwestern border.

After the Revolutionary War, settlements began to flourish along much of the 120-mile length of Lake Champlain, as did subsequent trade north to Canada. During the 19th century, both commercial and passenger steamboats—and later, railroads and the automobile—generated an efficient

NORTHWEST VERMONT & THE CHAMPLAIN VALLEY

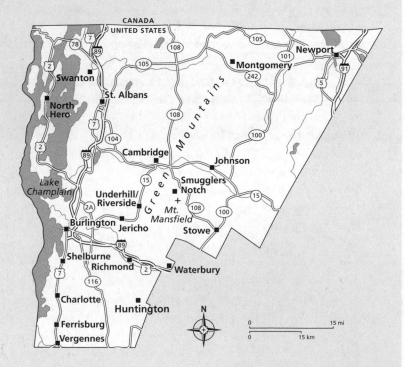

CANADA
UNITED STATES

Newport

Montgomery

Swanton

St. Albans

North
Hero

Green Mountains

Cambridge

Johnson

Lake
Champlain

Underhill/
Riverside

Smugglers
Notch

Mt.
Mansfield

Burlington

Jericho

Stowe

Shelburne

Richmond

Waterbury

Charlotte

Huntington

N

Ferrisburg

Vergennes

0   15 mi

0   15 km

transportation network. Together with the nearby fertile fields and plentiful forests, this fortuitous combination of diverse assets has led to rapid growth—and built the dynamic Northwest Vermont and Champlain Valley region that exists today.

Burlington

Burlington is about as cosmopolitan as Vermont gets; so much so, in fact, that people in other parts of the state sometimes joke that Burlington is not even part of their fair state! With five area colleges and frontage on Lake Champlain—not to mention a population of close to 43,000—Burlington is where many rural Vermonters head for a dose of urban activity. And they aren't the only ones. Only about 3.5 hours from Boston and 5 from New York, Burlington sees visitors from all over.

Burlington is a great city to explore on foot. It's small enough for slow walkers to manage, yet offers plenty of sights, shops, and eateries, so the adventurous need not be bored. From the waterfront, walk a few blocks up the hill on Main Street and visit *Mirabelle's* (198 Main St.; 802-658-3074; mirabellescafe.com), a bright, airy but small cafe with chintz tablecloths and seat covers, and food and drink to match, a la afternoon tea. At least 10 kinds of teas are available, as well as coffees and lattes. You can get your traditional two eggs and toast with delicious hash browns or satisfy a more refined palette with the breakfast scramble—eggs with spinach, mushrooms, roasted red peppers, and goat cheese (don't worry, this comes with toast and hash browns, too). There for lunch? Soups, salads (fresh, local ingredients), and sandwiches (ham and brie, avocado

BEST ATTRACTIONS IN NORTHWEST VERMONT & THE CHAMPLAIN VALLEY

Lake Champlain Maritime Museum	Sterling Falls Gorge
Montgomery County's covered bridges	Smugglers' Notch
	Centennial Woods

Curious Centennial Woods

Among Burlington's urbanization, there are still untapped places that offer a rare glimpse of mystery and perspective. **Centennial Woods** is 65 acres of oddly wild land sitting in the middle of Vermont's largest metropolitan area, and a lot of people don't realize it even exists. With a discreet entrance off a side street under the shadow of Fletcher Allen Health Care's herculean edifice, the park is marked by only a small green sign that is almost lost among the environment around it. But once you locate one of the trailheads, you find yourself in another world entirely.

At the entrance to Centennial Woods lies something that doesn't fit in with the gentle charm of the woods—a crumbling, graffiti-covered concrete bunker.

So what is it? The ruins of some sort of military installation? Some sort of early agricultural attempt to tame the steep hillside around it? Sadly, there doesn't seem to be any answers, and any information about it just doesn't seem to exist. But there are theories. Some say these ruins were once built by the infamous Green Mountain Boys for training exercises. However, that seems far-fetched, as concrete wasn't widely used in construction projects until after the Civil War. Others say this might have been part of some sort of unusual surveying attempts along the Burlington/South Burlington city line, which runs right through the middle of the woods. And another more mysterious theory is that this is the last remnant of a series of monuments that once were scattered throughout the woods. But if so, then a monument to what?

There are other odd artifacts in the area. Just down the trail from these sturdy ruins sits a city boundary survey marker. Its erosion and cracked surface show the

and cheddar, tandoori chicken, mushroom and goat cheese panini, and more) abound. Don't forget to save room for dessert, in which Mirabelle's is a gem. Choose from the likes of coconut-lime cake, chocolate-raspberry mousse cake, raspberry-blueberry brown butter tart, and oh-so-much more. Open 7 a.m. to 5 p.m. Mon through Fri, 8 a.m. to 5 p.m. Sat; and 8 a.m. to 2:30 p.m. Sun.

Chocoholics may want to skip lunch entirely and visit **Lake Champlain Chocolates** (750 Pine St.; 802-864-1807 or 65 Church St.; 802-862-5185 or 800-465-5909; lakechamplainchocolates.com). What started in 1983 on a dare has grown to a three-store enterprise with a nationwide reputation. You can visit their factory store (Pine Street) weekdays from 11 a.m. to 2 p.m. to see how their delectable treats are made (did we mention free samples?).

plaque's age, especially compared to its newer street sign replacements farther down the trail. "CITY OF BURLIN—C.B. 40" can be barely made out through its erosion and faded youth.

Centennial Woods' rocky ledges and serpentine marshlands hold another set of peculiar yet minimalistic ruins—a series of burned stumps, a rusted machine gear, and a beaten utility pole. Though the casual hiker would probably never guess it, these are the remains of the former South Burlington Kiwanis Ski Area. It opened sometime in the winter of 1963 and offered a 500-foot rope tow and lighted ski trails. However, the ski hill fell victim to arsonists in June 1967, and the fire destroyed the rope tow, tow shack, and machinery. The rest was looted by vandals, and all have been left abandoned and forgotten as Mother Nature reclaimed it. The burned foundation of the former tow shack still can be seen in the new-growth forest.

Any attempts to find the remains of the ski trail would be impossible; the area has grown wild and indistinguishable. However, walking down the hill behind the former tow shack, one will understand immediately why this site was chosen. The woods suddenly descend a very steep slope that makes its way down to a thick swamp along the fringes of I-89, the flash and blur of traffic seem like a dream through the soft spring canopy. This has become a favorite spot for mountain bikers—the steep and sandy slope carved into a series of dirt jumps with incredible elevation drops in between them, nothing for the faint of heart.

Centennial Woods is a wonderful place to get lost for a while underneath the red maples.

—Reprinted with permission of Chad Abramovich, *Obscure Vermont.*

The tours leave every hour on the hour with the last one starting at 2 p.m. It's free, but hours are subject to change, so be sure to check ahead.

When you're ready to make a purchase, head to the retail area at the factory store or to one of the other two locations (Church Street, nearby, or 2653 Waterbury Stowe Rd. about 30 minutes away in Waterbury) where you'll find more than 100 kinds of chocolates to choose from. Hours are different at all three locations and subject to change, so be sure to visit the website for the latest information.

Uncommon Grounds (42 Church St.; 802-865-6227; ugvermont.com) is a great little place to stop for a cup of something hot or not. Their selection of coffee and teas is mind-boggling. They also sell baked goods, a perfect complement. If you're looking for something cool, we highly suggest the

ANNUAL EVENTS IN NORTHWEST VERMONT & THE CHAMPLAIN VALLEY

JANUARY

Stowe Winter Carnival

various venues
Stowe
stowewintercarnival.com
Each year has a theme and is celebrated in late January at various venues throughout the area. There are ice-carving competitions, music concerts, a children's carnival, golf and volleyball in the snow, fireworks, and more.

MARCH

Smugglers' Notch Area Winter Carnival

Smugglers' Notch Resort
4323 Rte. 108
Jeffersonville
(802) 644-8851
Nordic ski races, snow sculptures, community breakfasts, snowshoe hikes, and social events.

APRIL

Vermont Maple Festival

various venues
St. Albans
vtmaplefestival.org
For almost 50 years, the Vermont Maple Festival has celebrated the state's leading commodity, with an antiques show, carnival, crafts, amazing specialty food, children's activities, and more. Some events are free and some require admission. Maps and schedules are available on the website.

MAY

Noon Music in May

Stowe Community Church
Main Street
Stowe
(802) 253-7792
stoweperformingarts.com
Sponsored by the Stowe Performing Arts and area businesses, these concerts are offered each Wednesday at noon. Anything from a piano duet or operatic selections to Polish dance music or chamber jazz. Concerts are free, but a donation is appreciated. Parking is available behind the church.

Stowe Farmers' Market

Mountain Road
(802) 472-8027
stowefarmersmarket.com
Held rain or shine every Sun, 10:30 a.m. to 3 p.m., mid-May through mid-Oct. You'll find everything from fresh-baked breads and goat cheese to country sausage and maple creams; plants, too—all locally grown and produced. The market is located a couple of miles from the intersection of Routes 100 and 108, next to the Red Barn Shops.

JUNE

Burlington Discover Jazz Festival

Main Street
Burlington
(802) 863-7992
discoverjazz.com
A 10-day festival held in late May to early June throughout downtown

that showcases local, regional, and international jazz musicians. Features meet-the-musician opportunities, classes, workshops, concerts, cruises, and more.

LCI Father's Day Derby

Lake Champlain
Burlington
(802) 879-3466
mychamplain.net
Held mid-June and filled with a variety of contests, weigh-ins, and awards.

LCI Little Anglers Derby

Windermere Way Access Area
Colchester
mychamplain.net/fishing-derbies/little-anglers-derby
This free mid-June event is sponsored by Ray's Seafood Market and is open to anglers 14 and younger, who must bring along an adult.

Frog Run Sap Beer Festival

Fiddlehead Brewing Company
6305 Shelburne Rd.
Shelburne
(802) 388-4964
vermontfolklifecenter.org/sapbeer/frogrunfest.php
A late June festival featuring Frog Run Sap Beer brewed by the Fiddlehead Brewing Company in Shelburne. This beer has its roots in the very soul of Vermont—sugar making. "Frog run" refers to the final run of sap suitable for making syrup, which is also the time when "peepers" (young frogs) begin their song. The festival also features

traditional Vermont and Quebec music. Admission is free, but all donations go toward supporting the Vermont Folklife Center in Middlebury.

Stowe Wine & Food Classic

Trapp Family Lodge
700 Trapp Hill Rd.
Stowe
(888) 683-2427
stowewine.com
A food and wine festival featuring talented chefs who offer wonderful pairings of farm-to-table food and delicious local wine. Proceeds benefit area charities. Held late June.

Vermont Quilt Festival

11 Pearl St., Suite 207
Essex Junction
(802) 872-0034
vqf.org
The oldest and largest quilt show in the region, this festival offers exhibits, appraisals, classes, contests, and best of all, shopping. Held late June.

JULY

Independence Day Celebration

Smugglers' Notch Resort
(855) 581-5906
smuggs.com/skivts
Old-fashioned Fourth of July celebration with a parade at 10 a.m., a carnival, a firemen's barbecue, and evening music before fireworks at dusk.

Music in the Meadow
Trapp Family Lodge
700 Trapp Hill Rd.
Stowe
(802) 253-7792
stoweperformingarts.com
Held Sunday evenings, late June through Aug. Bring a picnic and enjoy the sunset to music. The meadow opens two hours before the start of the concerts, which are usually around 7 or 7:30 p.m. Tickets are available online, through the mail, and at The Pizza Joint (383 Moscow Rd.; Stowe).

Great Race Triathlon/Duathlon
Route 36
St. Albans Bay
visitfranklincountyvt.com
The opportunity to run 3 miles, bike 12, and paddle 3 (or watch others do it). Live music and fun in St. Albans Bay in early July.

Annual Flynn Garden Tour
various areas in Shelburne
(802) 652-4507
flynncenter.org
Self-guided tour in mid-July that benefits the Flynn Center, with several outstanding area gardens open for the day and an elegant afternoon tea

Stowe 8 Miler
Stowe
locorunning.com
An 8-mile road race through the countryside and then the heart of downtown Stowe. Can't run the entire 8? Two people can split it and do a two-person relay. Starts at 9 a.m. at the Stowe town fields on Weeks Hill

Road and ends on the front lawn of the Golden Eagle Resort. Occurs mid-July. Cold beer and ice cream are served for the race at an area venue.

Gazebo Concerts
Stowe Free Library
90 Pond St.
(802) 253-7792
stoweperformingarts.com
Free concerts offered late July through early Aug on the lawn of the Helen Day Memorial Building, Tues 7 to 8 p.m.

Vermont Balloon & Craft Festival
Shelburne Museum
6000 Shelburne Rd.
Shelburne
(802) 425-3399
craftproducers.com/festivals
Balloon launching at sunrise and sunset and all sorts of arts and crafts in between. Adult admission. Held late July.

AUGUST

Burlington Sidewalk Sale
Downtown and Church Street Marketplace
(802) 863-1648
churchstmarketplace.com
Billed as one of Burlington's great traditions, this annual sidewalk sale is held early in August. Get there early (some merchants set their wares out around 8 a.m.) for the best bargains.

Festival of Fools
Church Street Marketplace
(802) 863-1648
churchstmarketplace.com

Also held early in August, this is a festival filled with street performers from far and wide. Acts range from musical to comedy.

Jeffersonville Festival of the Arts
Smugglers' Notch Resort
(802) 644-1960
cambridgeartsvt.org
Held in early August, this festival offers regional artists who display their creations along Jeffersonville's Main Street. There's also live music, children's activities, and food. Parking usually available at Cambridge Elementary School. 10 a.m. to 4 p.m.

Stowe Annual Antique Car Show
Nichols Field
Route 100
Stowe
vtauto.org
Peruse more than 800 antique and classic cars along with food concessions, giant automotive flea market, and antique car parade through Stowe. In the evening they close the streets to all but the antique cars. Held early Aug.

Stowe Mountain Resort Concert Series
Downtown and Church Street Marketplace
(802) 863-1648
churchstmarketplace.com
Thursdays from late Aug through late Sept, local bands perform outdoors at the marketplace. Grab a picnic lunch and enjoy. Sponsored by Stowe Mountain Resort.

SEPTEMBER
Darn Tough Ride
3576 Mountain Rd.
Stowe
(802) 253-9216
mmwa.org/darntoughride
A benefit bicycle ride for the Mount Mansfield Winter Academy. Options include 24-, 45-, 65-, and 100-mile rides through Stowe, Jay Peak, and Morrisville. As the name implies, it's not for the faint of heart.

OCTOBER
Stowe Foliage Arts Festival
Stowe Events Field
80 Weeks Hill Rd.
Stowe
(802) 425-3399
craftproducers.com/festivals
Held early Oct (usually Columbus Day weekend), rain or shine, under heated tents. Tons of exhibitors showing their arts and crafts. If you're staying the weekend, book early.

Oktoberfest
Jackson Arena
Park Street
Stowe
(802) 253-3928
stoweoktoberfest.com
Held in early October, this event sponsored by the local Rotary club offers a parade, live music and dancing, and children's activities. You'll feel as if you walked into a Bavarian village as you celebrate the harvest with plenty of food and libations. Proceeds from tickets and

ANNUAL EVENTS IN NORTHWEST VERMONT & THE CHAMPLAIN VALLEY (CONT.)

sales go to support local charities and scholarships.

NOVEMBER

Church Street Santa Parade and Lighting Ceremony
Church Street Marketplace
(802) 863-1648
churchstmarketplace.com
Parade starts at noon at City Hall and travels down Church Street, followed by a classic performance of *'Twas the Night Before Christmas*. Then carolers accompany the official tree lighting at 6:02 p.m. sharp. The man in the red suit has been known to make an appearance as well. Late Nov.

DECEMBER

Mountain Fireworks & Torchlight Parade
Stowe Mountain
7412 Mountain Rd.
Stowe
(802) 253-3560
stowemountainlodge.com/events/
mountain-fireworks-torchlight-parade
At 7 one night late in December, Stowe Mountain puts on a light spectacular that can be viewed from the comfort of the Spruce Camp Base Lodge patio.

lavender lemonade. Open Mon through Thurs 7 a.m. to 9 p.m., Fri to 10 p.m., Sat 8 a.m. to 10 p.m., and Sun 9 a.m. to 9 p.m.

If you like books, take your cup of deliciousness from Uncommon Grounds and head to **Crow Bookstore** (14 Church St.; 802-862-0848; crow bookshop.indiebound.com), where you can get lost in the stacks of new and used books in just about every subject. Open daily at 10 a.m. They close at 9 p.m. Mon through Wed, at 10 p.m. Thurs through Sat, and at 6 p.m. Sun.

Another great stop is the **Frog Hollow Vermont State Craft Center** (85 Church St.; 802-863-6458; froghollow.org), one of Vermont's largest nonprofit arts institutions. Dedicated to a love of the arts, Frog Hollow Craft Center was the brainchild of Allen Johnson. In 1971 he and a group of friends envisioned a program in which local young people could gain hands-on interaction with professional artisans. They made it happen. Local artists joined the cause and soon a gallery was set up to display their work. It was meant to be a friendly place where artisans and visitors could sit and while away an afternoon over coffee, and classes were offered on an informal basis to whomever was interested, with the idea of exposing as many people to as much crafts as was possible. Eventually the center expanded and added two galleries and offered organized educational programs in both Burlington and Manchester. But the economy wasn't kind to the center, and eventually all but the Burlington location were closed. But this location is doing well and currently exhibits the work of more than 200 Vermont artists (not all at once, but on a rotating basis), including hand-blown art glass, ceramics, fine pottery, furniture, jewelry, paintings, wood and metal work, and photography. The gallery is open daily but with changing hours, so be sure to check the website or call before heading out.

If you have had enough walking and are hungry, the *Red Onion* (140 Church St.; 802-865-2653; redonioncafe.webs.com) is a good choice for breakfast or lunch. They serve both hot and cold sandwiches, soups, salads, and fresh baked goods. We have it on good authority that the Red Onion Sandwich—layers of turkey, bacon, mayo, red onion, and cheddar cheese on thick, fresh yeast bread—is the only way to go. Whatever you choose, you can be assured it will be fresh. They roast their own turkey and bake their own bread daily. Choose to eat in at this funky little cafe, or take your sandwiches down to the waterfront. Breakfast is served Mon through Fri, 8 to 11 a.m., and lunch is served daily, 11 a.m. to 8 p.m.

If you've not had your fill of art, check out *The Flynn Center* (153 Main St.; 802-863-5966; flynncenter.org), a cultural institution that not only brings all forms of performance art—dance, symphony orchestras, Broadway musicals, theater, top vocal performers—to Vermont, but also offers a wide range of educational programs to enhance the love of the arts. Featuring a 1,411-seat auditorium, cabaret space, gallery space, and 2 educational studios, The Flynn Center serves more than 50,000 students annually and has hosted such musical greats such as Aaron Neville and Branford Marsalis as well as jazz and Latin bands and productions by national touring companies of Broadway musicals. The Flynn is also a sponsor of the annual Burlington Discover Jazz Festival, which takes place at the end of May into early June and has seen the likes of Ella Fitzgerald, Dave Brubeck, Dizzy Gillespie, and so many more.

If it's near supper time when your stomach starts rumbling, head over to *Trattoria Delia* (152 St. Paul St., just off City Hall Park; 802-864-5253;

trattoriadelia.com), an almost subterranean enclave of Italian dining. Go hungry if you plan to order both a *primi* and a *secondi,* since the pasta course is far from scanty. You'll find authentic dishes here not found easily elsewhere: *oricchiette* with *melanzane*—an Puglian-style fried tomato sauce with plenty of garlic—or *tagliatelle con ragu* with ground pork, local veal, and beef tenderloin. *Secondi,* priced from $20.50, may include a wood-grilled fish of the day, with a marinara of olive oil, lemon, parsley, and black pepper; or osso buco (braised veal shanks) over saffron risotto. Breads and pastas are made in-house, the wine list is extensive, and the menu changes

OTHER ATTRACTIONS WORTH SEEING IN NORTHWEST VERMONT & THE CHAMPLAIN VALLEY

Shelburne Museum
6000 Shelburne Rd.
Shelburne
(802) 985-3346
shelburnemuseum.org
Features folk art, paintings, quilts, and other items of New England history. Open mid-May through Oct.

Lake Champlain Ferries
1 King St.
Burlington
(802) 864-9804
ferries.com
Founded in 1826 and still runs 3 ferry crossings across Lake Champlain between Vermont and New York. Grand Isle to Plattsburg, New York, boat runs year-round.

Ben & Jerry's Factory Tour
1281 Waterbury-Stowe Rd.
Waterbury
(866) BJ-TOURS
benjerry.com/scoop-shops/factory-tours
Open daily year-round except for major holidays. Tours last for 30 minutes and leave every 30 minutes on a first-come, first-served basis. Hours vary with season, but are generally 10 a.m. to 6 p.m. Check website for specifics. Admission is charged to those 13 and older.

Cold Hollow Cider Mill
3600 Rte. 100
Waterbury Center
(800) 327-7537
coldhollow.com
Here you will find all things Vermont— homemade fudge, apple cider donuts (made on site), maple syrup, cider (of course)—and so much more. Open daily 8 a.m. to 6 p.m.

seasonally to offer the freshest ingredients. Two days in advance is not too early to call for a reservation here on weekends, but if you can't get a table, they also offer a take-out menu. Open 7 nights a week, 5 to 10 p.m.

Upstairs at the corner of Cherry and Winooski Streets, **Penny Cluse Cafe** (169 Cherry St.; 802-651-8834; pennycluse.com) serves breakfast and lunch daily, and offers the fine work of chef-owner Charles Reeves and his partner, Holly Cluse. This popular little place can get very busy, especially on the weekends. We've been told you can leave your name on a wait list if it's busy, leave to explore Burlington, and then return at a suggested interval of time to be seated quickly. Highly suggested are the popular gingerbread pancakes, or the crepes if you prefer. Of course it wouldn't be Vermont without maple-walnut cream cheese (smear it on just about anything). The lunch menu with its daily specials is varied and delicious. Open weekdays, 6:45 a.m. to 3 p.m.; weekends, 8 a.m. to 3 p.m.

While Lake Champlain is beautiful from the shore, it's even more so aboard a **Lake Champlain Shoreline Cruise** (Burlington Boathouse, 1 College St.; 802-862-8300; soea.com). Every day from mid-May through mid-October, scenic cruises leave at 10 a.m., noon, and 2 and 4 p.m., lasting about an hour and a half. You will hear historic tales of adventure, local lore, and geography all while enjoying the lake's stunning beauty. There are also special cruise packages available, including a pizza party, sunset, murder mystery, celebration, and picnic basket cruises. Check the website for all your options, of which there are many. Snack bar service (including a children's menu) and cash bar are available on most cruises. Reservations (made online or by calling) are recommended, but walk-ins are welcome and accommodated if possible. Prices range from $7 for children and $16 for adults up to almost $40 for some of the specialty cruises.

If you're looking for a place to let the kids run for a bit, head to **Waterfront Park** (10 College St.; 802-864-0123; enjoyburlington.com/parks/waterfrontpark.cfm), where you'll find gorgeous waterfront views along the park's 900-foot frontage along Lake Champlain, a boardwalk, and a section of the Burlington Bike Path, which actually runs for 7.5 miles from Oakledge Park in southern Burlington north to Winooski River (see sidebar). Also of interest at this park is the All American Series Display Garden, where you'll find the brightest and the best of new flowering ornamental plant varieties, blooming in profusion all summer.

Burlington Bike Path

Completed in 1986, the Burlington Bike Path runs along the original path of the Rutland and Burlington Railroad companies. Part of the Rails-to-Trails initiative that started 1973 and has since turned miles of railroad tracks into useable biking and walking trails, this bike path now meanders along the shore of Lake Champlain for almost 8 miles before connecting with the Colchester Bike Path in Colchester Causeway Park. While this path can get very busy during the summer months, the incredible views (especially the Adirondacks to the west) make it worth it.

Shelburne, the next town south of South Burlington, was chartered and settled early. The town charter was granted in 1763, and Shelburne was settled five years later by John Potter and Thomas Logan, early traders with Canada, although evidence of Native American presence has been discovered near Shelburne Bay. The town saw fits and starts for the next 20 years or so until the first town meeting of its 24 families was called in the spring of 1789.

Over the year, settlers were besieged by Native Americans and Tories alike, who at times worked together. Once such raiding party would have successfully burned an entire settlement if it hadn't been for a quick-thinking Vermonter with his large cask of home-brewed beer. Things are thankfully a bit quieter in Shelburne these days.

For example, at *Vermont Teddy Bear Company* (6655 Shelburne Rd. [Rte. 7]; 802-985-3001 or 800-829-BEAR; vermontteddybear.com) you can pick out your own teddy bear, stuff it just the way you want it, and someone will sew it up for you. No Tories in sight. And while it's not exactly off the beaten path, this showroom of cuteness is worth a stop when you're in the area. There are bears with just about every personality and theme. Half-hour weekday tours of the factory are also available but fill up quickly. If you're interested in a tour, check in first to see when the next one will depart; that way if there's a wait you can spend it exploring the showroom. Open daily 9 a.m. to 6 p.m. in summer, 9 a.m. to 5 p.m. in winter.

Shed Sales Antiques (3614 Shelburne Rd.; 802-985-8511) is like a huge household sale running through a half dozen rooms. The owners buy the contents of entire houses and bring them here for sale, the ultimate recycling. While you won't necessarily find many bargains here, you will have fun if picking is your game. There are so many things to see, it will boggle your mind. Please mind the owner's no-purse/no-smoking rules. Usually open Mon through Fri from 10 a.m. to 4 p.m. in the summer and 11 a.m. to 3 p.m. in the winter; don't be afraid to ring the doorbell if the door is locked. The owners live on the premises and will likely let you in. Saturday and Sunday are "catch us if you can," so call ahead before you make the trip.

The next town south on Route 7 is *Charlotte,* pronounced with the accent on the second syllable: Char-LOTTE. Charlotte is a quiet town that belies its close proximity to the bustling urban center of Burlington, a 15-minute drive away.

Take a right off Route 7 onto Ferry Road to reach downtown Charlotte. About a mile and a half down, you'll find the *Church & Maple Glass Studio* (802-578-0168; churchandmaple.com) of creative glass blowers, dedicated to designing and manufacturing art glass and sculpture. It's a fascinating place to visit but is open intermittently, so call ahead.

It's worth your while to find your way to *Authentica African Imports* (2190 Greenbush Rd.; 802-425-3137) in Charlotte. Follow the signs to the New York state ferry and turn right at the country store in Charlotte. Lydia Clemmons's unusual shop is ¾ mile up on the left. As you drive to her shop, keep looking west; the view of New York state is breathtaking.

Lydia has been operating Authentica African Imports for many years and is always bringing in new pieces of art, clothing, and jewelry from all over Africa. Check out the 5-pound ankle bracelets from Zanzibar. Drums, tapestries, pottery, and hand-woven scarves from Ghana are crammed into 2 rooms of Lydia's old Vermont farmhouse, while a woodstove keeps the rooms warm. The mixture of African items and old-style New England decor works well. Some of the more exotic items include Masai spears and a Yoruba ceremonial drum. Lydia also offers for sale unusual figurines that tell about daily life in Owo and are carved from 2- to 4-inch thorns that grow on egun and ata trees.

Hours are usually 2 to 6 p.m. Thurs through Sat, but several times a year Lydia heads to Africa to bring home great new treasures, so it's always best to call ahead before heading out. If her hours don't jibe with yours, you can make an appointment to visit her gallery Sun through Tues. For more information and a catalog, write to Lydia.

Ferrisburg is home to *Dakin Farm* (5797 Rte. 7; 802-425-3971 or 800-993-2546; dakinfarm.com), an 18th-century farm originally settled by

Timothy Dakin and run by the Cutting family for the past half century.

vermonttrivia

South Burlington, while slightly south, lies mostly east of Burlington.

Although time has passed, things are done very much the same as they always were at Dakin Farm, although some of the equipment may be a bit more modern. Meats are still slow smoked over smoldering corncobs and sap is still collected from the farm's sugar maple trees and boiled into delicious, sweet syrup. The farm eventually outgrew its local distribution and now delivers its smoke-cured meats, cheeses, and other products all over the US. Self-guided tours of the farms operations are available. Open daily 8 a.m. to 6 p.m. Dakin Farm also has a location in South Burlington at 100 Dorset St. and it's open Mon through Sat 9:30 a.m. to 6 and from 10 a.m. to 5 p.m. Sun.

If you are a history buff, don't leave Ferrisburg without visiting *Rokeby Museum* (4334 Rte. 7; 802-877-3406; rokeby.org). Rokeby holds twin distinctions. First, it served as the home of Vermont's most illustrious writer from the 19th century, Rowland Evans Robinson, author of *Uncle Lisha's Shop, In New England Fields and Woods,* and *Vermont: A Study of Independence and a True Hero of Ticonderoga.* His work also appeared in such publications as *Forest and Stream* and the *Atlantic Monthly.* Robinson was also an accomplished artist who successfully conveyed 19th-century Vermont to millions of people through his writing and pictures. His daughter, Rachel, was also an accomplished artist from a very young age and became well known for her work.

Many 19th-century houses in Vermont are frequently described as having been Underground Railroad stations—most often by zealous real estate agents who perceive every root cellar or hidden basement cubby space as having special historical significance. Usually these claims cannot be proved, since very little written evidence was kept by the owners of such homes for fear of prosecution.

Rokeby, though, is one house where ample evidence was kept, and the museum recently opened a new exhibit called *Free & Safe: The Underground*

Railroad in Vermont, which tells the story of slaves who were sheltered here and provides other information on the movement.

There's a lot to see here. The main house, which dates from before 1784, contains 8 rooms of clothing, furniture, and other artifacts from Robinson's family. There are outbuildings you can tour and hiking trails to explore. Open daily 10 a.m. to 5 p.m. mid-May through late Oct, Mon through Sun. Tours are conducted Fri through Mon at 11:30 a.m. and 2 p.m. Admission is charged. Their hiking trails are open year-round.

The city of **Vergennes,** one of only nine municipalities so designated in the state, is the third-oldest city in the nation and, at 1,152 acres, the smallest. Its boundaries form a perfect square. Vergennes is also a nautical city. The Otter Creek bisects it, flowing northwest into Lake Champlain.

One of the most striking displays at the **Lake Champlain Maritime Museum** (4472 Basin Harbor Rd; 802-475-2022; lcmm.org) in Vergennes is an exact working replica of the 53-foot, square-rigged gunboat *Philadelphia II,* which is so real it seems to have transcended time and come straight from the Revolutionary War.

Other exhibits that position Lake Champlain's impact on the area's history are housed in 6 buildings in a spacious setting on the lake's shore, including a number of boats that were recovered from its waters. Blacksmiths and shipbuilders demonstrate their skills, and exhibits show in detail the shipwrecks that ended the activities of many vessels in the lake's early days. Pageants reenacted by museum hosts representing the French, English, and Native Americans who lived and traded around the lake bring history alive.

Admission here is good for two consecutive days. The museum is open daily from early May through mid-Oct, 10 a.m. to 5 p.m.

All Things Maritime

The Lake Champlain Maritime Museum sponsors the Lake Champlain Maritime Festival with community partners to present a summer "festival of all things maritime." Concerts, demonstrations, and food and craft vendors line the waterfront as you stroll from venue to venue. General admission is free, but some concerts may require tickets.

The museum also has a Burlington location, the **Burlington Shipyard,** where you'll find the *Lois McClure,* a replica 1862-class schooner. For several years the museum sent divers to the bottom of Lake Champlain to take measurements of the *General Butler,* which was sunk by a winter storm in December 1876. They then re-created it as closely as possible and the *Lois McClure* (King St. Ferry Dock; 802-864-9512) was born. Visitors can board her May through Oct, and see firsthand an example of this popular 19th-century means of transportation. Although she is a fully functioning replica, she no longer sails the open seas.

If all this nautical history has made you hungry, check out the **Red Mill Restaurant** (4800 Basin Harbor Rd.; 802-475-2317; basinharbor.com/dining-red-mill.php) near the airport in Basin Harbor Club in Vergennes. Located in a renovated sawmill, this local landmark offers huge salads, burgers, panini, and delightful vegetarian dishes. The lamb shepherd's pie seems to be a favorite. Open daily for lunch, 11:30 a.m. to 3 p.m.; the pub menu is served from 3 to 5 p.m., and dinner starts at 5 p.m. Closing on weekdays is 9 p.m., 10 p.m. on the weekends.

Make Way for the Champ

Samuel de Champlain, discoverer of the lake named for him, was a down-to-earth man who reported things in his diary in a straightforward way. In July 1609 he reported a serpentine creature about 20 feet long, with a horselike head and about as big around as a barrel. As settlers began to establish farms around the lake, occasional other sightings were reported—one in 1819 in the *Plattsburg Republican* noted that several settlers were frightened by the appearance of a large creature close to Port Henry, New York—and other newspaper accounts have echoed similar descriptions. The largest group ever to report seeing "Champ," as followers of the phenomenon have named it, were on a sightseeing excursion boat when the creature surfaced.

The similarities to Nessie, the legendary monster of Scotland's Loch Ness, are remarkable, which has led interested scientists to note the similarities in the bodies of water: each large, deep, and cut off from a former connection to the sea. The chances of your seeing this shy beast, if indeed it exists, are pretty slim (unless you've brought along a lot of Long Trail Ale on your lakeside picnic), but you can bone up on the history, scientific investigation, and sightings at the nature center at Button Bay State Park, or in the Lake Champlain Maritime Museum.

If this sounds like something you might like, be sure to check out the special offered by the Lake Champlain Maritime Museum for museum admission, lunch at the Red Mill, and a cruise, all for one low price.

Shortly past the turnoff to Basin Harbor on Route 22A, you'll see the elegant *Strong House Inn* (94 W. Main St.; 802-877-3337; stronghouseinn .com) on the right. The completely restored federal mansion is listed on the National Register of Historic Places and is the home of Mary Bargiel and her husband, Hugh, who greet each guest. It's their personal approach and involvement that puts the capital H in "Hospitality" here, as well as their knack for creating beautiful rooms filled with the little details that make a stay memorable—thick robes matching the towels in each of the private baths, for example. Each room is different in size, shape, and style—ranging from the frilly Victorian Suite to the bright, spacious Vermont Room that affords beautiful Adirondack views. They offer weekend seminars such as creative writing and quilting, as well as interesting packages. Check out the Girlfriend Get-away or the Vineyards and Microbreweries Tour, among others.

The property is planted in gardens that you can enjoy from the gazebo or tables on the terrace. Cross-country, snowshoe, and walking trails begin from the backyard, and for winter fun a sledding hill (including sleds) is on the property, along with a skating rink. Whatever your desire, the Bargiels can help you plan it. Check out their website for the latest offerings.

Vermont Bicycle Tours (VBT; 614 Monkton Rd., Bristol; 800-245-3868; vbt.com) pedals clients all over the globe, so it's not surprising to find a trip right at home in Vermont. Their trips are typically 6-day, 5-night tours. One example is the Vermont and New York's Lake Champlain Valley Tour. It begins and ends in Burlington, touching Lake Champlain at Basin Harbor, Vergennes, and Fort Ticonderoga on the New York side. Along the way, clients pass through beautiful rolling farmland on the western side of the Appalachians, stopping at Shelburne Museum or Shelburne Farms. In addition to biking, there is an opportunity to kayak on Lake Champlain in an area where Revolutionary War–era gunboats fought it out. The rates (which start at about $1,400) include lodging (5 nights in historic inns), 5 breakfasts, 3 lunches, and 4 dinners, as well as use of a VBT bike, a helmet, maps, trip leaders, and a support vehicle for those who wither along the way. The terrain is rated moderate to easy, with expected mileage from 20 to 30 miles per day; optional routes available for longer mileage.

The Eastern "Suburbs"

As you head east out of Burlington on Route 2 (Williston Road), watch to the east for an interesting site. No, your eyes do not deceive you, those are whales' tails diving into the grass. Huh? This is **Reverence** (more often called the **Whales' Tails**), a sculpture of polished black South African granite that celebrates Vermont's commitment to environmental harmony. The statue is of two graceful, 13-foot whales' tails diving into a sea of grass, atop a slight rise in the land.

Artist Jim Sardonis created the work, which was sponsored by the Environmental Law Foundation in Montpelier and dedicated in 1990. Ten years later it was moved to its current location from Randolph, 60 miles to the south, where it had been commissioned by a British metals trader whose financing fell through. To see the sculpture up close, take Williston Road (Route 2) to Kennedy Drive (about 1.5 miles from I-89, exit 14). Turn right to Kimball Avenue, about 200 yards. Turn left to Community Drive, about a half mile. On the right you'll see Technology Park. Drive halfway around the circular drive. Walk across the field toward I-89. The sculpture is on the highest point of surrounding land.

If you're hungry after the whale watch, head back on Williston Road to where it intersects with Essex Road, and pop into **Cheese Traders and Wine Sellers** (1186 Williston Rd.; 802-863-0143; cheesetraders.com). Fine wine and cheese are expensive, but you can find the good stuff and skip the high prices here. You never know what specials you'll find, from Kenya AA coffee at half the regular price to creamy chocolate truffles, but you can depend on prices you won't see elsewhere. Some deals go fast and you might not see them again, so if you see something that strikes your fancy, grab it while you can. Some items are close to expiration date, but if you're going to consume it quickly, why not get it for a song. Other items may have damaged packaging and the owners were able to get it cheap and pass those savings on to you. Always be assured, though, that whatever might be offered, quality is guaranteed. If it's even slightly questionable, they don't sell it.

Shelves are stocked with a number of Vermont-made products, along with imports, many at serious discounts. Hot-sauce aficionados will appreciate Cheese Traders' selection of dozens of brands, including the locally made "Vermont Hots," that stands row on row. If you're especially lucky, you'll be visiting when they have their annual Garage Sale, where you'll find even more unbelievable deals. This generally happens in early June and also serves as a fund-raiser for a community organization. Cheese Traders is open daily, 10 a.m. to 7 p.m.

Food snobs can skip this, but those who long for really good fries, and maybe a corn dog or hamburger, should head to the shiny diner facade of *Al's French Frys* (1251 Williston Rd.; 802-862-9203; alsfrenchfrys.com). Lines are long at lunchtime, especially on weekends, and you may have trouble finding a spot in the parking lot, so Al's is clearly not undiscovered. Started in the late 1940s by Al and Genevieve Rusterholz, the place features Al's legendary fries, which made the stand a Vermont institution. Not a whole lot has changed. Al's is open 10:30 a.m. to 11 p.m. Sun through Thurs, and until midnight on Fri and Sat.

If you're looking to stay over in the area, you can't go wrong with *The Essex Resort & Spa* (70 Essex Way, Essex Junction; 802-878-1199; vtculinaryresort.com/accommodations). This inn on the grounds of the New England Culinary Institute (NECI) has all the warmth of a vintage country inn, without the squeaky floorboards and thin walls. Rooms are spacious and elegantly decorated, with quality furniture and nice touches, such as a woven lap robe on the rocking chair. Choose from 120 rooms and suites. Suites have fully equipped kitchens (complete with an apron), dining areas, and comfortable sitting rooms. Other rooms have fireplaces and whirlpool tubs roomy enough to share. The inn practices recycling and other earth-friendly and environmentally aware programs. A well-stocked library off the lobby provides travelers with books to curl up with. A variety of special packages are available; visit the website for details.

Because you are on the campus of a premier culinary institute, you'll be treated to some excellent food, with two venues in which to find it. Students and their instructor chefs create all the dishes for both *The Tavern,* a casual upscale pub, and the inn's more formal *Amuse,* at which you can reserve a seat at the Chef's Table for a "culinary adventure unrivaled in the region." This option is available only on Friday and Saturday evenings.

And if you're so inclined, check out the spa offerings at the sister *Spa at the Essex,* a full-service retreat offering such treatments as Reiki, Shiatsu, warm stone, and warm tissue massages; muscle melts; pure radiance resurfacing; deep detox; and a full array of salon services. Say "ahhhhhh."

The Richmond Downtown Fire

If you think the architecture in the downtown district of Richmond, Vermont, seems newer than that in the rest of Vermont, it's because it is. On April 23, 1908, a fire started in the basement of the Masonic Building on the corner of Bridge and Depot Streets. The fire spread and quickly raged out of control. Reinforcements were called in from neighboring Burlington. They arrived expeditiously, but unfortunately the length of hose available didn't reach the Winooski River, so brave firefighters were forced to use milk cans to transport water to the fire. It took more than four hours to douse the flames. By 4 a.m. on April 24, the whole of Richmond's business district was destroyed, including two hotels, the post office, the library, and several homes totaling more than $74,000 worth of damage.

Vermonters are resilient, however, and plans to rebuild began quickly. This time precautions against fire were taken, including the installation of thick firewalls within the two-story buildings. While occupants have changed often, the buildings you see on Bridge Street today are largely the same as they were in 1908.

Toscano Cafe & Bistro (27 Bridge St., Richmond; 802-434-3148), located in the rustic storefront, offers a Mediterranean-inspired menu rich in Italian influences. Chef-owner Jon Faith and his wife, Lucy, welcome guests into their bright and attractive dining room. A longtime musician in Vermont clubs, Jon changed careers and trained at New England Culinary Institute before working in several Vermont restaurants before finally opening his own. Some of his offerings include house-made ricotta gnocchi, dijon-crusted salmon fillet, Vermont maple brined pork loin, tortellini Mediterranean, and a full assortment of luncheon sandwiches and salads. Open for lunch and dinner Tues through Sat at 11:30 a.m.; brunch is served from 9:30 a.m. to 2:30 p.m. Sun, with light fare being served after that until dinner at 4:30 p.m.

Within walking distance of Toscano, *Richmond Victorian Inn* (191 E. Main St., Richmond; 888-242-3362 or 802-434-4410; richmondvictorianinn .com) sits grandly on a hillside. Voted Best of New England by *Yankee Magazine* in 2011, this inn is lovingly maintained by innkeepers Joyce and Frank Stewart. Guest rooms in this restored and turreted home are fresh and appealing, each different and nicely furnished. All have private baths. The tower room is particularly sunny, with large windows, pink walls, plum floor, and white wicker furniture set off by a gleaming brass bed. The beds all have pieced quilts and all rooms have comfortable bathrobes.

A full country-inn breakfast (including Vermont's famed Harrington bacon and sausage) is included in the reasonable rates, and from September through Mother's Day, guests are invited to join local people and other visitors to town for Sunday afternoon tea, served in the front parlor (there is an extra charge and reservations are suggested). While the inn does not accept pets, they will arrange pet boarding close by.

Richmond is also home to the **Old Round Church** (25 Round Church Rd., Richmond; 802-434-3654; oldroundchurch.com), one of the most unusual buildings in the state. It's not exactly round—it has 16 sides—but it holds the distinction of being the first community church in the country, since its construction in 1813 was the joint effort of five separate denominations: Methodist, Congregationalist, Universalist, Baptist, and Christian. In fact, it's rumored that 16 men each built one side of the church, and the 17th built the belfry, all under the direction of local blacksmith/carpenter William Rhodes.

vermonttrivia

There are a few theories as to why Rhodes chose a rounded design for the church, but our favorite is that the design eliminated any corners in which the devil could hide.

The congregations initially held joint services at the church, but they eventually broke away, and the church became the town hall and served in that capacity until 1973, when it was closed to the public out of safety concerns. It was then that the Richmond Historical Society was formed and stepped in to save the building.

vermonttrivia

It is said that Henry Ford once tried to buy the Old Round Church so that he could bring it back to Dearborn, Michigan, with him, but the town gave him a thumbs down.

Throughout the years the society has overseen extensive restoration efforts. Today the church is a National Historic Landmark, and is open weekends from 10 a.m. to 4 p.m. in summer and during foliage season. The building is also available to be rented for weddings and other events.

South of Richmond is the village of Huntington. Huntington abuts a parcel of land called **Buels Gore,** most of which is taken up by Camel's Hump State Forest. Gores are odd-shaped parcels of unincorporated land, usually rocky or otherwise worthless. They are not part of any town and are not often inhabited, but according to the 2000 census, the gore has a population of 12.

Buels Gore was named for Major Elias Buel, who back in 1780 wanted to start his own town of Montzoar in the gore, which totals 3,520 acres. He purchased all the existing land titles to the gore but neglected to have them recorded or to pay the taxes on them. To pay the taxes, the lands were seized and subsequently sold for a grand total of $11.02. Major Buel left the state and settled in New York.

Continue down the main road that runs through Huntington and turn west onto Sherman Hollow Road to reach the **Green Mountain Audubon Nature Center** (255 Sherman Hollow Rd., Huntington; 802-434-3068; vt.audubon.org). The center has an extensive trail system that is equally accessible to walkers and cross-country skiers. The small, slanting shack alongside the barn has trail maps inside.

Inside the main house is a nature museum occupying several rooms of the house. The Nature Discovery Room has a board with dates of recent sightings of common and not-so-common Vermont-based birds. Live turtles and garter snakes, a cubbyhole filled with 15 different birds'

Another Presidential Scandal?

Although President Chester A. Arthur is known to have been born in 1829, no one is quite sure where. Fairfield, Vermont, claims the honor, and a replica of his boyhood home was erected there in 1953. The town of Waterville, however, based on a memoir of a friend of his mother's, has staked a claim that he was actually born in that town and taken to Fairfield when he was five days old. But wait, there's more. His mother came from across the border in Dunham Flats, Quebec, and they claim that she went there for the delivery. If that's true, then he was not born in the US and shouldn't have acceded to the job of president in September 1881, after the assassination of President James Garfield. But no one in either Vermont town has much truck with that claim, and it's a little late to quibble about the validity of Arthur's presidency.

nests—the center calls them avian architecture—and matching games are in this room.

One of the upstairs rooms serves as a teachers' resource center and library. Steel yourself before you pull out the drawers of actual preserved bird species, from blue jays to pine grosbeaks and owls and swans. If you're at all squeamish, head out to the barn, which is filled with more exhibits and examples of taxidermy that are a bit easier to take.

While trails are open daily year-round from dusk to dawn, the center has office hours Mon through Fri 8 a.m. to 4 p.m.

Route 2 from Richmond to Waterbury pretty much parallels I-89, criss-crossing from one side to the other. About halfway between the two, at the town of Bolton, Route 2 crosses under the highway to the north side and immediately after the bridge is a road to Bolton Valley. For miles the road climbs upward until you reach **Bolton Valley Ski Resort** (4302 Bolton Valley Access Rd., Bolton Valley; 877-9-BOLTON; boltonvalley.com) at the end of the road.

This ski resort is family oriented, without the glitz of larger ski meccas to the south, but with all the amenities. In winter the resort is among the first to open and last to close because of the altitude and the way the mountain catches snow. Each year 300 inches of natural snow falls here, ensuring the best conditions on their 70 trails. Grooming is expert, the staff taking to the trails as soon as skiers have left for the day. The trails all face northwest, preserving the snow and giving skiers a wonderful view of Vermont's signature mountain, **Camel's Hump.** Be sure to save time to ski the Cobrass trail from the top of the Vista chair as the sun goes down—it's inspirational. But you don't have to stop skiing at sunset: They have night skiing as well.

But alpine is not all the skiing that goes on here. The resort also has an excellent cross-country program with more than 60 miles of trails.

Bolton has a respectable vertical drop of 1,704 feet and spreads out over 3 peaks, most all of the trails ending up back in to base area. Of the total 70 trails, 36 percent are labeled for novices, 37 percent are intermediate, and 27 percent are expert, making this a good place for family and recreational skiing. Six lifts serve the trails, including 2 quads, 3 doubles, and a new top-to-bottom quad. Boarders will also like the 1,500-foot fully groomed terrain park.

Bolton Mountain Resort has both hotel and condo lodgings available and offers some nice packages. Restaurants and other facilities, including a child-care center that can handle up to 30 children, are also available.

On the access road to the ski resort is the **Black Bear Inn** (4010 Bolton Access Rd., Bolton Valley; 802-434-2126 or 800-395-6335; blkbear inn.com), a rustic four-season bed-and-breakfast-style inn that reminds us of the cozy places where skiers used to stay before the days of condos and destination resorts. The roaring fire in the big fireplace in the ample lobby/guest lounge makes this a warm place in both senses of the word, and the innkeepers are most accommodating, not to mention the private outdoor hot tubs. Black Bear Inn is pet-friendly; call for details. A ski lift connects to Bolton Valley's trails and slopes, and the inn has a dining room.

While every traveler bound for Burlington on I-89 passes the Waterbury exit, and those bound for Stowe or Ben & Jerry's Ice Cream Factory join Route 100 there, not very many people go into the charming old town itself. We recommend you do. **Waterbury** has some very fine Victorian buildings (one house has a large horseshoe window overlooking Route 2), a charming little museum, and one of our favorite inns.

What is there about a checkered past that makes an inn irresistible—especially when it's been carefully restored and nicely furnished with unusual antiques and handmade furniture, and its innkeepers have a sense of humor? The **Old Stagecoach Inn** (18 N. Main St., Waterbury; 802-244-5056 or 800-262-2206; oldstagecoach.com) began as a coaching stop and town meetinghouse in 1826, and its Victorian facade with porches was added late in the century. Local opinion is divided from that point on, but most agree that the meetings that began to take place here were not of a civic (and certainly not public) nature, and a photograph the innkeepers have does seem to show a lot of women posed alluringly on the porches. Other local residents remember that the house was haunted, and the inn staff admits to some unusual encounters in Room 2, the one with the magnificent carved four-poster bed.

Today the inn is on the National Register of Historic Places. The guest rooms vary in size and shape, reflecting the architectural history of the house itself, a colonial-style building with significant Queen Anne overlays. The innkeepers love to cook, and guests are the beneficiaries, enjoying fresh, home-baked croissants for breakfast as well as their choice of hot entree as part of the full country breakfast included in the rates. If the weather's nice, the porch overlooking the garden is the place to eat.

A walking trail leaves from the inn's backyard, winding through a cemetery with stones from the 1700s and along the river. Just up the street is the town library, and upstairs is the *Historical Society Museum* (28 N. Main St., Waterbury; 802-244-7036; waterburyhistoricalsociety.org), a classic mélange of local history, curiosities, and treasures brought back by intrepid travelers. It has some excellent examples of miniature Berlin work, beading, and handmade lace; an interesting rocking butter churn, and an armadillo shell. Be sure to look at the photo album of the 1927 freshet, a flood that washed out much of Vermont's road and bridge system. Open when the library is open (Mon through Wed 10 a.m. to 8 p.m., Thurs through Fri 10 a.m. to 5 p.m., Sat 9 a.m. to 2 p.m. [winter], to noon [summer]) or by appointment.

Green Mountain Coffee Visitor Center & Cafe (1 Rotarian Place, Waterbury; 877-879-2326; greenmountaincoffee.com) is located in Waterbury's historic train station. Exhibits here tell the Green Mountain Coffee story f rom "tree to cup." Tours are self-guided and can be followed by a trip to the gift shop where you'll find treasures from the world over. After, why not relax with a wonderful cup of joe (check out their free samples before you decide to buy a cup). Open daily 7 a.m. to 5 p.m.

South of Waterbury, on Route 100, watch for signs to *Grunberg Haus* (94 Pine St., Waterbury; 800-800-7760 or 802-244-7726; grunberghaus.com), a three-story, hand-built chalet off the beaten path in the middle of everything. Each of the 10 guest rooms on the second floor has its own balcony, but not necessarily its own bathroom. Even though you'll be close to many of northern Vermont's more mainstream attractions, such as Ben & Jerry's Ice Cream Factory in Waterbury, Cold Hollow Cider Mill, and Stowe, you won't feel as if you're in the middle of everything. Be warned: Grunberg Haus is so pleasant a hideaway that you may have to consciously drag yourself out into the world, away from the queen-size beds with downy comforters. One of the guest rooms even has a tiny built-in alcove that houses a bed big enough for an 8-year-old, or maybe a couple of cats, or you, if you really want to get away from it all. Breakfast is accompanied by piano music.

Stowe's reputation as a top ski area undoubtedly owes much to Mount Mansfield's location in Vermont's Snowbelt. The first recorded descent of the mountain on skis was made in 1900 on barrel staves, but things moved slowly until the Great Depression years, when Stowe got its start as a major ski area. In 1932 the first skiers from New York City arrived in Waterbury to get to the top of Mount Mansfield—where Stowe's ski area is located—via an electric railway from Waterbury. Although it took the rest of the decade to cut trails and hook up rope tows, by 1940 Stowe could boast the first chairlift in the country. The town hasn't been the same since.

A quiet place to escape the crowds is the ***Helen Day Art Center*** (90 Pond St., Stowe; 802-253-8358; helenday.com), which exhibits the work of internationally and nationally recognized artists, as well as Vermont-based artists. The building itself was previously the town high school.

A variety of special events and discussions are also held every few weeks at the center, in conjunction with the current displays. In its special exhibits you may find hooked rugs, food labels, paintings, drawings, and other works of art covering the walls of the gallery. The gallery is open Wed through Sun, noon to 5 p.m. when exhibits are ongoing. Between exhibit showings the gallery is closed, so be sure to check ahead.

Although Stowe is not exactly off the beaten path, we'd be cheating you if we didn't mention a few of its attractions. Despite the number of tourists year-round, Stowe still manages to remain a real town, and one of its most appealing inns overlooks its main street. Rooms in the ***Green Mountain Inn*** (18 Main St., Stowe; 802-253-7301 or 800-253-7302; greenmountaininn .com) are all different, at least those in the original building, often with quirky, charming shapes. All are approached along corridors with an occasional up or down step. But there are no rough edges—look for carpeted corridors, original artwork throughout, canopy beds, whirlpool baths, fluffy towels, terry-cloth robes, premium bath amenities, electric fireplaces, and a host of other details of fine inn-keeping. In the afternoon everyone gathers for cider or tea and fresh-baked cookies, which you can take to a porch rocker to watch the comings and goings on Main Street. A pleasant dining room overlooks the street, and breakfasts are interesting and varied, including crepes filled with whole pistachios and ricotta. Rates include all the facilities of the health club and year-round outdoor heated pool; children 17 and younger stay free.

The *Blue Moon Cafe* (35 School St., Stowe; 802-253-7006; bluemoon stowe.com), located in an older home near Main Street, offers superb dining. The menu changes weekly, with an emphasis on local produce, lamb and beef, fresh fish, and bread baked in a wood-fired oven. Appetizers might include watercress and endive salad with Bayley Hazen blue cheese or smoked trout with apples, celery, frisée lettuce, and horseradish. The entrees might feature creative offerings such as grilled leg of lamb with roasted parsnips, dried cherries, and port wine or foraged mushroom and eggplant tart with sheep's milk feta, spinach, and roasted vegetables. There is an award-winning wine list and simple but excellent desserts. The Blue Moon is open 6 to 9 p.m. Sun through Thurs and until 9:30 p.m. Fri and Sat. Reservations are recommended.

On Main Street, behind Stowe Hardware & Dry Goods, is the beginning of the 5.3-mile *Stowe Recreation Path,* a paved multi-use corridor that follows the river through meadows and woodlands, roughly parallel with Mountain Road. Walkers, cyclists, in-line skaters, and cross-country skiers share the path, which leads past lodgings, dining establishments, gardens, a farmers' market, and endless views. If you want to take advantage of this beautiful path on wheels, stop at *Mountain Sports & Bike Shop* (580 Mountain Rd., Stowe; 802-253-7919) at the intersection with Weeks Hill Road and right on the path, where bikes are available for rent. Store hours are 10 a.m. to 6 p.m., Mon through Sat, 10 a.m. to 5 p.m. Sun.

Mountain Road is itself about as beaten as a path can get, lined with restaurants and lodgings of every stripe announced by a succession of signs lined up like street touts.

The Gables (1457 Mountain Rd., Stowe; 802-253-7730 or 800-GABLES-1; gablesinn.com) is a warm and welcoming family-owned inn without the pretensions of many of its neighbors, and loaded with just as many pampering comforts, including fireplaces, whirlpool tubs, and candlelight dining. Breakfast here is legendary and lasts most people through a full day's skiing or biking. The Gables is a particularly good place for people traveling or skiing alone, since the hosts make everyone feel as if they're visiting relatives and will make sure skiers have a ride to the slopes and arrive safely home.

For an experience truly off the beaten path, head out of the center of Stowe on Mountain Road (Route 108). Travel for about 1 mile, then turn right onto Weeks Hill Road. Head uphill to Percy Farm Road, on your right after about 2 miles. At the top of the hill, travel for about another mile before turning left as the road turns to dirt. If your car can make it, travel along this dirt road for another 2 or 3 miles until you reach the bridge. Turn left at the T right past the bridge and follow this road to its end. Watch for "Sterling Forest Parking" signs after you go up a big hill and pass a cemetery. Park here or in the next lot to the right, but please do not cross the bridge after the parking lot; this leads to private property. So, why have you come all this way? To see **Sterling Falls Gorge,** of course. This series of 3 waterfalls, 6 cascades, and 8 pools is within a short distance of the road. A walking path parallels them; from its dizzying height you can see how the stream carved its way through the schist, forming irregular potholes and swirly rock surfaces. Do be careful here, especially if the trail is wet, and don't lean over to take pictures (photographing the falls is nearly impossible, unless you're a bird). Don't look for the falls on any map—even some Stowe residents looked at us blankly when we asked about them. Now you know.

Back toward civilization, off the west side of Mountain Road, is the **Trapp Family Lodge** (700 Trapp Hill Rd., Stowe; 802-253-8511 or 800-826-7000; trappfamily.com), which overlooks rolling meadows, a valley, and the Green Mountains. The air is distinctly Austrian, and very von Trapp, but it's never overwhelmingly *The Sound of Music*. Music is often in the air, however, with Sunday morning jazz and coffee, evening sing-alongs, and a harpist in the dining room each evening. Rooms are beautifully decorated, and all overlook the valley views.

A full schedule of activities keeps guests busy year-round. In the winter you can enjoy cross-country skiing (the trails are open to the public and known as some of the finest in New England), snowshoeing, sleigh rides, and maple sugaring. Summer programs for families and for children of various ages include fishing, birding, hiking, nature walks, swimming, and llama treks. The dining room, serving European specialties such as wiener schnitzel along with game, is open to the public, but reservations are essential. There's even a fitness center and a brewery on the grounds.

vermonttrivia

The score from Rodgers & Hammerstein's *The Sound of Music,* which opened on Broadway in 1959, was unknown to the actual Von Trapp Family singers, who but rarely sang in English.

Head north on Route 108 toward Jeffersonville to find **Smugglers' Notch,** the actual notch, crossed by Route 108, not the resort (although that's nice, too; see below). The road through the notch is so narrow at the top that it is impossible to get plows through to keep it cleared of snow, so it closes until spring melts it clear. When it's open, however, the steep, winding road is one of the most interesting in the state, especially at the top, where it weaves among giant boulders. Trailers and large RVs are not allowed over it. (For more information on how this unusual notch was formed, see the book *Natural Wonders of Vermont,* by Barbara and Stillman Rogers.)

There's an old upcountry Yankee story that has since become an all-purpose bromide about the Flatlander who stopped to ask directions of a farmer, who replied, "You can't get there from here." He might well have been talking about **Smugglers' Notch Ski Resort** (4323 Rte. 108 South, Jeffersonville; 855-830-2112 or 800-419-4615; smuggs.com) in the winter. Getting there from Stowe in summer is a simple matter of driving straight uphill on Route 108 through the narrow rock-bordered passage, then dropping down the other side. When this unplowable road is closed in winter, you have to continue north on Route 100 to Morrisville, take Route 15 west through Johnson and Jeffersonville, and drive back along Route 108. If you are a skier, it's well worth the trip, however you manage it, and it certainly is off the beaten path.

Skiing is available on 3 separate mountains, and all of it is superb— with state-of-the-art grooming. We've arrived at midnight in a blizzard that dropped more than a foot of snow and awakened to perfectly groomed trails the next morning. The ski school is also tops—instructors tailor the lessons to your skills and weaknesses after watching you ski, even in group lessons. A special program

politicsispolitics andbusinessis business

From the time of the Jefferson embargo of 1808 through the War of 1812, Vermonters defied federal agents and continued to do business with Canada, their natural trading partner. The route through the notch was an important one for farmers seeking to sell their beef to the British in Canada, even while other Vermonters fought to keep British troops at bay—which is how it came to be named Smugglers' Notch.

is designed for adults who want to learn snowboarding. It's a family resort with all manner of accommodations for kids, including a day-care center toddlers won't want to leave. Not surprisingly, since the ski resort is designed especially for families, the children's learning program gets high priority. Unlike many areas, where the preschoolers' day includes mostly indoor play time with an hour's on-slope instruction twice a day, the practice at Smugglers' Notch is to put children as young as 4 or 5 on the slopes for at least two hours, morning and afternoon. Imagine a 5-year-old's pride at ending a weekend there proficient on the chairlift and able to ski down the mountain on real trails. Put them in the ski camp for a week, and they'll be leaving you behind in a cloud of fresh powder by Thursday.

The entire Smugglers' Notch complex is self-contained, with a shuttle bus between 2 base lodges and all lodgings. Slope-side condo units are huge, with many amenities. You can't ski right out your door and onto the slopes from the new North Hill lodgings, but they have their own activities center with a pool, hot tubs, and other facilities. Condos here have four-season sunrooms, multiple fireplaces, and a lot of extras: quality kitchen appliances, oversize whirlpool tubs, and a washer/dryer in each unit. Shuttle buses take skiers to the slopes from all the mountain lodgings. There's plenty to do here in the summer, too, with hiking, climbing, kayaking, nature programs, tennis, kids' camp, and more. Its secluded location and relaxed air make it seem like another world.

Smugglers' Notch Resort, long an environmental leader, has gone one step further. If you're in the neighborhood, stop in to see the *Living Machine Wastewater Treatment Plant.* The plant incorporates a three-stage process that includes use of a large greenhouse full of tropical and subtropical plants to purify wastewater from the resort. Odor-free, the greenhouse has a deck around it with signs that explain the treatment process. It is included on the several different property tours of the resort.

Farther along Route 108 at the junction of Routes 15 and 104 in Cambridge you'll find the *Boyden Valley Winery* (64 Rte. 104, Cambridge; 802-644-8151; boydenvalley.com). Set on a fourth-generation dairy farm in the Lamoille River valley, this winery might not be what you expect to find so far north. The owners of the winery use their own grapes, local berries, and apples along with maple syrup to make wines, cordials, and hard ciders. You can tour the winemaking facility to see the process and taste the results

---

Fun in the Snow: No Skis Required

While most people think of coming to Vermont in the winter only for skiing, an increasing number are discovering the joys of this active winter vacationland for its many other diversions. Non-skiing companions of skiers have long known this secret: While everyone is on the slopes, all the après-ski recreation facilities are nearly empty. There are opportunities for snowshoeing, sleigh rides, skating parties, igloo building, dogsledding, ice fishing, winter carnivals, and activities for those who prefer the warmer pursuits of shopping, museums, art galleries, and fine dining.

---

10 a.m. to 5 p.m. on weekends Jan through Apr, and 10 a.m. to 5 p.m. daily May through Dec.

While on Route 15, continue east past Jeffersonville and just a tad farther you'll come to Johnson, and in its center, *Johnson Woolen Mills* (51 Lower Main East, Johnson; 802-635-2271 or 800-635-WOOL; johnsonwoolen mills.com). The company goes back a century and a half, when local farmers brought their wool to the mill to have it spun and woven into cloth. In the late 1800s Johnson began making warm woolen trousers from the cloth. Meeting with the rousing approval of people who had to do farm chores in the dead of winter, a decade or so later the company added jackets, shirts, and vests. That's what it still makes, along with blankets, mittens, and hats, all of which are sold in a shop located in the original mill building. You'll find first quality at factory-store prices and seconds at unbelievable bargains. You also can buy wool yard goods for sewing or rug braiding. The store is open all year from 9 a.m. to 5 p.m. Mon through Sat, and on Sun from 10 a.m. to 4 p.m. You can also go online to purchase their products if you can't make it to the store.

If you return to Burlington on scenic Route 15 or the unnumbered, almost parallel route through Pleasant Valley, you'll travel through *Underhill*, which snuggles up against the western slopes of Mount Mansfield. If you happen along on the third or fourth Saturday in June, you'll find one of the last of the old-fashioned *Strawberry Socials* that used to fill the all-too-brief season when fields of strawberries ripen. Jericho-Underhill Lions Club members start picking just after sunrise on Saturday morning. By 10 a.m. they're back at the United Church of Underhill, washing, hulling,

He Certainly Picked the Right Place from Which to Be

Wilson Bentley of Jericho, known locally as Snowflake Bentley, had by the age of 21 developed a photographic microscope that was able to record the intricate patterns of individual snow crystals. The process was not a simple one, requiring a cold working area, great patience, and Bentley's ability to hold his breath for a full minute.

He discovered, after photographing thousands of snowflakes, that no two were alike, that they were all six-sided, and that each flake developed from a tiny nucleus into a hexagonal pattern. Today, more than a century later, much of what we know about snow is based on his research, and Bentley's photographs are among the prized collections of several museums, including the Fairbanks Museum in St. Johnsbury and the Peabody at Harvard. Although he never attended high school, Bentley was elected a fellow of the American Academy for the Advancement of Science.

slicing, and baking the biscuits. Real shortcake isn't made with sponge cake baked in little molds, or with pound cake; it uses "short" biscuits, and that's exactly what these are. From 5 to 8 p.m. the Lions hide these biscuits under juicy fresh berries and freshly whipped real cream and serve about 350 people, who stay until they've eaten their fill. No one asks how many bowls you've eaten, only if you'd like another—or a refill on the coffee, tea, or milk that goes with it. The price is reasonable and the money goes to a good cause. It's easy to see why the only advertising is the sign out on the village green.

Just down the street from the green is *Sinclair House Inn* (389 Rte. 15, Jericho; 802-899-2234 or 800-433-4658; sinclairinnbb.com), a striking Victorian with one of the loveliest gardens in the valley. When you follow the path from the front porch, you see only a part of the succession of flowerbeds that flow down the slope to the flat circle of lawn that just begs to have a bride and groom exchanging vows against a backdrop of Vermont farms and hillsides. The owners have lavished the same attention on the house itself, restoring its paneled interior and decorating its rooms in Victorian antiques and country furniture. We like the bright front rooms— one with a lattice window, the other with stained glass. Guests can buy lift tickets, rentals, and lessons at Smugglers' Notch, 18 miles away. One room is wheelchair accessible, even to the wheel-in shower and low closet hooks.

North of Burlington

The stretches of the Champlain Valley north of Burlington offer a flatter, more fertile landscape than many other parts of the state. This rich farmland played an important role in the early development of northwest Vermont.

Route 7 is a pretty stretch of highway as you wind your way into Milton.

If you're in the area at the end of April, head to **St. Albans** and its annual **Vermont Maple Festival** (vtmaplefestival.org). This three-day event held the last weekend of April signifies the official end of winter.

vermonttrivia

The town of Milton, Vermont, is said to have been named after the 17th-century English poet John Milton of *Paradise Lost,* but it is more likely that the name came from Viscount Milton, otherwise known as Carl William FitzWilliam.

There are many free and family-friendly activities, including sugar-on-snow, arts-and-crafts displays, relay races, an antiques show, face painting, a parade, cooking contests, and talent and variety shows. These and other town activities serve to wake up the townspeople in an area of the state where winter hangs on for a good five months of the year. And wake up they do—more than 50,000 people attend this event, which is quickly approaching its 50th anniversary in 2016 and continues to be staffed and run completely by volunteers. Wow. Their website offers detailed information and coupons for local merchants during this event.

On the green of St. Albans is **Jeff's Restaurant** (65 N. Main St., St. Albans; 802-524-6135; jeffsmainesea foodrestaurant.com), a gourmet-food

itwaswar,y'all

St. Albans was the site of the northernmost battle—more accurately, "event"—of the Civil War when, on October 19, 1864, a group of Confederate soldiers took over the town, robbed all the banks, blew up the Sheldon Bridge, and escaped to Canada. They were apprehended but were acquitted of any crimes because the jury felt they were acting on the basis of "legitimate warfare."

The St. Albans Bay Schoolhouse

There is a unique abandonment that greets passersby along the shores of St. Albans Bay. It failed as a schoolhouse and it failed in its second reincarnation as a gas station. But now, on its third try, it seems to have finally found success as a ruin. I've always been interested in this abandoned one-room schoolhouse, if not a little perplexed—sitting in the flash of busy summer traffic on their way to Kill Kare State Park, with its crumbling brickwork and sets of battered gas pumps resting out front on a grassy slope that seems to be mowed and maintained. Amusingly enough, it's almost as if this place had been pushed to the back of everyone's minds, despite its indiscreet hilltop perch and the constant flow of traffic along Route 36.

So, is there a story to be told here? I'm sure there is, but this is a story that only speaks in riddles, it would seem. I can only wonder what exists behind its boarded windows in claustrophobic darkness.

Thankfully for the residents of St. Albans Bay, there is a gas station just down the road that is very much not abandoned. —Reprinted with permission of Chad Abramovich, *Obscure Vermont*

and seafood shop and restaurant offering "fine food, stylishly Vermont." There are two dining rooms offering customers their choice of dining style and a market and wineshop next door that offers fish both uncooked and prepared, along with a large selection of ready-to-eat dishes like pesto lasagna, smoked bluefish, salads, sandwiches, and specials such as chicken burritos and spanakopita, and a large selection of French, California, and Italian wines.

Gourmet desserts are available both to eat in and to take out and include Toll House pie and chocolate hazelnut torte.

Jeff's is open Mon 11 a.m. to 3 p.m. and Tues through Sat 11 a.m. to 3 p.m. and 4:30 to 9 p.m.

Swanton on Route 7 is home to the largest number of Abenaki Indians in the state, who lived in Vermont long before Samuel de Champlain arrived in the early 17th century. The Missisquoi Abenaki village was established in 1682. The Abenaki people call themselves the "People of Dawn." To learn more about the Abenaki Tribe, visit tribal.abenakination.com/who-we-are for a wonderfully in-depth history.

Swanton has its own interesting history and the *Swanton Historical Society* (58 S. River St., Swanton; 802-868-2483; swantonhistoricalsociety .org) has compiled a walking tour of the town. Visit their website to print out a brochure that explains all the stops.

If you're not all walked out, or if nature is more your thing than history, head over to the beauty of the *Missisquoi National Wildlife Refuge* (29 Tabor Rd., Swanton; 802-868-4781; fws.gov/refuges/profiles/index .cfm?id=53520). Established in 1943, this 6,729-acre refuge is located on the eastern shore of Lake Champlain, where you'll find wetlands, open fields, hardwood forest, and river waters, all filled with large flocks of birds, deer, fox, and other mammals. Fishing is allowed, but all state regulations must be followed. Hunting is also allowed during designated periods in designated areas. Contact the refuge headquarters for more information. If your family likes to boat, there is an 11-mile loop down the Missisquoi past Shad Island, home to the largest great blue heron breeding area in the state. Please do not disturb these giant birds, though.

Miles of trails meander through the refuge for you to explore. If you visit in the summer, remember your insect repellent; if you visit in the winter, bring your cross-country skis or snowshoes; if you visit in the spring (generally April through June), shin-high boots are a good idea, as things can be a little soggy. This just makes it easier to see the tracks of the many animals that are sharing your trail. There are also many varieties of wildflowers and plants, so please stay on the trail to avoid damaging anything or encountering poison ivy (remember: leaves of three, let it be). While Fido will enjoy the outing, please keep him on his leash for the safety of those around you. The refuge is open daily from dawn to dusk.

An enjoyable stop in this area is *West Swanton Orchards, Cider Mill and Farm Market* (752 N. River St., Swanton; 802-868-9100), open daily, 10 a.m. to 5 p.m., from May through Nov. They offer 11 varieties of apples, including McIntosh, Cortland, and Red Delicious, which you can buy at the stand or pick yourself. As the name implies, the stand carries the trilogy of other Vermont products: honey, maple goodies, and cider, in addition to pies and baked goods and Vermont gift items. They also host an annual Harvest Festival in September.

If you have ever dreamed of living on a farm, now is your opportunity. *Berkson Farms Inn* (1205 W. Berkshire Rd., Enosburg Falls; 802-933-2522;

Things Are About to Get Rocky

As you head east from Swanton on Route 78, you'll most likely start to notice that things begin to look noticeably different. Route 78 parallels the Missisquoi River, a very wide, 86-mile-long rocky river that begins in the town of Lowell, heads north into Canada, and then swings back into Vermont by way of Lake Champlain.

Here, and elsewhere in Vermont, you'll see boulders and rocks in the fields, and you may wonder where they came from. The big ones came from nearby mountains, often quite some distance away. As the great glaciers of the last ice age moved over the mountains, they pulled off pieces of mountaintop and carried them along, dropping the rocks as they melted. These boulders are called "glacial erratics," and local settlers sometimes cut them up to use as building stones; more often they just plowed around them.

berksonfarms.com) offers guests the opportunity to stay for a night or two or for an entire week, participating in standard farm chores, from milking cows to bringing in sap buckets in the spring to helping to drive a fence post into the ground.

This working dairy farm on 670 acres is open year-round and in addition to a herd of milking cattle, is home to an assortment of sheep, swans, geese, chickens, and rams, as well as a friendly donkey named Jack.

Guests stay in one of 4 rooms in the 19th-century farmhouse. These rooms are furnished with handsome Victorian furniture, quilts, and large, comfortable beds. One room has a private bath, and all rooms come with a country breakfast. The kitchen and dining room are huge and welcoming and feature lots of antique furniture. One of the living rooms has an old pump organ and a Victrola. Now's your chance to live your farm vacation dream.

If you are in the mood for a drive, head east of Enosburg to Montgomery, lovingly referred to as the **Covered Bridge Capital** of Vermont, where you can take a tour of some of the country's oldest bridges still in use today. All the bridges we discuss below were built by brothers Sheldon and Savannah Jewett, two of eight children from the Jewett family, which has a long history in town. They are also all on the National Register of Historic Places. While these bridges are doing well, they are in constant danger of retirement. Remember, these bridges were built more than a hundred years ago and were not designed to handle modern traffic. In 2011 Hurricane

Irene ravaged many of the state's historic bridges, causing devastating floods that completely washed away some. Others sustained such damage that they had to be closed. Maintained by the state's highway department, the bridges sometimes require costly repairs that can be done by a select list of contractors who understand the original construction techniques. Sometimes the town just doesn't have the money to fix them the way they need to be. Community action is likely going to be the way these treasures are saved. In the meantime, there are still some you can see.

The first is about a 10-minute drive from Berkson Farms Inn. Head south on Route 108 (W. Berkshire Road). Turn left onto Route 105 and head east until you reach Route 118 (Montgomery Road). In about 2 miles you should see Hopkins Bridge Road; turn right and look for **Hopkins Bridge,** which should be on your right. Built in 1875, this lattice-type bridge is still in use today and spans Trout River. If you drive across this bridge, please reduce your speed to 10 miles per hour and respect this piece of history.

Back on Route 118 from Hopkins Bridge Road, turn right and head about 1.5 miles south/southeast until you reach Longley Bridge Road. Turn right and you'll see **Longley Bridge** on your right. This bridge also spans Trout River but was built in 1893. Some renovation occurred in 1992, and last we knew it was open to traffic.

From here, backtrack to Route 118 and travel south/southeast again for just a short distance. Take a right onto Comstock Bridge Road and you'll see **Comstock** covered bridge on your left. This is also a lattice-type bridge and was built in 1883.

Built in 1890, the **Fuller Bridge** is your next logical stop. Located just off the green past the post office on South Richford Road (a left off of Route 118), this bridge crosses the Black Falls Brook and is open to traffic.

Drive-by Scrooge

According to an article online, Fuller Bridge was the victim of a hit and run in 1982 when a logging truck struck it and destroyed the roof. The driver apparently didn't realize his truck had hit the bridge, but the evidence was indisputable—the holiday lights that had previously adorned the bridge and a few pieces of the bridge itself were seen dangling from the truck as it passed the town garage.

vermonttrivia

Creamery Bridge, according to town historian Bill Branthoover, completes a horseshoe-shaped route through the valley. One side of the horseshoe is called Hill West Road and the other is West Hill Road. Travelers used to be able to complete a closed circuit of the area, but due to the bridge closure, this is no longer possible.

If you're up for a challenge to find your next stop, head back to Route 118 and take a left onto Hill West Road. Travel about 2.5 miles to Creamery Bridge Road (which may be closed depending on the season) to find **Creamery Bridge.** You'll have to be diligent; road signs are not the best for this bridge, if they exist at all. Creamery Bridge is no longer in use and is blocked by large boulders. It really is a beautiful piece of history if you can find it, and offers great photo ops with fall foliage as a colorful backdrop. Creamery Bridge was built to allow farmers from area dairies to more easily transport their milk over West Hill Brook to a creamery to be processed, hence the name.

Heading back to Route 118 will put you on track for the final stop on your tour of bridges. Turn right onto Route 118 and travel about 4 miles until you see Hutchins Bridge Road on your right. Here, at the bottom of the slope of an unpaved road, you will find **Hutchins Bridge.** Built in 1883, this bridge crosses the Trout River's south branch and is still in use.

vermonttrivia

There used to be another covered bridge on Gibou Road, but it fell into such disrepair that it has been dismantled and placed into storage until funds can be raised to restore it. The 1883 Hectorville Bridge, alongside Route 118, used to span the Trout River but also fell into disrepair and was moved to sit alongside the road. It is now used for storage.

If you are now exhausted from your covered-bridge extravaganza, why not plan to stop for the night at the **Phineas Swann Bed & Breakfast** (195 Main St., Montgomery; 802-326-4306; phineasswann .com),where breakfast is not just a meal, it's an event, with home-baked breads and jams made from the berries grown in the backyard. And maybe the best part about this inn is that they are pet-friendly. In fact, they call themselves "New England's Most Romantic Pet-Friendly Inn." People apparently agree, since

TripAdvisor ranked them in the Top 10 Most Pet-friendly Hotels in the United States in 2012.

The entire place is welcoming (to both you and your pet), with well-decorated rooms and big-band music in the background at afternoon tea. But it's not a bit fussy, and you'll be perfectly at home here in your hiking boots or ski clothes. The owners are long on sense of humor and short on pretensions. If you're not a traveling-with-pet family, you can choose to stay in the beautiful main inn. If you brought along Fido or Fidoette, you may choose one of the suites in either the Carriage House or the River House. Room prices include a full gourmet breakfast, Internet access, and endless coffee, tea, spring water, and fresh baked goods. Remember, room rates listed on the website are per room, per night, not per person per night.

Jay Peak Resort (830 Jay Peak Rd., Jay; 802-988-2611; jaypeakresort .com), the state's northernmost ski area, is north of Montgomery along Route 242. Here, the snow falls deeper than in other parts of the state and the skiing is among the best in Vermont. Seventy-six trails traverse 2 peaks, and the alpine and Nordic trails cover more than 50 miles of territory. The longest run is 3 miles and the alpine trails are about 20 percent beginner with the balance split evenly between intermediate and advanced skier levels. Vertical drop here is 2,153 feet, making it one of the highest in New England. All of this territory is served by a multitude of double, triple, and quad chairlifts; 2 surface lifts; and 1 tram.

While Jay Peak's skiing is hard to beat, skiers are not the only ones who will love it here. Check out their huge indoor water park that boasts such things as the Double Barrel Flowrider, a lazy river, La Chute (a 65-foot drop that swimmers complete in 6 seconds), kids' play area, and more. Don't forget, too, that Jay Peak is a year-round resort. In the summer they offer an 18-hole championship golf course, hiking, tram rides, and summer camps. It's all on the website, so we won't go into detail here.

If you do decide to ride the tram in the summer, maybe check out the **Mountain Ecology Nature Trail**, a self-guided tour you can take back

jaypeaktrivia

Jay Peak's tram is the only aerial tramway in Vermont. Carrying 60 passengers, it makes six trips per hour (do the math—that's 360 people *per hour*) up to the almost 4,000-foot summit. The ride takes seven minutes one way.

down the mountain. Pick up the small guide to the nature trail at the resort welcome center. The trail winds down the mountain and takes about an hour and a half for the average hiker. At the upper end it passes through conifers and by an alpine pond, where the delicate ecosystem is explained. At lower levels the Forest Loop Trail travels past typical north-woods trees and plants. Look for the trees hollowed by woodpeckers, the tracks and droppings of moose and deer, and the headwaters of the Jay Branch. The upper end of the famed Vermont Long Trail passes through the area.

The heavy snows in this region also bring cross-country skiers to the trails of the **Hazen's Notch Association** (1423 Hazens Notch Rd., Montgomery Center; 802-326-4799; hazensnotch.org), a member-supported non-profit corporation dedicated to conservation, environmental teaching, and the responsible use of land. The association maintains 40 miles of trails in winter over conservation lands. During summer 15 miles of these trails are open for hiking and include short trails like the Beaver Ponds Trail and the longer and more strenuous Burnt Mountain Trail, which provides views out over neighboring mountains and valleys. Trails are mapped and explained on the website. Hiking in summer is free, but there is a charge for cross-country skiing (to defray grooming costs). A contribution to the association at any time of year is welcomed. This is truly spectacular country and there are trails at all skill and difficulty levels. All trails are closed to hiking during winter and spring mud season (mid-Dec through early May). Once the trails open in winter, the welcome center is open 9 a.m. to 4 p.m., Mon through Fri, and 9 a.m. to 5 p.m., Sat and Sun.

As you leave Montgomery Center, take a left onto Route 58 East, which climbs and twists and turns into a dirt road about a mile up from town. Great views soon abound. The road follows some parts of the **Bayley-Hazen Military Road,** which was originally planned to run from Newbury, Vermont, to St. John's in Quebec. Parts of the 54-mile portion that now runs from Newbury to Hazens Notch is still used today. The name Bayley-Hazen comes from the two major advocates of the road, Jacob Bayley and Moses Hazen, which are names you'll hear throughout New England history.

About 5 miles out of the town of Montgomery Center, you'll come across a huge rock outcropping—it looks as if you're going to drive right into the mountain. This is **Hazen's Notch** (also named for Moses Hazen), and **Sugarloaf Mountain,** with an altitude of 2,520 feet, lies directly behind

Fine Crop of Rocks This Year

The small stones in the fields actually grow there. Ask any farmer, who will tell you that even though a field is clear of stones in the fall, a new crop has grown there when plowed in the spring. It's the truth: As the ground freezes and thaws in the winter and spring, it heaves up rocks from below in a never-ending process. The original settlers, after they'd cleared the land of trees, moved the larger rocks to the edges and used them to build stone walls, which were more to contain livestock than to mark boundaries (although they served both purposes). As each winter turned up more rocks, the settlers would add them to the walls. In some of these fields, rocks are about the only thing that *will* grow.

it. Past the notch, the second left, where the sign says hazen's notch campground, leads to *McAllister Pond,* a beautiful body of water for fishing and swimming.

The Champlain Islands

A totally different landscape awaits if you travel northwest from Burlington instead of northeast. At times you'll forget and think it's a seascape, especially if haze obscures the Adirondacks across the lake. North of Colchester, take Route 2 toward South Hero, which you will reach via a long bridge. Just before you leave the mainland, you'll pass *Sandbar State Park* (1215 US 2, Milton; 802-893-2825), which, while great for little kids because the water never gets very deep, can be a little of a letdown for adults. Because the water level is low, the water can become stagnant and warm—not always the best combination. You might be better visiting this park in the cooler months than in the heat of the summer—just sayin'. Open 10 a.m. to sunset Memorial Day weekend through Labor Day weekend.

Even though you're not on the ocean, these island towns have a vague seaside resort feeling, but not quite as crowded. Vacationing families have been coming here for generations, primarily because not much changes in the islands from one year—or decade—to the next. Moreover, the islands are compact enough that you can spend the day exploring from South Hero to East Alburg, see about everything there is to see, and still have time to return to the mainland—or, after collapsing in one of the inns or B&Bs on the islands, still have enough energy to go for a long bike ride the next day.

If you decide to just stick to Route 2 and its immediate environs, you'll have plenty to explore, from the numerous antiques shops that dot the islands to the various historic sites. *Saint Anne's Shrine* (92 St. Anne's Rd.; 802-928-3362; saintannesshrine.org) on Isle la Motte has been attracting the faithful since 1893. The original shrine was part of a French fort built in 1666. It was here that the first known Mass was offered in the Northeast. But things changed and the fort was abandoned a few years later, and it wasn't until 1892 that the land on which the original shrine stood was acquired by the order of the Bishop of Vermont, Rev. Louis de Goesbriand. A new shrine was built and a large statue of Saint Anne, mother of the Blessed Virgin Mary and patron saint of Vermont, was accepted as a gift from the Breton Clergy of the Diocese. Today this beautiful statue still stands in the chapel at the shrine and welcomes thousands of faithful followers who make the pilgrimage to honor her. The shrine is looking to the future with plans for expansion to include overnight facilities in hopes of making the blessed place a year-round destination. Currently Saint Anne's can be visited from late May to mid-October. Service hours are listed on their website. There is also camping, a gift shop and cafeteria, and picnic area on the grounds. While admission is free, donations are always very welcome.

If you're a history buff like we are, you won't want to miss a visit to one of Vermont's oldest houses, *Hyde Log Cabin* (Route 2, north of Grand Isle; 802-828-3051). Built by Jedediah Hyde Jr. around 1783, this cabin is quite possibly the oldest log cabin remaining in the US (it's in the running with Nothnagle Log Cabin in Gibbstown, New Jersey). The Hyde family called this one-room cabin home for more than a century and a half. While it's not exactly where it was built (the Vermont Historical Society moved it 2 miles from its original location in 1946), it still appears much as it would have in the 18th century. It was restored in 1956 and again in 1985 and is now home to myriad period artifacts, including maps, furnishings, farm tools, and household paraphernalia. There is also an 1814 one-room schoolhouse on the grounds that you can visit. Open July through Labor Day, 11 a.m. to 5 p.m. Wed through Sun, or when the Open flag is flying. Very small admission charged for those older than 14.

In North Hero, the *North Hero House* (3643 Rte. 2, North Hero; 802-372-4732 or 888-525-3644; northherohouse.com) is a 26-room inn known for its rooms and its restaurant. It has been welcoming guests since 1891 and offers several choices for lodging, ranging from the restored inn house to the Cove House, which has rooms with screened porches that directly overlook the lake. These lakeside lodgings are popular with families, since the inn has its own sandy beach below and offers skating and cross-country skiing in the winter. In the main building, furnishings are often antiques or quality reproductions, and rates, which include breakfast for two, are reasonable.

If you plan to eat dinner at the North Hero House, either as an inn guest or as a visitor, be prepared for a wait, since the place is popular with locals and with some of the aforementioned families who have been coming here in the summers for decades. What's ideal is to dine on the porch, where large windows overlook Lake Champlain and the Green Mountains, on a late-summer night just as the sky turns to dusk. Reservations are highly recommended and can be made online if you choose. Be sure to mention that you'd like a table on the porch if that's what you desire. The menu offers meat, fish, and vegetarian dishes prepared simply but very nicely, and there's an award-winning wine cellar. The chefs have a way with seafood, and wow everyone with the maple salad dressing. If you see someone at the next table licking a salad plate, don't judge.

To explore the islands or delta on a day trip by sea kayak, reserve a space with *True North Kayak Tours* (offices: 53 Nash Place, Burlington; 802-238-7695; vermontkayak.com). This mother-and-son-run company has been operating on the Vermont shoreline for the past decade. They welcome all skill levels and almost all ages. They ask that children ages 7 to 12 double up with an adult in a two-person kayak. If you want to bring someone younger, give them a call and they'll work with you. While private tours and lessons are available, the group programs are certainly more economical. There are certainly enough to choose from, including inn-to-inn trips, overnighters, and fall foliage tours. They also offer a 5-day summer camp for kids in July and August.

Places to Stay in Northwest Vermont & the Champlain Valley

BURLINGTON

Lang House on Main Street
360 Main St.
(802) 652-2500 or (877) 919-9799
langhouse.com
Moderate to expensive
Eleven guest rooms offered in this 1881 former residence in the Hill Section of Burlington. Afternoon tea is served, and breakfast is created by a chef. Open year-round. Special rates available during special events.

The Inn on Trout River
241 Main St.
Montgomery Center
(802) 326-4391 or (800) 338-7049
troutinn.com
Moderate to expensive
An 11-room B&B in the newly restored 1890 mansion of the owner of the town's first automobile. Views of Trout River abound. Continental breakfast included in room rates. New owners as of 2012 have updated many aspects of this inn.

STOWE

Edson Hill Manor
1500 Edson Hill Rd.
(802) 253-7371 or (800) 621-0284
edsonhillmanor.com
Moderate to expensive
A 25-room inn on what was once the estate of a Colorado mining prospector. A summer base for hiking and horseback riding and in winter for tobogganing, sledding, or cross-country skiing. Award-winning dining and wine cellar. Complimentary afternoon tea and pastry.

Golden Eagle Resort
511 Mountain Rd.
Stowe
(800) 626-1010 or (802) 253-4811
goldeneagleresort.com
Moderate to expensive
Located on 40 acres in sight of Mount Mansfield and only 0.5 mile from Stowe Village, this resort is the finish line for the Stowe 8 Miler Run in July. Accommodations are affordable and clean.

Ye Olde England Inne
433 Mountain Rd.
Stowe
(802) 253-7558
Englandinn.com
Moderate to expensive
Award-winning rooms and suites, some with Jacuzzi tubs; all with private baths. Stay in the lap of luxury in their Bluff House Suites—maybe the penthouse?

VERGENNES

Emerson Guest House Bed and Breakfast
82 Main St.
(802) 877-3293
emersonhouse.com
Inexpensive to moderate
A comfortable 1850 Victorian home in downtown Vergennes with personal service that will make you feel at home. A full country breakfast is included with your room rate. Some bathrooms are shared.

WATERBURY

Stowe Cabins in the Woods
Route 100, Box 128
(802) 244-8533
stowecabins.com
Moderate to expensive
Modern, comfortable, and fully equipped cabins located in a beautiful pine-woods setting just off Route 100. Free Wi-Fi in all cabins.

Places to Eat in Northwest Vermont & the Champlain Valley

BURLINGTON

El Cortijo Taqueria & Cantina
189 Bank St.
(802) 497-1668
farmhousetg.com
Moderate
Open daily for lunch, dinner, and evening activities.

The Farm House Tap & Grill
160 Bank St.
(802) 859-0888
farmhousetg.com
Moderate
A "farm to table gastro pub dedicated to showcasing the many local farms and food producers." Open daily for lunch and dinner. Features live music in the beer garden on Thurs from 7 to 9 p.m., weather permitting.

COLCHESTER

Junior's Italian
85 South Park Dr.
(802) 655-0000; for the pizzeria, call (802) 655-5555
juniorsvt.com
Moderate

Authentic Italian cooking from a Bronx, New York, native. In operation since 1992.

ENOSBURG FALLS

Abbey Restaurant
6212 Rte. 105
(802) 933-4747
theabbeyrestaurant.net
Moderate to expensive
Known for hearty portions and Sunday brunch. Open daily at 11:30 a.m. for pub fare, Fri and Sat 5 to 9 p.m. for dining room service, and 9:30 a.m. to 12:30 p.m. for Sunday brunch.

FAIRFAX

The Country Pantry
951 Main St.
(802) 849-0599
countrypantrydiner.com
Moderate to expensive
Under new ownership and better than ever. Open Tues through Thurs 11 a.m. to 8:30 p.m., Fri and Sat 7 a.m. to 8:30 p.m., and Sun 8 a.m. to 3 p.m.

MONTGOMERY CENTER

Bernie's Restaurant
72 Main St.
(802) 326-4682
berniesrestaurantandbar.com
Moderate to expensive
Bernie's is chef-owned and -operated, so you know the food will be

good. Three meals daily from 6:30 a.m. to 11 p.m. Nightly specials.

NEWPORT

East Side Restaurant & Pub
47 Landing St.
(802) 334-2340
eastsiderestaurant.net
Moderate to expensive
With a solid menu featuring prime rib, pot roast, and seafood, it's also known for its chowder. Their salad bar comes with entrees. It overlooks Lake Memphremagog and offers dining on the deck in good weather. Mon through Fri 11 a.m. to 9 p.m., Sat and Sun 8 a.m. to 9 p.m.

RICHMOND

The Kitchen Table Bistro
1840 W. Main St.
Richmond
(802) 434-8686
kitchentablebistro.com
Expensive
A chef-owned bistro located in a historic farmhouse. Offerings change with the seasons and local food is used as often as possible. Some examples are pan-roasted wild king salmon, Maplebrook ricotta gnocchi, braised Boyden Farm pot roast, and more. Open for dinner Tues through Sat, 5 to 8:30 p.m.

TO LEARN MORE IN NORTHWEST VERMONT & THE CHAMPLAIN VALLEY

Church Street Marketplace
2 Church St., Suite 2A
Burlington
(802) 863-1648
churchstmarketplace.com

Franklin County Regional Chamber of Commerce
2 N. Main St., Suite 101
St. Albans
(802) 524-2444
visitfranklincountyvt.com

Jay Peak Area Chamber of Commerce
PO Box 218
Troy 05868
(802) 988-4120
jaypeakvermont.org

Lake Champlain Regional Chamber of Commerce
60 Main St., Suite 100
Burlington
(877) 686-5253
vermont.org

Smugglers' Notch Area Chamber of Commerce
PO Box 364
Jeffersonville 05464
smugnotch.com

Stowe Area Association
PO Box 1230
51 Main St.
(877) GO-STOWE
gostowe.com

Waterbury Tourism Council
PO Box 468
Waterbury 05676
waterbury.org

STOWE

Gracie's
18 Edson Hill Rd.
(802) 253-8741
gracies.com
Moderate to expensive
A good stop for mega-burgers, nachos, sand-wiches, and a general menu of moderately innovative dishes. Portions are generous, and they're open from 5 to 10 p.m.

The Pizza Joint
383 Moscow Rd.
(802) 253-4172
thepizzajoint.com
Moderate
Creative, delicious pies using fresh, local ingre-dients; salads; calzones; and traditional pies avail-able, too.

WATERBURY

Tanglewoods
179 Guptil Rd.
(802) 244-7855
tanglewoodsrestaurantvt.com
Moderate to expensive
Off Route 100 north of Waterbury, an outstand-ing New American menu with a penchant for the Southwest is offered here. Opens at 5:30 p.m. for dinner, Tues through Sun.

NORTHEAST KINGDOM

→

All of the Northeast Kingdom could be considered off the beaten path simply because it's so far removed from everything else. Some of the most sparsely populated areas in the East fall within the boundaries of the counties that make up the Kingdom: Caledonia, Essex, and Orleans.

Credit for the coinage of "the Northeast Kingdom" usually goes to Senator George Aiken, one of the most popular leaders in Vermont history (and who also loved to fish in the region). "Such beautiful country up here," he said in a speech in Lyndonville in 1949, "it should be called 'the Northeast Kingdom.'"

But according to *The Vermont Encyclopedia,* years earlier in the 1940s at least two other men so referred to their region. These were Newport newspaper publisher Wallace Gilpin and former Vermont senator W. Arthur Simpson. Additional legends crop up from time to time as well, a testimony to the uniqueness and beauty of the region, as well as to the fact that no other area of the state so far has been deemed worthy of its own moniker.

The Kingdom contains three of the four grants and gores in Vermont, land parcels that were left over when

NORTHEAST KINGDOM

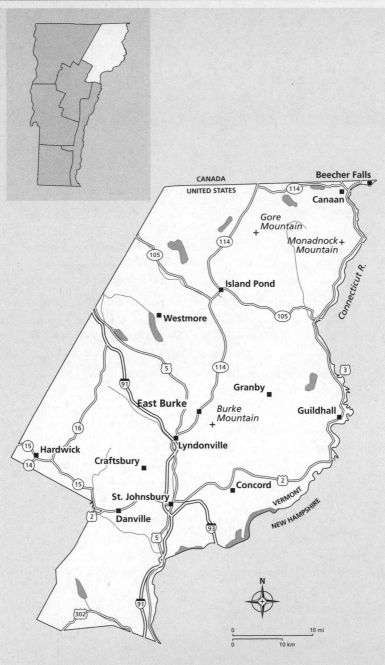

CANADA
UNITED STATES

Beecher Falls

114
Canaan

Gore
Mountain +

Monadnock +
Mountain

114

105

Island Pond

105

Connecticut R.

Westmore

5   114

91

3

Granby

East Burke

Burke
Mountain +

Guildhall

16

15   Hardwick

Lyndonville

14

Craftsbury

15

Concord

2

St. Johnsbury

VERMONT

NEW HAMPSHIRE

2   Danville

93

5

N

302

91

0   10 mi
0   10 km

town boundaries were set. The three—Warners Grant, Warren Gore, and Averys Gore—are nestled side by side in the extreme northeast, one town south of the Canadian border. Both Warners Grant and Averys Gore contain no roads, although Route 114 does cut through Warren Gore. All three, along with the adjacent town of Lewis, add up to a population of zero. In fact, most of the towns in the Kingdom have populations in the three figures, and sometimes less than that.

Towns in this northeastern frontier were settled later than towns in other parts of Vermont. While parts of southern Vermont attracted pioneers from "overcrowded" Connecticut and Massachusetts as early as 1764, much of northeastern Vermont was settled after 1785 and even well into the 19th century.

Some farms in Kingdom towns that front the Connecticut River—towns like Lemington, Guildhall, and Brunswick—still follow the boundaries of the settlement grants and charters of their first settlers. Farmland was laid out in long, narrow strips to allow every settler to have a little of the rich, fertile land that bordered the river, which also served as a water and transportation source.

The Kingdom holds a way of life that disappeared from other parts of the country long ago. Cherish this as you drive over its back roads.

Route 14 North

Route 14 gently climbs out of Montpelier and twists past farms and pastures, while the Kingsbury Branch River plays tag with the road, appearing first on the east side of the highway, then on the west, and finally feeding into Sabin Pond at the northern end of Calais (pronounced CAL-us) and the southern border of Woodbury.

After a gradual climb (this, by the way, is what Vermonters call flat), Greenwood Lake in the town of **Woodbury** appears, its shoreline a bustling community in summer and all but dead in winter. Here and there you'll see old abandoned houses, sagging barns, and granite block walls, remnants of earlier, more prosperous times. Woodbury holds at least two distinctive claims in the Vermont Hall of Fame: (1) The town affirms it sent more soldiers per capita to the Civil War than any other Vermont town, and (2) of the 28 lakes and ponds found in Woodbury, all of their streams and

BEST ATTRACTIONS IN THE NORTHEAST KINGDOM

Architecture on Main Street in St.
Johnsbury

Fairbanks Museum and Planetarium

St. Johnsbury Athenaeum and Art
Gallery

Burke Mountain Ski Area

Northeast Kingdom Country Store

brooks flow out of the town, not into it. (Farther north in Vermont, many of the rivers flow north into Canada, although the Lamoille crosses back into Vermont farther west.)

By contrast, **Hardwick** is a relatively busy center of commerce in the Kingdom. Hardwick served as the final destination for the Hardwick and Woodbury Railroad, which was built in 1896 to transport the mammoth blocks of granite from the quarries in Woodbury north to the mills in Hardwick. The railroad had the distinction of the steepest grades and most hairpin turns in the East. The tracks were taken up in 1940 when the quarries were abandoned.

In 2008 Hardwick landed on the national radar through a townwide move to create a sustainable economy based on local food production. The heart of that effort is the nonprofit **Center for an Agricultural Economy** (140 Junction Rd., Hardwick; 802-472-5362; hardwickagriculture.org), whose backers support community involvement for integrated and responsible agribusiness. They are making huge strides in this area and intend to spread this model beyond Hardwick's borders as they move forward.

The **Perennial Pleasures Nursery & Tea Garden Cafe** (63 Brickhouse Rd.; 802-472-5104; perennialpleasures.net) off Route 16 in East Hardwick is an extensive retail and mail-order nursery that boasts wonderful gardens with more than 900 varieties of flowers, herbs, and shrubs. While they tend to lean toward heirloom and medicinal plants, they have everything from catnip and lemon thyme to roses and lilies. They also have a gift shop with a large assortment of items as well as a seasonal tearoom that offers tea and light lunch in the gardens or conservatory. The nursery and gift shop are open early May to mid Sept, Tues through Sun 10 a.m. to 5 p.m. Tea is offered Memorial Day through Labor Day from 11:30 to 4 p.m., Tues through Sun.

Hardwick boasts fertile soil, as the nursery can attest. According to local legend, in 1796 pioneer Samuel Stevens was exploring what a year later would become the town of Hardwick, named after Hardwick, Massachusetts. He stabbed a spot in the ground with his walking stick near where the house currently stands, and the stick grew into a willow tree.

To drive along a piece of Revolutionary War history, take Route 16 north for 3 miles until you see a road on the left with a sign for Greensboro. Follow this road for 2 miles and continue straight past Tolman Corner until you see Caspian Lake on your right. This stretch of road is part of the aforementioned **Bayley-Hazen Military Road,** a 55-mile road originally authorized by George Washington in 1776 so that Revolutionary War troops could have easy access into Canada to launch surprise attacks against the British. A monument can be found on the east side of the road, overlooking Caspian Lake and just past the first road on the left past Tolman Corner. Colonel Jacob Bayley of Newbury directed 110 workers in building the road from his hometown on the Connecticut River to the town of Cabot, 20 miles away, in 45 days. He paid the laborers $10 a month and half a pint of rum per day.

After one month construction was halted when Washington realized that if the road made it easier for the colonists to reach Canada, then the British would reach the colonists quicker as well.

In April 1779 construction on the road began anew. This time Colonel Moses Hazen led his road builders 35 miles farther into Westfield. But work ceased again six months later when Hazen thought the Brits were gathering steam, and construction that was planned to go through Swanton and up to St. John, Quebec, ended for good. Two years later the war was over, and the road was used as a major artery for development by settlers.

Willey's Store (7 Breezy Ave.; 802-533-2621) in Greensboro Village has frequently been called the quintessential Vermont general store, as have many others around the state. Once you step inside, you'll see that it's the clear winner.

Willey's has camping gear, nails, hinges, fishing lures, greeting cards, toiletries, trashy summer paperbacks, a deli department, a selection of

ANNUAL EVENTS IN THE NORTHEAST KINGDOM

JANUARY

Northeast Kingdom Sled Dog Races
Island Pond
For dates and locations,
call (802) 723-6300;
islandpond.com

MAY

Annual Spring Festival
Hardwick Village
Hardwick
(802) 472-6555
Held in late May; offers a parade, craft fair, horse pulling, a barbecue, and fireworks to celebrate the coming of summer.

JULY

4th of July Celebration
Burke Mountain Ski Area
223 Shelburne Lodge Rd.
East Burke
(802) 626-7300
Visit the mountain for a barbecue, chairlift rides, live music—all topped off with a huge fireworks display.

AUGUST

Burke Mountain Bike 'N' Brew
Burke Mountain Ski Area
223 Shelburne Lodge Rd.
East Burke
(802) 626-7300
Usually the first weekend in Aug. Music, breweries, and bike jumping mania. Bikers can hit the trails all day and then relax around 4 p.m., when you can sample myriad local beers, enjoy a delicious barbecue, and relax to live music in the outdoors. Does it get any better than this? Oh, it does; there are also demos, contests, lessons, and more.

SEPTEMBER

Northeast Kingdom Fall Foliage Festival
Various towns
(802) 563-2472
Held late Sept to early Oct for 6 days throughout the towns of Cabot, Peacham, Barnet, Groton, Plainfield, and others, with one day's festivities (crafts shows, village tours, flea markets, community suppers) in each town.

DECEMBER

Torchlight Parade
Burke Mountain Ski Area
223 Shelburne Lodge Rd.
East Burke
(802) 626-3322
New Year's Eve on Burke Mountain features staff skiing down the trails with lighted torches, followed by dinner and dancing at the base lodge.

wines, phyllo pastry, and of course, maple syrup and Ben & Jerry's. Still run by the Willey family, as it has been for five generations, the store is open 7 a.m. to 5:30 p.m. Mon through Fri, and 8 a.m. to 5:30 p.m. on weekends.

Many consider **Craftsbury** to be the gold medalist in the picture-postcard division of Vermont attractions. But back in 1781, when the town was first chartered, not many of the original grantees could envision the town's promise. In fact, the grantees of most Vermont towns were residents of Massachusetts and Connecticut; a relatively tiny number of them actually acted on their land grants—typically 100 acres. Most sold the land to people who had little to lose by heading north and settling the wilderness. The original grantees were moderately wealthy men who did not want to forgo the luxuries of "civilization" for unknown territories.

The founder of Craftsbury, however, was one of the few exceptions. Ebenezer Crafts, one of the original grantees of Craftsbury, was from Sturbridge, Massachusetts, and served as an officer in the Revolutionary War after graduating from Yale University. He founded the village in 1788 (seven years after the town was chartered) and sent his son, Samuel, to Harvard. After Samuel graduated, he returned to Craftsbury to serve as town clerk and later was governor of the state for two terms.

People still follow Samuel Crafts's example by returning to Craftsbury, but unlike Sam, they stay only for the summer.

There's an old, immaculately kept cemetery right next to one of the buildings on Craftsbury Common. The gravestones of both Ebenezer and Samuel Crafts are in the graveyard, right up near the front. On summer evenings after dinner, stroll through the cemetery and read the inscriptions, some of which date from 1790.

The **Craftsbury Outdoor Center** was begun in 1976 in a defunct private boys' school. A variety of sports weeks are held here year-round, from running and sculling camps to walking weeks. You can stay here without enrolling in one of the special programs and participate in all sports. There are 140 acres, with 600 more acres serving as a nature preserve. Currently 65 miles of trails exist for skiers and hikers to explore, with a few more miles to be added during the next several years. The rooms are what you would expect of a former boys' school, but it hardly matters, since most of the guests spend their time outside being active. You can choose from a room with a private bath or opt to share one. There are also lakeside cottages

OTHER ATTRACTIONS WORTH SEEING IN THE NORTHEAST KINGDOM

Cabot Creamery
Main Street
Cabot
(802) 837-4261
cabotcheese.com
Tour their cheese-making operation
and sample Vermont cheddars.

Chandler Pond Farm
528 Burroughs Rd.
South Wheelock
(802) 626-9460
chandlerpondfarm.com
A 600-acre working organic farm.
Tours are available, as are farm-
fresh foods, including vegetables,
strawberries, maple syrup, sauces,
jams, pork, and dairy.

Great Vermont Maze
1404 Wheelock Rd.
Danville
(802) 748-1399
vermontcornmaze.com
Open Aug to mid-Oct. One of the top
10 mazes in the country.

Old Stone House Museum
109 Old Stone House Rd.
Brownington
(802) 754-2022
oldstonehousemuseum.org
Six buildings on 55 acres. The first
African American in the US to graduate
from college, Alexander Twilight, built
Athenian Hall, which is one of the
buildings.

Stillwater State Park
44 Stillwater Rd.
Groton
(802) 584-3822
vtstateparks.com/htm/stillwater.htm
Located in Groton State Forest, which
offers more than 17 miles of hiking
and more than 20 miles of multi-use
trails. Tent, trailer, and lean-to camping
available.

and apartments available. The daily rate includes a room, some sports fees, and 3 all-you-can-eat, buffet-style meals a day. The food is delicious, with the emphasis on complex carbohydrates to fuel all the exercise you'll get at the center. Vegetarians are amply accommodated, and during summer the vegetables are from the center's own gardens.

The center is open year-round and can accommodate large crowds (think family or high school reunions); just call ahead and discuss your needs with them.

Newport, just south of the Canadian border, is a utilitarian kind of town, blending touches of the 21st century and bilingual traffic signs with the ambience of an old Vermont town. Even though Newport has always depended somewhat on border trade, it's not especially geared to tourists; it's more for Canadians and Vermonters who need to get their business done as quickly and cheaply as possible.

The town—it's actually a city, the only incorporated city in the Kingdom—rises from the shore of Lake Memphremagog, which means "beautiful waters" in the Algonquin language.

St. Mary of the Sea (191 Clermont Terrace; 802-334-5066; materdei vermont.com/St.html) is a Catholic church with a fine view of Lake Memphremagog from its commanding position high on Prospect Street, on the west side of town. This church with twin granite towers is a mariners' church, uncommon so far inland. The dedication stone reads may 1904, and an inscription reads *Ave maris stella,* a statement that combines Mary and the nautical reference point of the North Star. An anchor is carved into the stone, and a lighted figure of Mary stands between the two towers. This landmark is made almost entirely out of local granite and is visible from most of the town at night. The church is open to the public only for Saturday and Sunday services.

Since 2001 **Lago Trattoria** (95 Main St.; 802-334-8222; lagotrattoria .com) in Newport has earned three *Yankee Travel Magazine* Editor's Picks in a row, and has ranked in the top five farm-to-table restaurants in Vermont for 2013. All of the pasta, bread, sauces, and dessert items are home-made and scrumptious. Says *Ski Vermont* magazine, "Chef Frank Richardi has quickly become a ski country star for his thin-crust grilled pizzas, homemade ravioli, and signature dishes like shrimp and clams Amalfi with linguini, dramatically served right in the pan." The seafood is fresh, and all Italian products are imported. A different steak is featured every night. Choose from a pasta *quattro formaggio,* for example: a bit of gorgonzola, fresh Parmigiana Reggiano, romano, and fontina, served with fresh baby peas, cream, and fresh herbs; or maybe the rack of lamb: marinated with a little Vermont maple syrup, fresh rosemary, and Dijon mustard, and grilled to perfection. Frank offers not only specialty martinis, but also an extensive wine list, featuring many fine Italian wines. Open Mon through Sat, 5 p.m. to closing.

The Northeast Corner

Snuggled into the far corner of the state, this region north of St. Johnsbury and bordered by Canada, New Hampshire, and I-91 is to many people the heart and soul of the Northeast Kingdom. While its border with New Hampshire is pretty easy to identify—in all but one tiny spot, you must cross a river to change states—crossing into Canada is less obvious.

What about border guards? When you cross on a road that actually goes somewhere in Canada, there will be the usual border formalities. But at other places, back roads may stray across the line and back again without your even being aware of it. The rule is that if you can't get anywhere from the road, no one cares much. Or so it seems. In reality, however, the entire boundary between the two countries, which is the longest undefended international boundary in the world, is closely watched. Surveillance cameras alert authorities on both sides to any unusual crossings, even on foot. These illegal crossings are investigated, so the casual appearance of the border on remote roads is misleading.

The border is even more fun in *Derby Line.* As you might guess from its name, the town sits right on the boundary line, with residential streets wandering back and forth randomly. The colors of street signs change at the line, but it is otherwise invisible. The *Haskell Free Library and Opera House* is an impressive building that ties Derby Line firmly to Stanstead, its neighboring town in Quebec. The international border is marked by an inlaid wooden strip across the center of the reading-room floor. You can read a book there while sitting in two countries. Upstairs, the theater has the stage in Canada, while the audience applauds from the US. Anyone who plays there instantly becomes an international star.

nowi'mhere, nowi'mnot!

Some homes were built astride the Canada/US border, so one portion of the house is in Canada, and the other in the US. Imagine what fun this was for revenue men during Prohibition. Guests could enter through a "dry" front door and drink quite legally in the kitchen.

Westmore, south of Derby Line, is a popular summer camp area. Westmore was chartered in 1781, but its grantees decided not to organize until 23 years later. Since then the population has grown at a snail's pace, still totaling only a few hundred. If it wasn't for *Lake Willoughby,* there might not even be that much. Virtually all of the tiny town's industry is geared toward summer visitors, from the campground and two restaurants to the six inns and clusters of cottages that overlook the lake.

For all its proximity to tiny Vermont towns—East Haven and Victory—*East Burke* is a relatively sophisticated area and has been named among the 101 Best Outdoor Towns in the US by *101 Best Outdoor Towns.* While *Burke Mountain Ski Area* is not exactly on the top of the list when the topic of Green Mountain ski areas comes up, things may be about to change. In 2012 the owners of Jay Peak purchased Burke Mountain. They assure the public that they are definitely not going to make Burke Mountain anything like Jay Peak. Burke Mountain will stand on its own—literally. It's not part of a mountain range; it is a lone mountain, which makes it different already. Its trails are narrow and tree lined, and the plans are to keep it that way. The owners have decided to embrace the natural attributes of Burke Mountain, and work with them to give skiers a truly Vermont experience.

With that in mind, the owners have pledged to spend more than $100 million over the next several years. Plans include a new 116-room hotel and conference center, the first of 4 new lodges, as many as 60 trails, and new lifts. Other amenities being discussed include an indoor bike park, a tennis center, organic farming, and other innovative ideas. Time will tell where this resort is about to go, but we are sure it will be exciting and totally Vermont.

In the summer and fall, you can drive almost all the way to the summit on the *Burke Mountain Toll Road* (802-626-3322), which is a long novice ski trail in the winter. At any time of year, the views are lovely and include the ridges of Mounts Pisgah and Hoar, with Lake Willoughby between them. From this distance, they look like a single ridge with a giant bite chewed out of the center. The road opens at 8 a.m. and stays accessible until a half hour after sunset, Memorial Day weekend through Oct. The toll money is collected at the entrance to the road and access is always weather permitting.

Located minutes from Burke Mountain Ski Area is the *Northeast Kingdom Country Store* (466 Rte. 114, East Burke; 802-626-4611; nekcountry store.com), where you can browse antiques, fine gifts, Vermont country crafts, pottery, candles, artisan gifts, and more. You can also pop over to The Cafe, the store's restaurant, where you'll find fresh baked breads, gourmet

Visit an Artist's Studio

The Vermont Crafts Council (1344 State St., Montpelier; 802-223-3380; vermont crafts.com) sponsors an annual Memorial Day *Open Studio Weekend,* which gives visitors an opportunity to go into the studios of more than 200 artists and fine craftspeople all over the state. In addition to artists in many media, studios include those of makers of fine reproduction and contemporary furniture, potters, glassmakers, ironworkers, and photographers. Some of the studios offer demos and special talks and exhibits throughout the weekend. You can get a map of the arts tour from the Vermont Arts Council website, by visiting the Vermont Tourist Information centers, and at all the participating galleries and studios.

salads, and simply savory sweets. But that's not all—the building itself is worth the stop. Built in the mid-1800s, it recently underwent a renovation to restore the original woodwork and bring back its former glory. The decor is very much in keeping with the building's history. You will feel as if you've stepped back in time. Stop by for a visit Mon through Thurs, 7 a.m. to 7 p.m., Fri until 8, Sat 8 a.m. to 8 p.m., and Sun 8 a.m. to 6 p.m., year-round.

The Northeast Kingdom Country Store is located on the ***Kingdom Bike Trail*** (PO Box 204, East Burke; 802-626-0737; kingdomtrails.org), part of a multi-use, nonmotorized trail system recently voted Best Trail Network in North America by *Bike Magazine.* Take your pick of mountain biking, trail running, hiking, cross-country skiing, and snowshoeing on miles of trail. The trails are overseen and managed by the Kingdom Trails association, a group of volunteer business owners and citizens who work together to create legal access to these trails (all of which are currently on private land) and to manage their use. The idea was born in 1994 as a way to ramp up economic growth and promote the use of Vermont's beautiful resources in a nondamaging, nonthreatening way. The concept has breathed new life into the area. The association is very conscientious about the use of the trails and lists specific information on their website, especially where to and where not to park. They also sponsor special events throughout the year; see our Annual Events section for more information.

On property that was once part of the 8,000-acre farm of Elmer A. Darling, an enormously successful hotelier in New York and a major benefactor of the town, sits the ***Inn at Mountainview Farm*** (3383 Darling Hill

Rd., East Burke; 802-535-7617; innmtnview.com), a perfect home base from which to explore the Kingdom Trails. Although the farm no longer produces cream, butter, or crops on what at 953 acres was once the largest farm in Vermont, its 440 intact, quiet acres hold farm buildings that will entice you to explore them. So surrounded by beautiful country, you will feel as if you are in the middle of nowhere, when in fact you are only three hours outside of Boston, Massachusetts.

The stately brick main house, which once served as the creamery for the farm, offers 9 rooms or suites and the farmhouse offers 3 more; each room or suite has its own bath. There's an understated, casual elegance to the inn that owner Marilyn Pastore has worked hard to attain. There are several sitting rooms downstairs, an ice chest in the lobby, and braided rugs on all the floors, which are painted cement. The breakfast room still contains the old steam engine that provided the power to run the creamery machines; today antique furnishings are found in the common areas and in each bedroom.

vermonttrivia

You can see Elmer Darling's mansion and huge main barn down the road from the Inn at Mountainview Farm. Both are now privately owned.

A number of restored farm buildings are scattered across the land, and the weather vane atop each tells its purpose: The dairy barn has a cow weather vane that measures 5 feet in length, and on top of the creamery is a butter churn. The clock on top of the 1912 post-and-beam barn chimes on the half hour, and the structure was a model for 19th-century agricultural efficiency. Upstairs, hay was stored. Farmhands would spread hay evenly throughout the barn, almost up to the rafters. When it was time to feed the horses, they'd rake the hay over to what look like half-moon hot-tub structures at the sides of the barn, lift up the covers, and let the hay drop. The horses kept here were about 16 hands high, and you can see where they chewed on the bottom of the barn's windows.

The inn operates as a bed-and-breakfast from mid-May through Oct. During the rest of the year, they offer their town houses for rent for the weekend or an entire week.

About 20 minutes south of East Burke is the town of *Lyndonville,* where you'll find the warm and hospitable *Wildflower Inn* (2059 Darling

Hill Rd, Lyndonville; 802-626-8310 or 800-627-8310; wildflowerinn.com), situated on more than 500 country acres with views over the mountains. When innkeepers Jim and Mary O'Reilly purchased the property in 1984, they set about creating a family-friendly resort. They've succeeded—TripAdvisor recently awarded them the 2013 Certificate of Excellence. Travelers love this place. The grounds are like a village in themselves. Stunning gardens frame every view in the spring, summer, and fall, while autumn brings a panorama of brilliant foliage. The swimming pool is set in the gardens, with a view of its own.

Rates include a delicious country breakfast, complete with homemade maple granola. Yum. You can choose to eat in the farmhouse's dining room or on the porch. You start with a wonderful cold buffet and then move on to hot creations from the kitchen. Afternoon snack is also included in your rate. Don't miss the to-die-for chocolate chip cookies while you sip hot cider or cold lemonade, depending on the season. Dinner isn't included in the rate, but is offered at the inn's restaurant, Juniper's at the Wildflower Inn, with its varied and extensive menu. Reservations can be made online.

There are a bunch of packages you can choose from that offer a variety of activities. You'll also find a barn full of animals to pat and watch, bunk beds in many of the rooms, a sledding hill (with sleds) and lighted skating rink, playground equipment, a batting cage, a pitching machine, a basketball court, a playhouse, and a playroom with games and a trunkful of costumes. A dozen miles of cross-country ski trails (free to guests) wind through the property, and weekend winter carnivals in March bring skating parties, contests, and dogsledding. Sleigh rides and hayrides are available regularly.

On the same property is **Vermont Children's Theater** (2283 Darling Hill Rd.; 802-626-5358; vermontchildrenstheater.com), which for over 20 years has produced two musicals each summer, one a Broadway show and the other written especially for 8- to 13-year-old actors. Performances are held in mid-July and Aug; tickets are inexpensive, or you can watch rehearsals in the afternoons in the 200-seat barn theater.

The **Miss Lyndonville Diner** (686 Broad St. [Route 5]; 802-626-9890) is related to the Miss Vermonter Diner down in St. Johnsbury, but it's not as big as its sister, and there are fewer out-of-state plates in the parking lot.

The original dining car has been enclosed but is still very much in evidence. The just-greasy-enough burgers are served plain and simple or as the

Vermonter, a hamburger-and-thick-steak-fries combo with gravy spooned over both, with a side of slaw. Locals on lunch break hang out at the counter, read the paper, and catch up on local news and the weather. Portions are large and consistently tasty. The Miss Lyndonville is open from 6 a.m. until after supper, whenever the last person leaves.

If it's something sweet you're looking for, head to **Carmen's Ice Cream** (1000 Broad St.; 802-626-1174) for delicious Vermont-made, organic frozen confections. Located within the Lyndon Freighthouse, Carmen's offers more than 80 flavors of ice cream, yogurt, and sorbet, including gluten- and dairy-free varieties—and it's all made locally on a small family farm. They'll even serve Fido a doggie dish or cone with a homemade canine treat. Open daily from 9 a.m. to 8 p.m.

We're not sure how **Trout River Brewery** (58 Broad St., Lyndonville; 802-626-9396; troutriverbrewing.com) got its name, since there is no Trout River that we know of in East Burke, where the brewery used to be, nor in Lyndonville, where it is now. But the name inspires some clever titles for the excellent brews: Hoppin' Mad Trout and Rainbow Red. Hoppin' Mad is an IPA, and Rainbow Red is their flagship brew with a nutty malt flavor and hints of fruit. Scottish Ale is always on their list, as is the Chocolate Oatmeal Stout, which is hearty enough to substitute for dinner. Speaking of which, the brewery serves good pizza (hand-tossed sourdough) from 4 to 9 p.m. Fri and Sat. It doesn't get any better than beer and pizza, does it?

If you need to walk off the pizza or the ale, head over to **The White Market** (128 Main St.; 802-626-5339; whitemarketvt.com) on the green (open daily from 7 a.m. to 10 p.m.) and ask for directions to the 6-mile **Lyndon Covered Bridge Walk,** or download a map of this and other Lyndonville walks from https://secure.bcbsvt.com/files/LyndonvilleWalking Map2012.pdf. This walk takes you by 4 covered bridges. The terrain is mostly level, but there are few sidewalks and some traffic challenges, so be prepared. To learn more about the history of the bridges, visit lyndon-vermont.com/covered-bridges.php.

The town of **Glover,** to the north on I-91, was settled in 1797 by General John Glover, who was granted the town in gratitude for his service in the military during the Revolutionary War. But today Glover's most popular residents are a 180-degree turn from the town's military founder. Near the Glover General Store, turn onto Route 122 to find social commentary at the **Bread and Puppet Museum** (753 Heights Rd., Glover; 802-525-3031; breadandpuppet.org), less than a mile up the road on your left.

Bread and Puppet is a theater troupe that travels all over the world presenting its political ideas to eager audiences. It was established in 1963

The Pond That Isn't There

The well-named Mud Pond was the source of the Barton River, which flowed north, providing power for the grist- and sawmills of Barton and Glover. But in dry summers, such as that of 1810, even the mud dried up, and the mills lay idle. About a mile south, but almost 100 feet higher, was the larger Long Pond, with plenty of water year-round. With his mill idle, owner Aaron Wilson did a little investigating in the mile of marshy brush between these ponds and discovered that their ends were really only 700 feet apart.

A little information can be a dangerous thing, so Wilson persuaded the men of Glover to dig a trench between the two, allowing some of the ample water in Long Pond to spill out and fill Mud Pond, providing water to run the mills downstream. Enough were convinced (possibly by his promise of a keg of rum when the work was done) that a group assembled on June 10 with picks and shovels. By noon, a trench was finished through the soft sand, and most of the men were sampling the rum as a few dug through the last few feet at the north end of Long Pond.

What no one knew was that inside the mound of fine sand holding the lake's end was a lining of packed clay, like the rim of a pottery bowl. When the first pickax broke that rim, the water quickly washed away the supporting sand, and the rim shattered. By the time the one billion or so gallons of water had reached Lake Memphremagog seven hours later, only one house was left in Glover, a few more in Barton, and the fields and pastures were 6 feet deep in sand and mud. Wilson's mill and all the other mills were gone. Trees and boulders were swept away by the wall of water, along with houses, barns, mill machinery, dams, and livestock. Water rose as high as 75 feet above river level in narrow places.

When the pond broke loose, several men ran ahead to warn people to run for high ground, so not a single life was lost. Everyone lost crops and livestock, but they had more than five tons of fish to salt for winter, which they found stranded along the shore, pulled from the mud, or caught in tributary streams into which the fish had fled as the turbulence entered the lake.

Foundations of the church and other buildings you see in Glover are built of stones cut from a 100-ton boulder swept into the village by the flood. And up on Route 16, look for a small sign on the west side of the road marking the low muddy area that was once the 300-acre surface of Long Pond.

on New York's Lower East Side by an artist-actor named Peter Schumann. He began Bread and Puppet by traveling around New England with a stick-puppet show telling stories from the Bible. Then the organization became more radical, using life-size puppets and performing in parades in New York. Schumann moved his troupe to Plainfield, Vermont, in 1970, then to its present location in Glover in 1974.

You'll never mistake them for conservatives, but all types of people used to show up at Bread and Puppet's annual Domestic Resurrection Circus, a two-day event that thousands of people participated in on the theater's pastures.

But the big annual show—so famous that several alternative restaurants as far away as Brattleboro used to close for "Bread and Puppet Day"—is no more. Instead, smaller shows are performed throughout the summer. A list of performances and workshops is provided on the website. The museum is open all summer through October, and if you've never seen the theater's actors perform, the museum can be a little overwhelming. The sign reads enter at your own risk. Don't say you haven't been warned.

Bread and Puppet makes its point using 12-foot-high, larger-than-life puppets with huge heads and tiny bodies. But the exhibits do what a museum should do: make you think. Downstairs in the former horse stable—this is the former Dopp Farm—are montages of previous performances.

If downstairs is striking, then upstairs is an absolute assault on the senses, for everything hangs from the ceiling—a visual cacophony of papier-mâché globes, 12-foot-tall Ben Franklin look-alikes, and more. There's also a box of puppets for adults and kids to play with if inspiration hits.

Across the road is the ***Cheap Art Bus,*** an old school bus filled with art and prints ranging from 10 cents to $15, though most go for around $5. The museum and shop are open every day from 10 a.m. to 6 p.m. June through Oct., and the museum is open the rest of the year by appointment.

St. Johnsbury

St. Johnsbury developed as a busy northeastern Vermont outpost due to its location at the confluence of three major waterways: the Passumpsic, Moose, and Sleeper's Rivers. The Fairbanks family from Massachusetts also influenced the growth of the town. Yes, we said "town"—despite its appearance,

St. Jay, as it's commonly called, is a town, not a city. By building a factory, Thaddeus Fairbanks, inventor of the lever scale, made good on the initial patent he was awarded in 1830.

Today the town seems to have two separate parallel main streets running through it, each with a totally different atmosphere. The lower one, Railroad Street, is the commercial area with facing rows of brick business blocks. But if you have any architecture aficionados in your family, it's the second one, Main Street, you'll want to explore. A great way to do this is to follow the *Historic St. Johnsbury Walking Tour,* which takes you past fine Victorian residences, churches, and public edifices, several of which were designed by the architect Lambert Packard. Some of these are based on the Richardson Romanesque style (which Bostonians know well from the imposing Trinity Church on Copley Square). Maps of the walk are available at the welcome center on Railroad Street or at the St. Johnsbury Athenaeum on Main Street. A podcast can also be downloaded from discoverstjvt.com.

The centerpiece of Main Street (and the tour) is the red sandstone *Fairbanks Museum and Planetarium* (1302 Main St.; 802-748-2372; fair banksmuseum.org), a classic of Richardson style, which contrasts with the Victorian (and also Lambert Packard) but much more perpendicular Gothic style of the North Congregational Church opposite it. This wonderful Victorian "cabinet of curiosities," which began as the private collections of the town's favorite son and benefactor, has an oak barrel–vaulted ceiling with an arcade of cherry and oak display cases forming an upper gallery. The building is as fascinating as its exhibits, which range from an interactive examination of Vermont's wetlands and the creatures that inhabit them to a bizarre collection of Victorian "bug art" portraits of Washington, Lincoln, and others. Be sure to stop at the wildflower identification table, where you will see fresh examples of wild plants in bloom locally during the current week. The requisite stuffed birds are from all over the world, as are the other natural history collections, although the wildlife displays concentrate on Vermont habitats.

Upstairs are old toys, dollhouses, books, and stone tools from an Abenaki grave in Swanton. The "Vermont in the Civil War" exhibit shows everything from medical and dental implements to a saddle used in battle. Downstairs is for the kids—a hands-on nature center complete with wasp hives, frogs, iguanas, and turtles, as well as machines that show some of the basic properties of physics. The museum also serves as an official US weather observation station, and its planetarium offers in its 50-seat theater informational programs on the weather and sky above St. Johnsbury.

The museum is open year-round. Its hours are 9 a.m. to 5 p.m. Mon through Sat and 1 to 5 p.m. Sun, Apr through Oct. From Nov through Mar, the museum is closed on Mon. Planetarium shows are scheduled during open hours, but you should check ahead for days and times. Admission is charged and planetarium shows are extra. A family rate is available.

Although Lambert Packard did not design the *St. Johnsbury Athenaeum and Art Gallery* (1171 Main St.; 802-748-8291; stjathenaeum.org), he did supervise the building of the art gallery, which was constructed to house Albert Bierstadt's *The Domes of Yosemite,* still displayed there.

The building, which is a National Historic Landmark built in 1871, recently underwent renovations. It serves as the town's public library, and welcomes visitors into the athenaeum, an immense dark room with a lone skylight overhead and quietly whirring ceiling fans. The sign at the door says welcome to the nineteenth century, which is true if you ignore the current best-sellers out in the main part of the library.

The paintings include several religious subjects from the Italian school, as well as classic ships-at-sea and others. The art is a mix of American and

They Carried It to the End of the Earth

When Albert Bierstadt's monumental painting *The Domes of Yosemite* was brought from New York to the St. Johnsbury Athenaeum in 1873 to be displayed in its specially built gallery, New York critics lamented it as a "profound loss to civilization." The 10-by-15-foot painting is one of the largest landscapes in the US and is appropriately (well, maybe not, according to 19th-century New Yorkers) housed in the country's oldest Victorian art gallery still in its unadulterated original form. Most other galleries have been modernized, but like the neighboring Fairbanks Museum, the Athenaeum remains a pristine monument to the age of great public museums.

This appropriation of things from the Big Apple didn't end with the painting, however. The street clock at the corner of Main Street and Eastern Avenue in front of the Athenaeum was formerly in the old Grand Central Station and was placed here in 1910, where it has told time (but not always the correct time) ever since.

European styles, and the collection, as well as the building, was financed by Governor Horace Fairbanks. The showcase at the entrance has books and ephemera from the early days of St. Johnsbury.

The athenaeum is open Mon through Fri 10 a.m. to 5:30 p.m., and Sat 10 a.m. to 3 p.m.

One of the more interesting dining spots in St. Johnsbury is **Kham's Thai Cuisine** (1112 Memorial Dr. [Route 5]; 802-751-8424; khamsthai.com). The chef-owners are from Thailand, and the dishes they prepare are wonderful. They use really fresh veggies and you have your choice of vegetarian, chicken, fried or steamed tofu, beef, pork, shrimp, squid, or scallops in all of the dishes served. You also have a choice of degrees of "hot"—one to four stars—one of the few restaurants anywhere that will actually make it hot enough for true Thai fans. The atmosphere is pleasantly upscale. It's open Mon through Sat 11 a.m. to 9 p.m.

theartistwillnot seeyounow

In the 19th century, a self-educated artist named Russell Risley lived in the town of Kirby, which lies north of Route 2 as you head east out of St. Johnsbury. Russell and his sister devised a series of levers, pulleys, and trapezes to transfer full and empty milk pails between their house and the barn. They lived as virtual hermits; instead of visiting with real people, Russell painted pictures of neighbors and prominent figures on the side of his barn. Although people came from all over to see his creations, Russell was, after all, a loner at heart; thus, he painted a sign that said SMALLPOX and thereby solved his problem.

If you are in St. Johnsbury on a Monday night from mid-June through mid-August, you can attend the **Courthouse Park Band Concerts** held in the town center. If you thought these outdoor band concerts had gone the way of the Edsel, guess again. Hosted by the **St. Johnsbury Band** (stjohnsburyband.org), the concerts begin at 7:30 p.m. and are free.

Another good place from which to explore the Kingdom is Lower Waterford, which lies close to the Connecticut River along Route 18, a meandering country road between I-93 exits 1 and 44 (in New Hampshire). It's a cozy settlement of very few buildings, surrounded by beautiful hills. It is here you will find **Rabbit Hill Inn** (48 Lower Waterford Rd; 802-748-5168; rabbithillinn.com), one of the premier small inns in the state, and indeed the entire country, as well as one of the friendliest. Its white-columned facade dominates the town and is perhaps why the town is reputed to be the most photographed in the state. The inn is country elegant, beautifully appointed but as comfortable as a visit to your best friend's house. Each room is furnished with quality antiques or reproductions and plenty of reading lights. Little details include lighted vanity mirrors, a silent heating system (no roaring blowers or clanging radiators), and coffeemakers. Most have spacious sitting areas (the smallest room has space for two large wing chairs), and each is different in style.

The public rooms for guests are just as comfortable and are plentiful. A big fireplace invites guests to curl up in front of it, and an intimate lounge is well stocked with wines as well as a full bar. Hospitable innkeepers Brian and Leslie Mulcahy pay attention to every detail and always seem to have time to chat unhurriedly with guests and suggest places for them to visit in the area. This thoughtful couple has assembled neat packets of brochures to accompany travel instruction sheets for a variety of special interests, from antiques and shopping to outdoor sports.

Rabbit Hill excels at working with local attractions and businesses to give guests real Vermont experiences, several of which they offer as midweek or weekend packages. You can choose from biking tours, guided ATV and snowmobile tours, a zipline adventure package, or mountaintop picnic or lazy river paddling packages—so many from which to choose. Browse their website for details. Don't forget to check out their mid-week specials for some great deals.

Concord, on Route 2, claims the distinction of being home to the first school in America specifically founded to train teachers. The **First Normal School,** as it was called, was founded in 1823 by the Reverend Samuel Read Hall. The house is 2.5 miles south of Route 2; follow the signs to Concord Corners. The house is not open to the public.

From Route 2, follow signs to Granby and Victory, a left turn as you're headed east. The first few miles of the route are paved, and lots of hardwoods line the road, which follows the curve of the Moose River. At the Victory town line, the road turns to dirt as you enter the **Victory Basin Wildlife Management Area,** almost 5,000 protected acres where deer, bear, grouse, and woodcock roam freely. This is Vermont's largest boreal forest, and the fruits of Fred Mold's labor. For many years Mold worked to have this management area created. Mold was also the director of the Fairbanks Museum and Planetarium from 1948 until his death in 1975, and worked diligently to, um, mold the museum into what it is today. He had a love of the outdoors and a great respect for preserving it; his two jobs went hand in hand.

A couple of miles into the bog, if you're sharp-eyed, you'll see to your left a boulder with a plaque that reads: IN MEMORY OF FRED MOLD, WHO WORKED TO PRESERVE VICTORY BOG. IN HIS ROUND OF DAILY LIFE, HE GAVE OF HIMSELF. HE CARED ABOUT THE 'LEAST OF HIS BRETHREN' AND TOOK THE TIME TO EVEN FEED THE BIRDS. WHERE HE MET A STRANGER, THERE HE LEFT A FRIEND. 1921–1975.

This area was the site of a huge and long-running logging operation. In the beginning, the river was the way to transport the logs out of the forest. Sometimes logs were piled along the river until the snowmelt allowed them to float down to sawmills. Often there were log trains that were miles long, all coming from different places, but heading to the same one. In 1927, however, Comerford Dam was built across the Connecticut River, effectively cutting off the water supply to this area. But Vermonters weren't to be discouraged. The railroad replaced the river as the main type of transportation. Small railroad tracks gave way to larger ones the closer to town you came. Today remnants of these tracks can be found throughout the wildlife area. There is even said to be a small steam engine hidden in the vines and tree cover, but not many have been able to find it.

It's a nice place for a picnic, surrounded by a quiet pine forest and giant spruce trees. There are miles of old logging roads and unmarked trails to explore, and we suggest you stay to these trails. This is a vast area and it would be easy to become lost. Never hike alone and always tell someone where you're headed and when to expect you back. The area is managed by the Vermont Fish & Wildlife Department (1 National Life Dr., Montpelier; 802-241-3700; vtfishandwildlife.com).

On the other side of the bog, a right turn in the village of Gallup Mills (which is still part of the town of Victory) brings you through little Granby, the last town in Vermont to get electricity. That was in 1962. As you head on toward Guildhall, watch the right-hand side of the road for an old garage covered with license plates—literally covered. There are plates from Vermont and other states and from many years—1962, 1959, Maine, California, New York, New Hampshire, Nevada, Connecticut, Washington. Old vanity plates read salty, topcat, teach, chess. The sign on the garage reads no trespassing, so feel free to look, but please don't stop and linger.

Guildhall is the only town in the world with this name. The Essex County Courthouse is here, along with more houses than you've seen for many miles if you arrived here via Victory Basin. Route 102 wends its way north, playing tag with the Connecticut River to the town of Maidstone. This is prime hunting country, and landowners are pretty liberal about allowing hunters on their land. Instead of the posted NO TRESPASSING/NO HUNTING signs that are common in the southern part of the state, HUNTING BY PERMISSION signs abound. Often the landowners offer themselves out as hunting guides to people who don't know the territory.

youmightaswell hearitfromus

It's a classic border tale, one of many told along the Connecticut River, and you're bound to hear it if you hang around long enough. When the exact location of the border was finally established, the local selectmen went to visit an elderly Vermonter whose home, according to the new line, was now in New Hampshire. They feared that the shock would be too much for him and took the local doctor along just in case. But they needn't have worried. A happy smile broke out on the old gentleman's face at the news, and he replied with fervor: "Good, b' God, I don't think I could've survived another one of those Vermont winters!"

The entrance to **Maidstone State Park** (5956 Maidstone Lake Rd.; 802-676-3930; vtstateparks.com/htm/maidstone.cfm) is in the town of **Brunswick.** This is the most remote of Vermont's state parks, and has been since 1938. The 5-mile dirt access road proceeds to Maidstone Lake, a clear, cool glacier-made lake, and the park, which even in summer is uncrowded throughout its 469 acres. There are 71 campsites (tent, trailer, and lean-tos). There is a sanitary dump station, but no hookups. Once you're settled, you won't be bored; you can boat (rentals available), fish, swim, hike, mountain bike, picnic, and, most important, relax. There are hot showers in 3 out of 4 bathhouses, but bring along your quarters to use them. Listen for the loon cries from the lake. The park is open daily Memorial Day through Labor Day from dawn to dusk.

In Lemington the **Columbia Covered Bridge** crosses over into Colebrook, New Hampshire. The bridge was built in 1912 by Charles Babbitt to replace a previous one that had been destroyed by fire. It stood for almost 70 years before being renovated to the tune of more than $100,000 in 1981. Today it stands proud as the most northerly bridge to span the Connecticut River and connect Vermont and New Hampshire. It is listed on the National Register of Historic Places. Also of interest is the granite US/Canada boundary marker on the slope of the river on one side of the bridge.

The land that surrounds this bridge is sparsely populated, and appears to revel in its isolation. It has thrived for years, hidden away from the rest of the world and from most human influence, with scarcely more than 100 residents in the 20,532-acre town.

This makes **Canaan,** the next town north, seem like a metropolis by comparison, with a number of Christmas tree farms, dairy farms, and a couple of restaurants in town. One place that consistently gets wonderful reviews as a home away from home in the middle of the wilderness is **Jackson's Lodge and Log Cabins** (213 Jackson's Lodge Rd., Canaan; 802-266-3360 [in season], 802-266-7053 [off season]; jacksonslodgevt.net). Located on the eastern shores of crystal-clear Lake Wallace, Jackson's Lodge has been welcoming travelers since 1926, but not necessary under the same name. A man named Harry Marshall first built the camps along the pristine lake to accommodate fishermen and their families who wanted a place to fish and relax. Marshall successfully operated his camps until 1958, when Elmont Jackson purchased the property and turned it into Jackson's Lodge and Log Cabin Village. He and his wife and eventually their six daughters all worked together in the business and added a successful restaurant that hosted live bands on Saturday nights. In 1986 daughter Gloria purchased the business from her parents and has been running it with the same attention to detail ever since.

The cabins are pet- and family-friendly. While they are rustic and technology-free, television, phones, and Internet are available at the main lodge, which is pet-free for those seeking a non-Fido vacation.

isthatfish americanor canadian?

It's interesting to note that the US/Canadian border is somewhere in the middle of Wallace Pond. If you can find the exact point with a boat, you can fish in two countries at once.

While you are there, you won't be bored. There's always swimming and relaxing at the lakeside beach, or you can hunt, fish (rowboats and lifejackets are available), golf at the nearby country club, hike, bike, play tennis, kayak, and explore neighboring Canada if you wish. There are inside activities, too, if it should happen to rain. So many guests return year after year, the Jacksons must be doing something right.

Just north of Canaan is the one tiny place where New Hampshire and Vermont share a land border. The Connecticut River turns due east at **Beecher Falls,** while the border continues to run generally north. Canada is directly north, and although the line of the US-Canadian international boundary was set in the 1800s by the Webster-Ashburton Treaty, the two states continued to dispute the exact location of the line for many years. The issue finally went to the supreme court of the US Boundary Commission in 1934, and the definitive line was drawn.

You can cross it on a road that leaves Beecher Falls and follows the river to the right, while the main road continues left to the international line and the customs control point. The river is a lazy stream here, and as you follow it, you can see cars on Route 3 in New Hampshire on the other side. After the pavement ends, and just as you're sure you must have strayed over into Canada by mistake, you'll see a *granite boundary marker* set at an odd angle on the left side of the road. Its position is skewed because

Really Do Be Wary of Moose

As you drive in this part of the state, especially along Route 114, which parallels the international border, you'll see an increasing number of signs warning MOOSE CROSSING or MOOSE NEXT 12 MILES or MOOSE NEXT 5,000 FEET. These are not tourist advertisements to tell you the best sites for wildlife watching. They are serious warnings to sharpen your peripheral road-scanning skills to avoid a collision with the most dangerous animal in the northern woods. Slow down when you see these signs, and be especially watchful on overcast days, in the early morning and evening, after dark, and early in the spring. Moose don't dent cars, they total them—and often the driver and passengers as well. Nearly everyone up here knows a family that has lost someone to a moose collision, a more frequent occurrence as the moose population increases. Take a good look at the stuffed moose in the Fairbanks Museum in St. Johnsbury, and picture it flying over the hood of your car. You'll understand why you should slow down in moose country.

it sits directly astride the border, and on one half is carved: Town/Canaan, Vermont and on the other, Line/Pittsburgh, New Hampshire. Cross that line and you'll need a copy of *Off the Beaten Path New Hampshire* to guide you.

The town of *Averill* is large, with an area of 24,320 acres, and was one of the first towns in the Kingdom—not to mention the state—to be chartered, in 1762. But the town was never organized and today has only a dozen or so year-round residents.

Nestled within this community, however, you'll find **Quimby Country Lodge and Cottages** (1127 Forest Lake Rd.; 802-822-5533; quimbycountry .com), Vermont's oldest sporting camp at more than 100 years old. Today Quimby's is a rustic, 1,000-acre resort tucked into the woods on the shore of Forest Lake, but still a favorite with sportsmen (and -women) and their children. The best way to describe this unique place is as a summer camp for families. Guests are close to Great Averill Pond and Little Averill Pond, remote bodies of water that are superb for fishing, swimming, and boating. Meals are family-style and feature food sourced locally when possible; lodging is either in the big lodge or in one of 20 rustic cabins. There are no televisions, but Wi-Fi access is available.

Quimby's motto is "Where nothing ever changes," and apart from the addition of a more dependable electrical system, that's quite true. During the summer, rates (which include meals) are a bit higher than in the spring and fall, but include a full program, with counselors, for children (Quimby's is open from mid-May through mid-Oct). Cottages with kitchens begin with a base rate per person with significantly reduced rates for each additional guest, but without meals. In the spring, these cottages are popular with fishermen and birders, who enjoy seeing the migrating flocks that stop around the lake. Wildflowers are at their best in June, with lady's slipper carpeting the ground in places. In September the lakeshores are painted in bright leaves. All the kayaks, boats, tennis courts, and other facilities are available off-season as well, but you have fewer people with whom to share them.

Norton's claim to immortality is that, while it was the first town to be granted a charter in the state, it was among the last to be settled, in 1860. To reach Norton from any other part of Vermont, travelers first had to travel north into Canada and then travel south into the town center, which straddles the international boundary line. This route, understandably, caused the delay in settlement.

Travel about a half an hour south down Route 114 and you come to the town of **Brighton,** which incorporates the village of **Island Pond**—a place with quite an illustrious past. A religious group known as the Twelve Tribes came to town in 1977 to escape opposition it was facing elsewhere, but it wasn't peace its members would find here. Amid allegations of child abuse, the group struggled to maintain their beliefs in a town where it wasn't understood. In 1984 state police and state social workers conducted a raid and retrieved more than 100 children from the group. Upon further investigation, the children were immediately returned, and the raid deemed unconstitutional. The group continues to live in town, some say peacefully; others say they have struck a balance with the townspeople by merely tolerating each other. Mystery writer Archer Mayor, who lives down near Brattleboro, based his 1990 novel *Borderlines* on the religious group.

About 12 miles east of Island Pond on Route 105 you will find the headquarters and visitor center for the **Nulhegan Basin Division of the Silvio O. Conte National Fish and Wildlife Refuge** (Route 105, Brunswick; 802-962-5240 or 802-962-5396; fws.gov/r5soc/come_visit/nulhegan_basin_division.html). Named after Massachusetts Congressman Silvio O. Conte, this refuge was established in 1997 and boasts the state's only "viable population" of spruce grouse. Bird enthusiasts will delight in a possible glimpse of such rare species as Wilson's warblers, gray jays, olive-sided flycatchers, rusty blackbirds, black-backed woodpeckers, and three-toed woodpeckers. More than 100 species of birds use this area as a breeding ground; that's paradise to birders everywhere. Others who call this refuge home include moose, black bear, white-tailed deer, snowshoe hares,

canyouhearit?

Stand on the shore of Island Pond, close your eyes, and listen for the long-ago bustle of a town where the most valuable resource in the midst of the Industrial Revolution was this body of water. The pond once served as the outlet for the tributary off the Pherrins River that was used as a transport for floating logs from Norton and Canada. Island Pond—the village—was also known as the halfway point between Montreal and Portland, Maine, on the Grand Truck Railway, part of the larger St. Lawrence and Atlantic Railroad, the first international railroad. The railroad station still stands today as a testament to the town's important role in history.

squirrels, beavers, fisher cats, coyotes, snakes, turtles, frogs (lots of them), and all sorts of fish in its rivers.

There are a number of ways you can explore the basin. There are 40 miles of gravel roads that will take you through the area. These are open to cars for most of the year with the exception of winter (roads are not plowed) and mud season (you'll just get stuck and make a mess of things). You can, however, take your properly registered snowmobile, snowshoes, or cross-country skis across the network of groomed trails in the basin when it's covered in snow. Be aware that when conditions are right, you will be sharing these roads with logging trucks: Keep to your own side and stay vigilant. Bicycles, ATVs, and horses are not allowed on these roads. If in doubt, call (877) 811-5222 for road conditions.

we're talking huge

Wrap your brain around this tidbit from the refuge's website: "Currently the Refuge is over 34,000 acres in size and includes six divisions and seven units in the four-state area that includes portions of Connecticut, Massachusetts, New Hampshire, and Vermont." That's huge.

Prefer exploring under your own steam? Then the Nulhegan River Trail is for you. This 1-mile loop leaves from the visitor station in Brunswick and travels over stone steps and bog bridges. More trails are planned, but for now if you want to go farther, take to the roads, but again, be vigilant.

Have little ones or slower walkers with you? Then check out the boardwalk through the Mollie Beattie Bog, named for the Vermont native and former director of the US Fish and Wildlife Service. This 200-foot self-guided walkway is fully wheelchair accessible, too. You'll be able to see wildflowers, wildlife, and more from this boardwalk, and it has informative signs along the way.

Hunting and fishing are also allowed within the basin. Please check the website for details and always follow all pertinent state guidelines.

Wildlife Division offices are normally open weekdays from 8 a.m. to 4:30 p.m., but staff are often out in the field, so if you need to talk to one of them it's best to call ahead to make sure someone will be in the office. Maps of the basin are available at the entrance kiosks as well as online. Same rules apply here: Never hike alone and always tell someone where you're going and when you expect to be back.

South of St. Jay

The valley south of St. Johnsbury is a pretty, rural area where many artists have been inspired to call such towns as Peacham and Barnet home. Farms are interspersed with crisp white Capes and rolling vistas of the mountain ranges and lakes that characterize Vermont.

At the **P&H Truck Stop** (2886 Rte. 302, Wells River; 802-429-2141) in the north end of the town of Newbury, *thick* is the watchword, whether you order omelets, meat loaf, pork chops, fish chowder, or onion rings. This is an old-fashioned kind of truck stop where locals, truckers, and travelers all converge to chow down on delicious and hearty real food. The truckers have their own section upstairs to eat in and relax, while families sit downstairs.

The menu is written in both French and English. Don't pass up some of the homemade bread at P&H: white, oatmeal, whole wheat, or cinnamon raisin. Called a "rare gem" by Roadfood.com's Michael Stern, P&H Grill is open from 6 a.m. to 10 p.m., 7 days a week. More than a few southern Vermonters have been known to drive up to Wells River for a piece of Reese's Pie—made with chocolate cream, chocolate pudding, and peanut butter, an exact replica of the candy—or maple cream pie.

The **William Scott Sleeping Sentinel Monument** is just down the road about 5 miles west of Groton Village. During the Civil War, Groton native William Scott enlisted in the Union army as a member of Company K of the Third Vermont Infantry Regiment. He drew night duty one evening, then stood in again the next night for a fellow soldier who was ill. Private Scott fell asleep and was court-martialed; however, President Lincoln stepped in and pardoned him, rescuing him from the firing squad. Scott went back into battle and died on a Virginia battlefield seven days after his 23rd birthday, on April 16, 1862. This monument to Scott was carved by the James W. Main Granite Company from Groton. On June 25, 1936, it was dedicated by the Grand Army of the Republic on land not far from the house where Private Scott had lived, now only a cellar hole.

Route 232 North cuts through **Groton State Forest** (802-584-3822) just west of the village. More than 37 miles of hiking trails and gravel roads traverse this forest's 26,000 acres. Mountain bikers and equestrians also enjoy these trails. Campgrounds are scattered around the forest as well.

In **Danville** is the headquarters and bookstore of the **American Society of Dowsers** (184 Brainerd St.; 802-684-3417; dowsers.org), which is open to the public. Dowsing is the ancient art of locating underground water sources using simple tools, and you can take free lessons here Mon through Fri between 8 a.m. and 4 p.m. There are also weekend workshops; check the website for the latest information. The store here carries tools and books on dowsing and other New Age subjects. The society's annual convention is held in late July or early August at Lyndon State College, where you can sit in on basic, expanded, and specialized classes and a wide variety of lectures on dowsing and related topics, including earth energies, feng shui, and labyrinths. Behind the headquarters building is a labyrinth of raised earth that you are welcome to visit whether the society headquarters is open or not.

If you leave Danville on Brainerd Street, where the Society of Dowsers is located, you will see some of the state's finest views of its neighbors, the White Mountains of New Hampshire. To the left is the Killkenny Range; to the right is Cannon Mountain and Franconia Notch, where Mounts Lincoln and Lafayette are located, with Loon Mountain showing in between their peaks. If you continue straight at the fork, along the top of the ridge, you will enjoy more mountain views before dropping to the **Greenbanks Hollow Covered Bridge.** Built in 1886, it spans Joe's Brook, which is actually a rushing river that drops a significant distance as it cascades past the stone foundations of old mills. The sides of this small, one-lane bridge are open, not enclosed, as most others are.

If you bear left onto Joe's Brook Road, however, you will come to the **Danville Morgan Horse Farm** (1906 Joe's Brook Rd.; 802-684-2251) stretching along a hillside with more White Mountain views. You can visit the farm any day between 9 a.m. and 3 p.m. Small signs point the way from Danville or from Route 5, where you will end up if you continue along Joe's Brook Road.

Places to Stay in the Northeast Kingdom

GLOVER

Rodgers Country Inn Bed & Breakfast
584 Rodgers Rd.
(800) 729-1704
rodgerscountryinn.com
Inexpensive
Situated on 350 acres, this year-round inn offers 5 guest rooms in the main house, all with shared baths. There are also 2 cabins available for guests to rent. Rates cover 2 meals, including a full breakfast.

ISLAND POND

Lakefront Inn & Motel
127 Cross St.
(802) 723-6507
thelakefrontinnislandpond.com
Moderate
Overlooking Island Pond, in the center of town, this is a nicely kept property where snowmobilers congregate in the winter, and people who enjoy water sports can moor their boats or beach their canoes.

ST. JOHNSBURY

Comfort Inn & Suites
703 Rte. 5 South
(802) 748-1500 or (866) 464-2408
vermontvacationland.com
Inexpensive to moderate
Fifteen minutes from the White Mountains, this hotel offers 107 guest rooms and suites. Complimentary hot breakfast buffet served every morning 6 to 10 a.m. Large indoor heated pool, sauna, whirlpool, and fitness center.

The Fairbanks Inn
401 Western Ave.
(802) 748-5666
stjay.com
Moderate
Forty-five rooms and suites close to Burke Mountain. Golf, Ski, and Romance packages available.

WESTMORE

WilloughVale Inn and Cottages
793 Rte. 5A South
(802) 525-4123 or (800) 594-9102
willoughvale.com
Moderate to expensive
Views from each of its 7 unique rooms and 4 lakefront cottages, all furnished in handcrafted Vermont furniture. The inn is closed in Nov and Apr. Overlooking Lake Willoughby.

Places to Eat in the Northeast Kingdom

BARTON

Brown Cow Restaurant
900 E. Main St.
(802) 334-7887
Inexpensive
A great little place serving breakfast.

DERBY

Roasters Cafe & Deli
4267 Rte. 5
(802) 334-6556
Inexpensive
Serves traditional breakfast and lunch comfort food.

HARDWICK

Claire's Restaurant & Bar
41 S. Main St.
(802) 472-7053
clairsvt.com
Moderate
Open Mon and Tues through Sat 2:30 to 10 p.m., Sun 11 a.m. to 9 p.m., serving local ingredients from a menu of fresh ideas. This is truly a hidden gem; you won't go wrong with any choice.

TO LEARN MORE IN NORTHEAST KINGDOM

Barton Area Chamber of Commerce
1296 Cook Rd.
Barton
(802) 239-4147
centerofthekingdom.com

Lyndon Area Chamber of Commerce
14 Depot St.
PO Box 886
Lyndonville 05851
(802) 626-9696
lyndonvermont.com

Northeast Kingdom Chamber of Commerce
Green Mountain Mall
2000 Memorial Dr., Suite 11
St. Johnsbury 05819
(802) 748-3678 or (800) 639-6379
nekchamber.com

Northeast Kingdom Travel & Tourism Association
466 Rte. 114
PO Box 212
East Burke, VT 05832
(802) 626-8803 or (800) 884-8001
travelthekingdom.com

Heart of Vermont Chamber of Commerce
PO Box 111
Hardwick 05843
(802) 472-5906
heartofvt.com

Vermont's North Country Chamber of Commerce
246 The Causeway
Newport 05855
(802) 334-7782
vtnorthcountry.org

EAST BURKE

River Garden Cafe
427 Rte. 114
(802) 626-3514
rivergardencafe.com
Moderate to expensive
In the center of East Burke, the cafe serves lunch and dinner year-round Wed through Sun (closed Tues in winter) in an upbeat setting. Jamaican jerk chicken with black beans, fajitas, pesto salmon, or lamb may be on the menu.

NEWPORT

Baan Thai Cuisine
156 Main St.
(802) 334-8833
Inexpensive to moderate
A pleasant surprise if you like Thai food. The dumpling soup gets high marks, as does the Thai chicken curry.

CENTRAL VERMONT →

Central Vermont has long been defined by its massive granite quarries. This is partly because of the many Scottish, Irish, and Italian granite workers who flocked to the area during the last half of the 19th century. Just as important, though, was the rough topography, which determined where residential areas cropped up, where the best access routes to the quarries were, and where the railroad tracks were laid. Vermonters in this central area had to learn to rely on themselves to a greater extent and in different ways than people in other parts of the state.

But this region of Vermont also has its own particular rugged beauty that is unlike the Green Mountain range to the west or the almost-nautical air of the towns that skirt Lake Champlain. Central Vermont's beauty stems from the rocky riverbeds of the first, second, and third branches of the White River, branches that eventually wind their way down and through the mountains to empty into the Connecticut River. The region's beauty also comes from the stands of second- and third-growth forest that line the sides of the state highways through towns such as Chelsea and Corinth. And it's hard to miss the beauty in the wide valleys

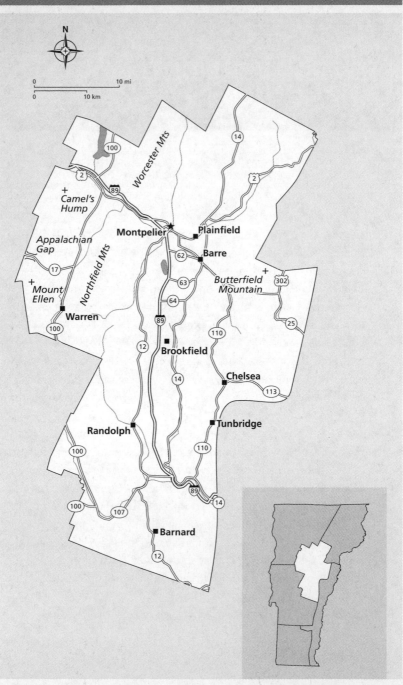

N

0   10 mi
0   10 km

100

14

Worcester Mts

2

89

2

Camel's
Hump

Montpelier   Plainfield

Appalachian
Gap   Barre

Northfield Mts   62

17   63   Butterfield
                                Mountain   302

Mount   64
Ellen
                                         25
Warren   89
100
                           110
              12
                 Brookfield
                            14   Chelsea
                                      113

Randolph   Tunbridge

100   110

                    89
100   107   14

Barnard

12

that cut a swath along Route 12 in Braintree and Brookfield. Only occasionally does a house pop up in some of these spots.

So drive down an unmarked dirt road on impulse, or follow the signs to the quarries in Barre, to see a part of Vermont that is unlike any other.

Barre/Montpelier

The Barre/Montpelier area is the thriving, active heart of this central region and of the state. Barre has been home to thousands of immigrants over the years, from the Italian stonecutters who came to Vermont via Ellis Island to work in the granite quarries to the Irishmen who were recruited in droves to work on the railroad, first to lay track and then to operate the trains.

The granite quarries were founded shortly after the end of the War of 1812. Three grades of granite are still taken from the mountains: a coarse stone ideal for millstones and doorsteps; a less sandy stone for house foundations, much like the stone used to build the state capitol in Montpelier; and the beautiful, almost flawless stone that is used for gravestones and monuments all over the world.

Despite the retail development both downtown and on the Barre-Montpelier Road, *Barre* has managed to retain its working-class, melting-pot flavor for more than a century.

Hope Cemetery (201 Maple Ave., Barre; 802-476-6245), a 75-acre cemetery that dates back to 1895, is on Route 14 just north of Route 302. The cemetery is known for its elaborate carvings of Vermont's early 20th-century stonecutters. New stones are interspersed with old ones, and Italian names are plentiful. When you first enter Hope Cemetery, turn right and drive around its perimeter to see some remarkable granite statuary stones.

BEST ATTRACTIONS IN CENTRAL VERMONT

Hope Cemetery	Brookfield Floating Bridge
Covered bridges in Tunbridge and Randolph	Mad River Glen
	Joslyn Barn
Northfield Falls's covered bridges	

The lifelike sculptures of some of the grave markers are the attraction at Hope Cemetery. Far left and back look for the Brusa stone: A brooding angel, with legs crossed, trumpet on lap, sits beneath a Greek pillar and balustrade sculpture. Here, so as not to detract from the elegance and detail of monuments, small stones with the name of each family member are placed in front of the sculpture.

Also look for Elia Corti's stone, a life-size monument at the crossroads near the back of the cemetery. Corti was a stonecutter who died in 1903. His stone shows his full-size likeness sitting and gazing at the surrounding forest. A few stones away from Corti's is the Cole/Spence stone, complete with contemplative Greek goddess.

Another Brusa monument—located in another patch of stones downhill and secluded from the main yard—depicts a wife comforting her dying husband, who succumbed to silicosis, a lung disease many stonecutters contracted from exposure to stone dust. Directly in front is a sculpture of Gwendolyn and William Halvosa, a husband and wife holding hands, with the inscription, set me as a seal upon thine heart, for love is strong as death.

Heading back out of the cemetery, stop to walk among the stones that don't face the road. Look for a chair that serves as a grave marker, a soccerball stone, and another with a classic Green Mountain view—complete with fence posts, a rifle, a fishing rod, a dune buggy, and lots of trucks. One shows a Shell Oil truck driving through the mountains; another serves as a belated advertisement for the Benedini Well Company, depicting a truck in the process of digging an artesian well.

You will notice a number of Art Nouveau and Art Deco influences in the designs on stones and on the bronze doors of the family vaults along the back row. On the Calcagni monument, an Erté-like angel stands in a colonnade. You will also notice that all the flowers are fresh, not plastic. Bouquets of cut flowers and carefully tended blooming plants decorate many of the burial places, and on weekends you're likely to see families tending these. Since people from the area still bury their loved ones here, Hope Cemetery is not a historical icon from bygone days. It is an active cemetery where Vermonters come to remember their dead, whether they died a century ago or last week. A cemetery is a place to pay one's respects, so remember to show courtesy to people who might not like to be reminded that visitors are taking a casual, interested stroll through the cemetery's grounds.

Population Burst

Barre holds the distinction of having the largest increase in population in Vermont to occur within a decade: With the opening of Ellis Island in New York City and the great influx of skilled granite workers from Scotland, Italy, and Scandinavia, the population of Barre increased from 2,060 in 1880 to 6,812 in 1890. Social unrest soon followed, when the underpaid granite workers got together to demand better working conditions and higher pay.

Though today Barre looks like the solid, conservative, working-class town that it is, back in the late 19th century the politics in town were quite radical. Long before Vermont sent Bernie Sanders, the only independent in the US House of Representatives (and later, the US Senate), to serve in Washington, DC, Barre elected a socialist mayor to serve its people. Early 20th-century anarchist Emma Goldman was arrested in Barre and charged with aiding and abetting the murder of a mayor.

As you might expect, Barre has a lot of public statuary. One such memorial honors 18th-century Scottish poet Robert Burns. More than 10,000 people attended the statue's unveiling on July 24, 1899. Carved by Samuel Novelli and Eillia Corti, the *Robert Burns Memorial* overlooks the lawn of the former Spaulding School building, now home to the Vermont Historical Society, at 60 Washington St. (Route 302).

On North Main Street at the intersection with Washington Street is the *Soldiers' and Sailors' Memorial.* Carved from Barre granite by Gino Enrico Tosi, Enrico Mori, and John Delmonte, the statue takes center stage at Vermont City Park. The statue was so loved that it was adopted as the seal for the city of Barre. If you have a chance to visit this statue, take note of the graceful bench, created by John Mead Howells, that surrounds the memorial. Have one person sit at one end of this bench and whisper. The sweeping curve of the granite will carry the sound all the way to the other side, earning the bench the moniker of the "whispering wall." Be sure to give it a try.

Also on North Main Street at the corner of Maple Avenue is the long-deserved tribute to Barre's Italian heritage. Erected in 1985 in Dente Park is the 23-foot-high statue of a sculptor with a kindly face, so well sculpted that his character seems to shine from within the stone. Designed by Elmo Peduzzi and sculpted by Philip Paini, the statue is dedicated to *Carlo Abate,*

carvedinstone

As you drive around Barre, notice the numerous business signs—real estate offices, the credit union—carved in granite. It's a tradition.

a sculptor who arrived in Barre from Italy and established one of the first art schools in the state.

Speaking of granite, in downtown Barre, about a mile from Hope Cemetery, is the *ReSource Household Goods & Building Material Store* (30 Granite St.; 802-477-7800; restorevt.org). This shop recycles a bit of everything and sells it to local craftspeople, schoolteachers, and others with a little imagination.

Everything at the ReStore is considered to be clean industrial scrap from Vermont businesses. And since the ReStore receives new shipments every week, the inventory is always changing.

All types of fabrics, wooden beads, polished marble bases, packing materials, and clay flowerpots are accepted from businesses. The ReStore also accepts items from local homeowners—old lamps, bubble wrap, magazines, cookie tins, office supplies, and the like, items that would otherwise end up in Vermont landfills. Most of the items are unpackaged and displayed in large bins so that you can pick as few or as many as you need. Open Mon through Sat 9:30 a.m. to 6 p.m.

that'ssomerock band

Rock of Ages quarry (560 Graniteville Rd.; 802-476-3121; rockofages.com) in Barre is 550 feet wide, 0.25 mile long, and 450 feet deep, the largest in the world. The high-quality granite is used for monuments and headstones because its exceptionally fine grain makes it the perfect medium for finely detailed but long-lasting, durable outdoor sculpture. The quarry is the basis of a $200 million-a-year industry that employs more than 1,500 Vermonters. It is also a popular tourist destination with tours available. Visit their website for details.

In East Barre you can visit quarries; the hills that surround the town are actually tailing piles from the quarries. In the center of this town, where the quarry workers lived, is a large antiques mall, a craft center, and the factory store of *Vermont Flannel* (128 Mill St.; 802-476-5226; vermontflannel.com), where you can get good bargains on flannel clothing and fabric. They have a half-price sale in April.

East Barre also has one of the largest multidealer shops in the state. The **East Barre Antique Mall** (133 Mill St.; 802-479-5190; eastbarreantiquemall .com), with more than 12,000 square feet of display space, features antiques and collectibles from glass to furniture, which is one of their strong points. A basement-level area is set aside for bargains. Open Tues through Sun 10 a.m. to 5 p.m. (summer); closed Wed in winter.

Though they're joined at the hip, Barre and Montpelier could never be mistaken for twins, fraternal or otherwise; they're hardly even siblings. Their temperaments are too different. From January through April Vermont's state legislature is in session in Montpelier. Elected representatives from all over the state come to the capital to decide how their state will run for the rest of the year. Then, in May, representatives in both the House and the Senate turn back into their regular selves for the rest of the year—farmers, office workers, and homemakers among them.

Montpelier is a dynamic state capital and the smallest in the nation, with a population of under 10,000. Several colleges are located here; and students, teenage skateboarders, conservative lawyers, and activists who live on nearby communes all know one another and frequently share the enjoyment of a dish of Ben & Jerry's on Main Street. It's not unusual to see men with long hair and batik clothing sitting next to women in suits and high-heeled shoes.

The **New England Culinary Institute** (necidining.com) is one of the foremost in the country, and as part of its training program, it operates 3 dining rooms in Montpelier: NECI on Main, Chef's Table, and La Brioche Bakery and Cafe.

Located on street level and open for breakfast, lunch, and dinner, **NECI on Main** (118 Main St.; 802-223-3188) boasts a sleek, modern, and attractive dining room, with big sliding windows overlooking the street and alfresco dining on the

musicalcapitals

Montpelier was established as the state capital in 1805, with the first statehouse completed in 1808. Previously the capital had rotated throughout the state, its legislators meeting in towns from Burlington to Randolph. In 1838 another, more regal statehouse was constructed and Vermonters thought the matter was settled. But the debate flared up again in 1859 after the second statehouse burned down, leaving only the shell. Montpelier remained the capital, however, rebuilding the statehouse in the same location.

ANNUAL EVENTS IN CENTRAL VERMONT

JULY

Free Summer Band Concerts
Statehouse lawn
Montpelier
Wed at 7 p.m. through July and Aug

AUGUST

Lippitt Country Show
1 Fairground Ln.
(802) 235-2264
lippittcountryshow.com
Old-fashioned horse show in mid-Aug that includes in-hand, under-saddle, and in-harness performances displaying western, English, jumping, and trail skills. Located in the same town where the famous horse Figure is buried. Great family-oriented fun.

SEPTEMBER

Tunbridge World's Fair
1 Fairground Ln.
Tunbridge
tunbridgeworldsfair.com
(802) 889-5555

Held mid-Sept when about 30,000 people cram into this tiny town, creating the state's longest and worst traffic jams on record, but it's worth it for all the festivities.

DECEMBER

Live Nativity Pageant
Joseph Smith Birthplace
357 LDS Lane
South Royalton
(802) 763-7742
lds.org/locations/joseph-smith-birthplace-memorial
During Thanksgiving weekend a live nativity is presented, including live animals, followed by a lighting ceremony and free cider and donuts. The grounds are decorated for the holidays and visitors are invited to explore.

portico in good weather. As expected from a culinary school, the menu is interesting and the fare well prepared with a dedication to farm-to-table selections. Soups and starters include such things as cream of zucchini soup (served hot or cold), creamy chicken fritters, and prosciutto and green bean salad. If you want a sandwich, you can choose from an open-face barbecue brisket served with sweet potato chips, or a grass-fed beef burger served on fresh-baked ciabatta role with hand-cut fries. Entrees include such creations as jerk pork loin served with apple cabbage slaw, potato gnocchi with fresh tomato, zucchini-basil oil, and Parmesan *tuile,* or an interesting and creative daily special. Open Tues through Sun for lunch 11:30 a.m. to 2 p.m., for light fare 2:30 to 5:30 p.m., and for dinner or lounge menu 5:30 to 9 p.m.

Sunday brunch is offered 10 a.m. to 2 p.m.; reservations are suggested and can be made online.

Chef's Table (118 Main St.; 802-229-9202) is the domain of second-year students. A bit more formal, its innovative dinner-only menu is always changing to incorporate the freshest in-season ingredients with an emphasis on Vermont products, including native lamb, duck, hams, and cheeses. Chef's Table is open 7 days a week, 8 a.m. to 9 p.m.

Located diagonally across the street from its two sister restaurants, *La Brioche Bakery & Cafe* (89 Main St.; 802-229-0443) is a European-style bakery, a good place for a light continental breakfast or a soup and salad lunch. A great place for a sugary concoction any time of the day. There are tables indoors and outdoors on a plaza raised just above sidewalk level. Arrive early for the best selection; the students get there at 4 a.m. to start the baking. The doors are open Mon through Fri 7 a.m. to 5 p.m., Sat 7 a.m. to 3 p.m.

While not exactly off the beaten path, the *Inn at Montpelier* (147 Main St.; 800-223-2727; innatmontpelier) is still a very cool place to stay, and very much steeped in history. Throughout the years, the houses that compose the inn have been home to the well-known proprietor of the Union House Tavern but unsuccessful gambler, a US senator, a prominent if unkempt doctor, a wealthy businessman and later his daughter, and a successful construction business owner and builder of the city's first brick apartment building. The in-depth history is explained in more detail on the inn's website.

Both houses were built in the 1800s and have often been linked together throughout their history. Today they offer a total of 27 guest rooms, all with private baths and individually decorated and furnished in antiques and reproductions. The rest of the interior is also warm and comfortable, with fireplaces, fine woodwork, and grand staircases. Plan to be there long enough to enjoy the wraparound front porch overlooking the shady street. It is one of the nicest you'll sit on anywhere, and the relaxing atmosphere of the inn will make you want to do just that. There's even a little in-house bar, so you can enjoy a glass of wine on the porch. The inn is only a block from the center of Montpelier, but in a town so small, this means you're still in a quiet residential neighborhood. Rates are moderate to expensive, but include a large continental breakfast complete with baked goods from Labrioche Bakery & Cafe. Yum.

1927flood

In late fall of 1927, the yellow house on Main Street was severely damaged in a flood—the worst in the town's history. Waters rapidly rose while owner Bertha Baird and her children scrambled to second floor. They refused offers of rescue and waited out the floodwaters, which reached within 2 feet of the first-floor ceiling.

Located near the Inn at Montpelier, the *Vermont State House* (2 Gov. Aiken Ave.; 802-828-0386; vtstatehouse.org) is an interesting stop, with its ornate halls and floors of—what else would you expect?—marble. Flags from the Civil War decorate the walls, along with portraits and other paintings. You can wander on your own (we suggest using the audio tour, which you can pick up at the Sergeant of Arms office), or take a more formal tour with a guide, offered weekdays July through Oct on the hour and half hour from 10 a.m. to 3:30 p.m. and Sat from 11 a.m. to 2:30 p.m. During this time, the legislature is not in session, opening more of the building for you to see. From Nov through June, tours must be scheduled in advance by calling (802) 828-1411. The building is open year-round weekdays from 7:30 a.m. to 4:15 p.m., and on Sat from 11 a.m. to 3 p.m. from July to Oct only. Admission is always free.

Downtown Montpelier presents a remarkable architectural heritage, and a walking tour is the best way to admire all the buildings that line it. As you leave the statehouse, look to the right, across the street at the *Edward Dewey House* (128 State St.). As Queen Anne as you can get, this is the first of 12 stops on the *State Street Walking Tour.* With all the variety this late-1800s style embodied, notice the different shingles, rooflines, and windows. Turn left and walk down State Street, past the flamboyant Romanesque *Department of Agriculture* building. Nothing could be further from the simple lines of the farms this agency represents; like the Queen Anne house up the street, it seems never to repeat anything, with a potpourri of different windows and roof styles. A tower, bay, and turret further complicate its design, which is even more embellished with a carved wooden frieze above the front door.

The clean, symmetrical lines of the 1870 building next door are a nice contrast with their tall windows and straight columns. This building houses the *Vermont Department of Personnel.* Opposite is the elegant reconstruction of the *Pavilion Office Building,* which once housed legislators during sessions and now houses state offices and the Vermont Historical Society (see description later in this section). Its bricks were made from molds dating from the 1800s, and some of the original architectural ornaments, such as keystones and spindles on the porch, are originals from the earlier building.

Three buildings on the same side of the street in the next block represent different stages of the federal period, with its clean, well-balanced shapes based on the Georgian style then popular in England. Number 107, behind the service station, shows more of the Georgian lines in its steep roof and balanced chimneys. Number 99 is more federal, with the characteristic recessed doorway topped by a fanlight. Number 89, next to it, is quite similar and may have been one of the first houses on State Street. On the corner is the Greek revival *Washington County Courthouse,* and behind it on Elm Street is the *old brick jail,* which was transformed in the early 1900s to a flat-roofed business block; you can see where the new brickwork began.

OTHER ATTRACTIONS WORTH SEEING IN CENTRAL VERMONT

Sugarbush Ski Resort
1840 Sugarbush Access Rd.
Warren
(802) 583-6300
sugarbush.com
Huge four-season resort that is a skier's paradise but offers summer adventures as well.

Joseph Smith Birthplace Memorial
357 LDS Ln.
South Royalton
(802) 763-7742
lds.org/locations/joseph-smith-birthplace-memorial
The birthplace of the first latter-day prophet and church president Joseph Smith.

USS *Montpelier* Museum
39 Main St.
Montpelier
(802) 229-4619
A museum showcasing the naval history of ships that carry the Montpelier name.

Vermont History Center and Library
60 Washington St.
Barre
(802) 479-8500
vermonthistory.org
Extensive collection of artifacts and books.

Across the street from the courthouse is the ***Episcopal church,*** a Gothic design built of local granite. Inside you can see its vaulted ceiling and a rose window. The ***bank building*** across Elm Street from the courthouse was built in 1874, but the mansard roof and round dormers were added about 20 years later.

The ***Walton Block,*** next to it, is a beautifully restored 1870s commercial building decorated in cast-iron columns and stamped sheet metal, a style popular in that period. Opposite, on the corner of State and Main Streets, is Montpelier's only remaining example of a federal-period commercial building. You can recognize its federal lines in the steeply sloping roof and the gables at the ends.

To see more fine examples, most of them Victorian, wander up Main Street to your left, past the residences that show Greek revival and federal origins—often mixed at about the same time the earlier federal homes were modernized. Some of the "newer" homes are more purely Victorian, built after two fires in 1875 destroyed many older ones.

To learn more about the distinguished public and business buildings and the beautiful Victorian residences that line Montpelier's streets, visit the ***Vermont History Museum*** (109 State St.; 802-828-2291; vermonthistory .org) and pick up tour brochures for a small fee. Located a few doors down from the capitol toward the center of town, the museum operated by the Vermont Historical Society features an extensive library. Fortunately, you don't have to be a member of the society to visit—people travel here from all over the country to conduct genealogical research, for which the library has a treasure trove of old papers, letters, and reference works.

The museum also has exhibits about the numerous stages of the state's history, and these exhibits change about once a year. The museum's feature exhibit is the award-winning "Freedom and Unity: One Ideal, Many Stories," showcasing the state's more than 400-year history. It includes a full-size Abenaki wigwam, a railroad station, and other reproductions and fills about 5,000 square feet of museum space.

Located on the first floor of the Pavilion Building, the museum is open Tues through Sat 10 a.m. to 4 p.m. Admission is charged to both the museum and library, but allows entry into the Heritage Galleries in Barre as well.

Manghi's Bakery (28 School St.; 802-223-3676) (pronounced "Mang-high") bread is available fresh in general stores and markets around the

Barre-Montpelier area, but it's best to buy it direct from the source. Manghi's bakes bread Mon through Fri. The bakery is open from 7 a.m. to 4 p.m. Mon through Thurs and from 7 a.m. until 2 p.m. on Fri. The best times to stop in are from noon to closing on Mon, Wed, and Thurs, or you can call ahead to order a special loaf. Manghi's offers anadama, maple walnut, six-grain, cracked wheat, onion herb, challah, and whole-wheat oatmeal breads, as well as special breads at holiday times, like hot cross buns at Easter and stollen at Christmas. Manghi's Bakery is located off Main Street, 2 blocks northeast of its intersection with State Street. Or just follow the aroma of baking bread.

The *T.W. Wood Art Gallery* (46 Barre St.; 802-262-6035; twwoodgallery .org) was founded in 1896 to give Vermonters access to the art of their time, and it still fills the mission with changing exhibits of contemporary artists. But you will also see art from earlier times, including the work of the 19th-century artist T. W. Wood, who endowed the gallery. Permanent collections feature a selection of Depression-era work. Admission is free, but hours are by appointment only.

Montpelier is nothing if not compact; everything is either within a long 2-block or a short 2-block radius of everything else. Tucked away a few steps from the main drag is *Angeleno's Pizza* (15 Barre St.; 802-229-5721; angelenospizza.com), a local favorite for pizza and pasta. Situated in an old Victorian house, Angeleno's makes the best pizza in Vermont. The pizza has a thin crust, and the tomato sauce is just a little bit spicy. You can choose from 31 different toppings, with the more obscure ranging from peanut butter and pickles to turkey and eggplant.

All the pasta is homemade, and daily pasta specials include baked mostaccioli and linguine tossed with olive oil and shrimp; one side of the menu is devoted to heart-healthy dishes and suggestions for diabetics. Wine and beer are available, and the desserts are variations on traditional Italian themes. The frozen tortoni is made from a slice of rum-soaked pound cake with vanilla and chocolate ice cream and rum custard between the layers and a thick, hot, bittersweet fudge sauce ladled on top.

And of course, Angeleno's has cannoli, a crunchy shell with a light ricotta filling that tells you it was prepared seconds before arriving at your table.

Angeleno's is open from 11 a.m. to 9:30 p.m. Mon through Thurs, to 10 p.m. Fri through Sat, and 1 to 9 p.m. Sun.

Sarducci's (3 Main St.; 802-223-0229; sarduccis.com) overlooks the river, with an enclosed porch for dining on the waterside. Low walls separate the large dining room into several smaller areas without obscuring the view of the big wood oven or the flamboyant chef show with the pizza dough in the open kitchen. But pizza, however good and tender of crust, is only part of the menu. Pasta dishes usually have more meat than pasta, a refreshing change from the usual. Nice pairings may include mussels and Italian sausage with roasted onions in a white-wine sauce or sea scallops with tomatoes and asparagus in a basil broth. The menu balances well between the haute of northern Italian dishes and the red-sauce circuit. Sarducci's doesn't make pretenses and provides a thoroughly satisfying dinner, cheerfully served in a most pleasant atmosphere at a very reasonable price. Who can ask for more? Sarducci's is open for lunch Mon through Sat 11:30 a.m. to 4:30 p.m., for dinner Sun through Thurs 4:30 to 9 p.m., and for dinner 4:30 to 9:30 Fri and Sat. Reservations are suggested.

Maple syrup and its relatives—maple sugar, candy, and cream—are perhaps the quintessential Vermont products. A good place to see these made the old-fashioned way and to experience the pleasures of a maple grove is ***Bragg Farm Sugarhouse and Gift Shop*** (1005 Rte. 14; 802-223-5757 or 800-376-5757; braggfarm.com) in East Montpelier. Take the personal guided tour of this family operation, or watch it all on the 20-minute video. The farm shop sells candy, syrup, and Vermont cheeses, and can ship your items home for you if you want. They claim to have the "World's Best maple creemees, shakes, and sundaes." Guess you'll have to try them to find out. On Sat and Sun from Mar to mid-Apr, Bragg's makes sugar-on-snow from noon until 5 p.m. The farm is open daily at 8:30 a.m. They stay open until 8 p.m. June through Aug, but close at 6 p.m. Sept through May.

Sugar-on-Snow

Although it's called sugar-on-snow, it's really hot syrup poured onto snow. Contact with the cold causes the syrup to solidify quickly into a sticky strip of sweet, chewy candy. It's so sweet, in fact, that the traditional accompaniment for it is sour pickles. Sugar-on-snow is a New England rite of spring, and it should not be confused with a maple snow cone, a warm-weather treat at county fairs that involves pouring cold syrup over finely crushed ice in a paper cup.

Winter has other pleasures in Montpelier, one of them at the *Morse Farm Ski Touring Center* (1168 County Rd.; 802-223-0560; skimorsefarm .com). Main Street in town passes the Culinary Institute of America buildings and shortly thereafter becomes County Road. Two and a half miles from the roundabout you will find Morse's, a beautiful location with views of Camel's Hump and the Hunger Mountain Range, and 15 miles of professionally designed and machine-tracked trails for all levels of experience. There are also 2.5 miles of snowshoe trails as well. Voted Best Cross Country Skiing Location by the *Barre-Montpelier Times Argus,* the facilities include a warming hut where skiers can enjoy cider and coffee, and they have a well-stocked rental shop. Trails are open daily 8 a.m. to 4:30 p.m. with rentals available until 3 p.m.

Also on site is the *Morse Farm Maple Sugarworks* (1168 County Rd.; 800-242-2740; morsefarm.com), open daily year-round, 8 a.m. to 8 p.m. Free sugar house tours and samples, a nature trail, country store, farm museum, and great wood carvings by Burr Morse are all at the farm, not to mention the requisite sugar-on-snow, available weekends in Mar.

North of the Capital

The town of *Plainfield,* on Route 2, was a mecca in the 1960s for communes and hippies of all stripes. We suspect many of them are still here. In fact, when you visit this wonderful little town, you might have the urge to check the calendar to make sure you haven't traveled back in time a decade or five. A large contribution to this groovy-feeling town comes from *Goddard College* (123 Pitkin Rd.; 802-454-8311; goddard.edu) and its graduates. This progressive, private liberal arts college was founded in 1863 as, ironically, a seminary. It was later chartered as a college in 1938 and in 1963 became the first American college to offer adults the opportunity to earn their degrees. A woman named Evalyn Bates founded this program after she proposed the idea in her own college thesis. The basis, she believed, of such an education should be to encourage students to "become who they truly are, expand their potential, and increase confidence with peers, allowing for continual life growth benefiting the individual and society." Goddard embraced this idea and has always been on the cutting edge of education and life in general. School founder Royce "Tim" Pitkin was Goddard

Seminary graduate and believed in the liberal values he had learned there. He guided the college through its growth, which included being the first university to offer single parents on public assistance admission into the college's residency programs. Today the college continues to provide an education to its students through its low-residence program, which means students design their own study in an area of interest each semester. They spend an intense eight days in residence at the college, and then 16 weeks working independently but in conjunction with a faculty member to reach their goals. The school offers both bachelor's and master's degrees.

During their hours of self-reflection, many students (and others) spend time at *"the wall,"* a stone wall near a beautiful waterfall that has become a popular gathering place in town.

Oftentimes they will stop at **The Country Bookshop** (35 Mill St.; 802-454-8439; thecountrybookshop.com) and browse through its 30,000 books, old postcards, and other very cool stuff throughout the first floor of a 100-year-old house. Open daily 10 a.m. to 5 p.m. year-round.

Another great nearby place is the **Plainfield Co-op** (153 Main St.; 802-454-8579; plainfieldcoop.com), where you can find fresh local and organic food and great company. The co-op was created in the 1960s as mistrust of packaged foods and a desire to have fresh, unaltered food increased (much like today). It had modest beginnings but has grown through the years and thrives today. While still offering fresh, healthy food, the co-op is also active in many community events, from pasta dinners to film showings and political gatherings. Located in the former Plainfield Grange Hall, the co-op is located right before the firehouse on Main Street, around the back of the buildings. Open daily 9 a.m. to 8 p.m. except for holidays.

The **Maple Valley Cafe and Gift Shop** (8195 Rte. 2; 802-454-8626) only enhances the aura of its town. Do not be fooled by the humble look of this mom-and-pop store. Don't even be fooled when you enter to an interesting mix of Vermont ephemera (there are actually some very cool things to be found in the gift area; if you have time, take a look around). Keep walking to the back for the diamond in the rough that locals have known about for years—the food. The breakfast is delicious. The baked goods are wholesome and homemade. You'll find everything here from bacon and sausage to avocado and sprouts. There menu is creative, and gluten-free and vegan options are available as well. There is also really good Vermont coffee (but of course). Open daily except for Wed, 6 a.m. to 3 p.m. Closed for the winter.

Back on Route 2, continue east into Marshfield and to **Rainbow Sweets** (1689 Rte. 2; 802-426-3531) in the village. Ask owner Bill Tecosky if the empanadas have just come out of the oven. These Mexican turnovers, stuffed with onions, green and red peppers, raisins, and spicy beef, all wrapped up in a slightly sweet, flaky crust, come with a side of chips and hot salsa. Rainbow Sweets also offers stuffed brioche, which is its trademark; smoked salmon; and gnocchi.

People of lesser willpower and greater determination come in, sit down, and cut right to the sugar. The chocolate tart is light, sweet, and chocolaty, a three-layer cake liberally strewn with almonds and cocoa-butter cream. The almond meringue tart is mild, with a thin layer of sweet almond filling on top. There's a big display case filled with that day's desserts, and the staff patiently describes each one to you.

For those who visit and can't wait until next time, several offerings can now be shipped to your door. Linzer torte, walnut caramel kirsch torte, English fruitcake, almond chocolate butter crunch, and chocolate cherry almond torte are the delectables from Rainbow Sweets that travel well on a UPS truck, and many patrons take advantage of this service.

Rainbow Sweets is open summers from 9 a.m. to 7 p.m. Mon, Wed, and Thur. and from 9 a.m. to 9 p.m. on Fri and Sat. On Sun the restaurant is open from 9 a.m. to 5 p.m.; it's closed Mar and Apr. During the winter, they are closed Mon and Tues, opening at 10 a.m. the rest of the week, closing at 5 p.m. on Wed and Thurs, 9 p.m. Fri and Sat, and 3 p.m. on Sun.

From the town center of Marshfield, take the road west that leads to East Calais and Route 14. Follow the signs to Kent's Corner. At the Kent's Corner crossroads, turn right onto Robinson Cemetery Road. A short way up on the left is **Robinson Sawmill,** a reconstructed sawmill with original parts that were used to build the mill back in 1803. A display gives the history of the mill and shows the development of the area with photos that date from 1875. Set on the Aldrich Nature Preserve at Mill Pond, the sawmill still has its old turbine, saw blades, and machinery intact.

Robinson Sawmill was a busy place in its heyday. One miller wrote out his invoices on shingles that were milled here, kids floated on sap pans in the pond, and local farmers and merchants traded gossip and news. The mill sits on extremely thin fieldstones as pilings, one atop another. You're almost afraid to sneeze, lest the impact set the mill tumbling down. But the mill can take a lot more than is obvious, as it was in full operation from 1803 to 1958.

The Mad River Valley

Camel's Hump, a 4,083-foot mountain that straddles the borders of Duxbury and Huntington, is the third-highest mountain in the state, after Mount Mansfield and Killington. It has variously been known through the years as the Sleeping Lion, the Couching Lion, and Camel's Rump. The Long Trail passes by Camel's Hump, and trails to access the mountain's summit run through Huntington and Duxbury.

South of Duxbury on Route 100 are Waitsfield and Warren. This is prime tourist country, very busy in summer and winter. The ski resorts Mad River Glen and Sugarbush are in the area.

To say that *Mad River Glen* (57 Schuss Pass, Fayston; 802-496-3551; madriverglen.com) is a skier's mountain is a bit of an understatement; it is, in fact, the only ski mountain in the country that is actually owned by the skiers. Founded in 1948 by Fred Palmedo, it was not primarily a business but rather a place for people who loved the sport. That philosophy stuck with the next owners, Truxton and Betsy Pratt. When Betsy decided to retire, she almost closed the place down because she didn't want it to become like the other areas. That's when the skiers who loved it got together and bought it.

The vertical drop of about 2,000 feet is among the greatest in the state. Mad River has such a reputation among avid skiers that many beginners hesitate to try it. That's a mistake, because beginners have their own separate section of the mountain with their own lift. Intermediate trails run from the tops of two of the peaks of the ridge, as do expert trails. One of the really nice things about the trail layout here is that you won't get a nasty surprise if you start down a beginner or intermediate trail. Trails here either keep their own rating or merge into trails of the next lower category, so you won't suddenly find yourself over your head (literally or figuratively). For experts, the terrain here is probably the most challenging anywhere in the East, over natural snow covering wild bumps and down through narrow trails and glades. Located on 3,600-foot General Stark Mountain, Mad Glen sees an annual average natural snowfall of about 250 inches per year,

The Great Green Mountain Pumpkin Show

While most of the spring and summer *Ellie's Farm Market* (952 Darling Rd, Northfield; 802-485-7968) sells plants and fresh produce from their stand on Route 12, south of Montpelier, it is in October that half the population of Vermont (or so it seems) appears at Ellie's. On October 30 and 31 every year, the staff carves more than 1,000 jack-o'-lanterns, which are then placed about the property, even in the trees. Come after dark, preferably after 9 p.m., to avoid the crowds. Admission is free, but donations are taken to benefit a local charity.`

which tends to keep the 45 trails well covered. Ten of the trails are novice, 16 are intermediate, and 21 are expert. Most of the trails are groomed, but the snow is all natural.

Their "ski it if you can" motto ought to tell you something. Remember, this place is for skiers—there's no huge lodge with a big bar and lots of snow bunnies. But if you like it, you can become an owner. Details are on their website, as is an application for ownership. If you're a snowboarder, however, pass this one by, because snowboarding is not allowed, a policy that suits most skiers just fine.

The *Joslyn Barn* overlooking the valley in nearby Waitsfield is a local landmark, one of very few remaining round barns in the state of the 24 known to have been built. The barn was in use from 1910, when it was built by Clem Joslyn, until 1986, when Jack and Doreen Simko bought it and the surrounding farm and buildings from Clem's cousin Ralph and his wife, Marge. The Simkos were not dairy farmers, however, and set about fulfilling their plans to turn the farm into the *Inn at the Round Barn Farm* (1661 E. Warren Rd; 802-496-2276; theroundbarn.com).

The renovation was a success. The inn fits so well into the rambling home with its attached carriage sheds that you'd never guess what guest luxuries await inside. The large rooms are beautifully designed and furnished, with windows big enough to make the mountain views part of the decor. Hearty breakfasts are filled with home-baked breads and served in a bright sun porch overlooking the gardens below. In the winter the inn has its own cross-country ski center for guests and the public. Hosts are relaxed about everything but the maintenance of the inn, which is meticulously cared for, and they enjoy conversations with their guests.

Once the house renovations were complete, the Simkos turned their attention to the barn. It took them two years to restore it, from the time they began jacking up the entire structure and pouring a new foundation until it was insulated and reroofed. Then they had to decide what to do with it. When a couple asked to be married at the inn, they had part of their answer. The rest of it came when they held a music festival there, and it was a success, and the **Green Mountain Cultural Center** was born. Now with more than 200 members, the barn is a venue for performing and visual arts and hands-on workshops year-round, with the Vermont Mozart Festival, soloists, ensembles, and an annual art show filling its schedule.

On Route 100 in Warren cross-country enthusiasts will find **Ole's Cross Country Center** (2355 Airport Rd.; 802-496-3430; olesxc.com), with about 30 miles of trails traversing gently rolling hillsides, forests, and fields with views of Sugarbush. Group and individual lessons are available, as is equipment rental. Snowshoe rentals and trails add another dimension of snow sports. All of the trails are machine groomed and tracked, but ski skating is available as well. Warm up in the hut with hot beverages, fresh soups, and sandwiches.

Many of Ole's ski trails traverse the 125 acres of the **Warren-Sugarbush Airport** (2535 Airport Rd.; 802-496-3473), which is also beautiful in the warmer months. While it might sound odd, the airport—well, *this* airport anyway—is perfect for a spring, summer, or fall day's outing. Especially since the airport is home to **Sugarbush Soaring** (802-496-2290; sugarbush

itmadesense atthetime

The tiny town of Washington is part of Orange County but not of Washington County, its immediate neighbor. Washington—the town—was named for George Washington. Washington—the county—comprises the towns of Barre, Montpelier, Plainfield, and Waitsfield, among many others, and was originally called Jefferson County (in 1810) after Thomas Jefferson. Four years later, however, the locals and many other Vermonters turned against Jefferson for his influence on the Embargo Act and the War of 1812. The name of the county was therefore changed, but the name of the town—which, again, is in Orange County—wasn't. Got it?

.org), a flying club that offers flight instruction and scenic rides in their 5 gliders. Flight in one of these sleek, long-winged beauties is unlike any other flight experience. It's soundless and has the sensation of freedom from the earth. The soaring season at Sugarbush begins in mid-May and ends the last week in Oct.

Those remaining on the ground are free to enjoy the Sugarbush Soaring Clubhouse, where the club's main office is located, and *Sugar Mama's Restaurant* (802-496-7842), which offers breakfast and lunch Thurs through Sat as well as a Sunday brunch. From the clubhouse and beautiful outdoor patio, you can watch the planes fly in and out, and if you're lucky, watch the skilled pilots perform amazing aerial acrobatics.

notacornerto hidein

Designed by the Shakers, round barns are a classic example of the Shakers' inventive and practical improvements on farming. The farmer could drive a team in, load or unload, and circle around and drive out. The raceway, a ramp to the loft, led directly into the top, where hay was stored. The middle level was for dairy cows, which were also easier to herd in and out in a circle and whose straw litter and manure could be removed by trapdoors to the ground floor. There it could be removed easily — or even allowed to fall directly into the wagons.

The White River Valley

The first and second branches of the White River rise in the hills south of Barre, paralleled by Routes 110 and 14, respectively. Either route takes you through rolling farm country, and at the southernmost end of each, past covered bridges. A third north–south road, Route 12, parallels these to the west of I-89. To make the choices even more varied, Routes 64, 65, and 66, as well as several unnumbered back roads, go east–west between these. You could spend a couple of days wandering about in these hills and valleys and see a Vermont that even most Vermonters have never explored.

Route 12, the westernmost of these roads, goes through Northfield Falls, where four covered bridges cluster in a group. Three of these bridges are within a quarter mile of each other on Cox Brook Road and all cross Cox Brook, which is a tributary of the Dog River. To find these bridges from

Route 12, head west on Cox Brook Road. The first one you'll come to is **Northfield Falls Covered Bridge.** Built in 1872, this town lattice truss bridge is the longest, at 137 feet. While it was damaged by Hurricane Irene in 2011, it survived and was repaired. It is also known as the Station Covered Bridge and First Bridge. Keep heading west on Cox Brook Road toward Horse Lane to find the next two—the **Lower** and **Upper Cox Brook Covered Bridges.** These two were also built in 1872, but after the Northfield Falls Bridge and are of queen post truss construction. This is the only place in the state where one can stand in a covered bridge and see the portal of another one. The Lower Cox Bridge is also known as the Newell Covered Bridge. Back on Cox Brook Road, head southeast until you can take a right onto Route 12. Take your next right onto Slaughterhouse Road, of which some portions are unpaved. Here you will find **Slaughterhouse Covered Bridge,** also of queen post truss construction, spanning Dog River to the abandoned site of a former slaughterhouse, hence the bridge's name. Head back out to Route 12 and turn right just past Overlook Drive onto Route 12A. Travel a little over a mile and a half to Stony Brook Road. Turn right to find **Stony Brook Covered Bridge,** an 1899 kingpost truss bridge and the last to be built on a Vermont public highway. All these bridges remain open to traffic and all are listed on the National Register of Historic Places.

When you've had your fill of covered bridges (is that even possible?), hop on Route 110. This easternmost road in the White River valley goes through Washington, and from here it is only a short trip east—on unpaved but good road—to **East Orange Village** and its unique **mosaic church**. A needlelike spire, pointed windows with stained glass framing the panes, and a riot of fancy-cut shingles identify this structure as atypical of Vermont village churches. A nice four-bay carriage shed and a small schoolhouse complete the ensemble in the center of this tiny town.

From here, hop on Route 14, the center option, which passes through Williamstown, where you should look on the southern end of the village for a sign to **Knight's Spider Web Farm and Gift Shop** (124 Spider Web Farm Rd; 802-433-5568; spiderwebfarm.com). Yes, you read that right. It's a farm. Where they raise spiderwebs. One day Will Knight decided to maximize the beauty of the spiderwebs he saw in his barn. He devised a system of spraying a spiderweb with a combination of white paint and glue before mounting it on a wooden plaque and allowing it to set.

Knight initially scouted out webs in his own and neighbors' barns, then opted for mass production by constructing a series of frames protected by a roof where spiders could spin their webs in peace and where you can watch them at work. Some of Knight's designs incorporate painted flowers onto the plaque for an additional decorative touch. The farm and gift shop are open daily mid-June through mid-Oct, then every weekend through Christmas 9 a.m. to 6 p.m.

Farther south on Route 14, a right turn onto Route 65 will bring you to the town of **Brookfield,** home of the 320-foot-long **Floating Bridge.** To reach the bridge, you'll first come to a dirt road, then take a right. Floating Bridge is a one-lane bridge that floats on 380 tarred wooden barrels and is connected to the land by hinges that allow for variations in the water's depth. Although the bridge is no longer open to vehicle traffic, you can walk across it. Floating Bridge spans what is called at various times Sunset Lake, Mirror Lake, and Colts Pond.

The bridge, which is part of Route 65, is located in a tranquil spot with lots of trout. As if to attest to the bridge's popularity as a fishing spot, fishing lines and sinkers hang suspended from the phone lines and power lines that cross over the lake, parallel to the bridge. There are some boggy areas to the lake. Depending on water levels, water can come up between the wooden planks. Puddles of water gather in strategic spots on the bridge. Because of this, it's often under repair, or might be closed.

In the late 1800s and early 1900s, Brookfield was known as one of the best sources of high-quality ice, and harvesting ice from Sunset Lake was one of the town's primary businesses. The general store had a large icehouse near the floating bridge and stored enough ice there to supply the town. The rest was sent to nearby Randolph, where it was used to cool the milk train to Boston.

For more than a quarter century, the people of Brookfield have revived this industry for one day each winter at the **Brookfield Ice Harvest and Winter Carnival** (802-276-3959). On the last Saturday in January, weather permitting, they haul out all the old ice-harvesting tools and equipment, which visitors and townspeople alike can use to cut, saw, and haul ice blocks. As one local said, "After you see all the work involved, it makes you want to go home and hug your refrigerator." So unusual is this activity, which takes place at the Floating Bridge, that 200 people may show up to watch and participate.

Within a stone's throw of the bridge is *Green Trails Inn* (24 Stone Rd.; 802-276-3412; greentrailsinn.com), whose several buildings range from federal to Greek revival style. Of the 13 guest rooms, some have private baths, some shared, some with whirlpool baths. Trails originally cut for the inn's stable of riding horses now serve as hiking trails in summer and cross-country and snowshoe trails in winter. Winter also brings sledding and skating.

coolfacts

It took 5,000 pounds of ice a year to cool food for an average family.

It took 1,500 pounds of ice to cool the milk produced by a single cow during a year.

A cube of ice measuring 1 square foot weighs about 57 pounds.

Brookfield ice was so clear that people claimed they could read the *Boston Herald* through a piece 16 inches thick.

Ice blocks stored in sawdust would keep through the summer.

Farther south and on the west side of I-89 is *Randolph,* a busy, thriving town with farms and manufacturing plants, and home of Vermont State Technical College.

Randolph was chartered in 1781, and the origin of its name is somewhat confusing. General John French, an early settler in the town, was born in Randolph, Massachusetts, but the town was not named by or for him. The first settler in Randolph was known to be from New Hampshire; although there is a Randolph, New Hampshire, as well, local history has it that Randolph, Vermont, was named by Vermonters, without any outside influence. Incidentally, early towns in Vermont were named by the governor of New Hampshire, Benning Wentworth, when Vermont was part of the New Hampshire grants.

In the village of Randolph, the *Chandler Center for the Arts* (71 to 73 Main St.; 802-728-9878; chandler-arts.org) serves as the area's cultural oasis for locals who don't want to travel to either Montpelier or Dartmouth College in Hanover, New Hampshire, for their dose of art.

The music hall holds several performances each month, ranging from works by local theater groups and children, to swing bands, to Broadway musicals. The music hall season begins in September and runs through May with concerts generally held Friday and Saturday evenings and Sunday afternoons. In July they sponsor the Summer Pride Festival, in August look for a multiday Chamber Music Festival, and on the last Sunday before Labor Day the New World Festival, an all-day event. Tickets can be ordered online or by calling the box office (802-728-6464) between 3 and 6 p.m. Mon through Fri, and from 11 a.m. to one hour before show time on days of performances.

The Chandler Gallery (802-728-9878) next door presents exhibits centering on the history of Vermonters' use of art. Past offerings have included displays of decoys, children's art, antiques, stenciling, and art from the Abenaki; workshops and demonstrations are often conducted on the theme of a given month's exhibit.

The gallery opens when there are performances at the music hall. It is also open Fri, 3 to 6 p.m., and Sat and Sun from noon to 3 p.m., or by appointment during the week.

Route 12 leads from Randolph to **Bethel,** the first town chartered by the erstwhile Republic of Vermont. One of the most unusual street signs in the state is located in Bethel. If you're headed north on Route 12, the state highway makes a sharp left turn over a bridge. If you miss the turn and instead go straight, you'll soon discover your error, for there is a big red-and-white sign on the right that says THIS IS NOT ROUTE 12. The residents got sick of answering travelers' questions after too many wrong turns and remedied it with the sign.

If you follow Route 107 east from the village of Bethel, you'll reach **Vermont Castings** on your right. You've probably heard of this maker of woodstoves, since the company ships its stoves all over the world. Some of its models—the Defiant, the Vigilant, and the Resolute—have been responsible for Vermont Castings' reputation for powerful, reliable stoves that go all night. The company has kept up with technology by introducing gas-powered stoves as well as the pellet stoves that cut down on pollution and wood use. They also run their foundry on renewable and clean energy sources, and their cast iron, is produced only of recycled materials. If you've never considered owning a woodstove, a visit to a Vermont Castings showroom will make you yearn for a cold winter's night even if it's the middle of summer.

South of Bethel, as Route 12 heads toward Woodstock, Barnard sits on the shore of Silver Lake, with a quintessential village store in its center. **Barnard General Store** (6231 Rte. 12; 802-234-9688; friendsofbgs.com) has stood on this corner since 1832. Locals call it the "glue that holds the community together," and they almost lost it a few years ago when the owners were forced to close the doors due to financial difficulties. But this community couldn't let that happen and townspeople rallied and came up with a solution—almost a half a million of them, actually. That's right, the community so loved this town fixture that they raised close to a half million dollars to purchase and reopen the store. Joe Minerva and Jillian Bradley took over the operation of the store in 2013, though it is owned by a community trust. The couple bring years of grocery experience to the store and plan to keep much of what makes the general store so special, but also have plans to add some modern improvements. No doubt the Barnard General Store will resume its rightful place in the community. We wish them luck. The store is open Mon through Sat 7 a.m. to 8 p.m., Sun 8 a.m. to 6 p.m.

The store is also a good place to provision for an impromptu alfresco meal, with picnic tables on the lakeshore and in the **Dorothy Thompson Memorial Common,** on the other side of the store. Dorothy Thompson was a longtime Barnard resident, the first internationally syndicated female journalist, and wife of famed author Sinclair Lewis. Lewis is best known for his 1920 novel *Main Street,* which brought him commercial success. In 1922 he hit gold again with *Babbitt,* which was recognized when Lewis became the first American to receive the Nobel Prize in Literature.

The couple purchased a home in Barnard, Vermont, in the late 1920s, although they were both traveling extensively for their careers. They lived happily in this sleepy little Vermont town, enjoying their success. It is said that Sinclair Lewis would seclude himself in a sugarhouse on the property when the writing mood struck him. In April 2012, this same sugarhouse was relocated to his wife's memorial common with future plans to turn it into a Sinclair Lewis Museum. It took two years to raise enough money to relocate the sugarhouse, but plans are already moving forward for the museum. Those interested in donating to the cause can write to the Barnard Silver Lake Association/Sinclair Lewis Museum Comm., PO Box 124, Barnard, VT 05031.

Across the street from the common is the entrance of the 35-acre **Silver Lake State Park** (20 State Park Beach Rd; 802-234-9451; vtstateparks .com). Open Memorial Day through Labor Day 10 a.m. to sunset, this state park offers 49 tent and trailer sites and 7 lean-tos for camping. There are restrooms with running water and coin-operated hot showers. There is a sanitary dumping station, but no hookups for RVs. At the beach you'll find restrooms, play area, sandy beach, changing rooms, and boat rentals. Pets are allowed, just not on the beach, and they must be on-leash at all times.

Just up the street (which in this case is Route 12) from the lake and the Barnard General Store is a charming, small B&B, *The Fan House* (6297 Rte. 12; 802-234-6704; thefanhouse.com), where you will be greeted with an indefinable Tuscan feel, despite the wide-board floors, Victorian claw-foot tub, American antiques, and oriental rugs. The low ceiling has been opened to reveal every quirky angle of the eaves, but the space overhead is relieved from any cavernous feeling by cappuccino-colored paint and a skylight over the bed, through which you can count stars in the night sky. Gallery lights illuminate an original Gobelin tapestry on one wall. On the opposite wall a wood mantel, stripped of a century of paint layers, surrounds a working fireplace. There is no artifice, and no decorator-magazine Tuscan embellishments, but the feeling is unmistakable.

Owner Sara Widness has restored and decorated this Victorian revival house skillfully, incorporating family heirlooms with art she has collected throughout her extensive travels. Very knowledgeable about this area of Vermont, she can guide your travels well and help you plan your day over a full country breakfast, which is included in your room rate.

For those who enjoy wildlife, The Fan House has teamed with a local Audubon Society leader and an expert animal tracker to introduce guests to local birds and animals. These wildlife walks can be planned for a half or full day, with snowshoe rentals available locally for winter tracking trips. Seasonal birding events include hawk-watching in September, the breathtaking sight of thousands of snow geese migrating in October, and the Christmas bird count in December. May is the prime month, however, with sightings of as many as 50 species possible in an afternoon ramble. Ask at the inn for details.

A short distance past the entrance to Silver Lake State Park is an unpaved road that takes you to the gallery of well-known artist *Sabra Johnson Field,* who works and sells prints at her studio (75 E. Barnard Rd., South Royalton; 802-763-7092; sabrafield.com). Many of her themes are inspired by Vermont's landscapes, and the Vermont Land Trust commissioned her to create a commemorative poster. Be sure to call first if you plan to visit the gallery, since it is not always open.

Just east of Bethel, Routes 14 and 110 follow the respective branches of the White River, joining in the Royaltons, where their streams also meet the main body of the White River. A trip up either one of these or, better yet, a loop that combines the lower ends of each by a road over the ridge that lies between them will show you another cluster of covered bridges. Heading up Route 110 you will pass, in turn, the Howe Bridge (on the east side of the road), the Cilley Bridge (on the left), and the Larkin Bridge (on the right). The next is the Flint Bridge, on the right.

A Fine Horse Indeed

If you cross Flint Bridge, turn right and follow the dirt road up the hill until you come to a small grassy triangle at a fork, to your right. Beside the right-hand road (which turns into a driveway here), you'll see a granite stone marking the grave of the Morgan horse Lippitt Mandale. Now look downhill to find another stone monument, which was erected by the Morgan Horse Club and reads as follows: ON THIS FARM LIES THE BODY OF JUSTIN MORGAN, FOALED 1789 DIED 1821 PROGENITOR OF THE FIRST ESTABLISHED AMERICAN BREED OF HORSES.

Are you as confused as we were? Okay, let us clarify. The horse's name was actually Figure. He was a bay stallion born in West Springfield, Massachusetts in 1789 and became the standard by which all Morgan horses are measured. He came to be owned by Justin Morgan, a teacher and former town clerk of Randolph, Vermont, who owned him until 1795, and after whom the breed would be named. After that, Figure passed from owner to owner, sometimes being hired out as stud, sometimes winning at the track as a racehorse, and sometimes working as a farmhand. But throughout his 32 years of life, he was consistent in that his offspring always bore a very close resemblance to him, both in looks and in performance. He was well sought after, and Morgans became a very popular horse breed of the 19th century.

The name Lippitt comes from a man by the name of Robert Lippitt Knight, who owned a farm in Randolph, Vermont, near where Justin Morgan lived. In the late 1920s through the early 1960s, Knight was a major player in breeding Morgans, and valued the attributes that Figure had passed to his offspring. He worked hard to keep the lines clean and undiluted; therefore, these "old-type Morgans" are referred to as "Lippitts."

In 1954 Marguerite Henry wrote a fictionalized account of Figure's life called *Justin Morgan Had a Horse*.

Okay, once you're back on the road, you'll have to look carefully for the next bridge, which is not visible from Route 110. You can find it if you follow the riverside road instead of recrossing the Flint Bridge. You will cross the 1883 Moxie Bridge and return to Route 110, just before the left turn that will take you over the ridge (with nice mountain views) to Route 14 at East Randolph. About a mile south of the intersection is Braley Covered Bridge Road on your right, at the bottom of which you will find a small covered bridge. Farther along Route 110 is the Gifford Bridge on the left and the Hyde Bridge on the right. Not far south of the last bridge, Route 14 joins Route 107 to complete the loop.

As you travel along Route 110, you will pass through the town of Tunbridge, site of the ***Tunbridge World's Fair*** (1 Fairgrounds Ln.; 802-889-5555; tunbridgeworldsfair.com), which has been going strong since 1867. It missed only twice: in 1918 because of the terrible influenza epidemic, and during World War II, when so many men were away that it was impossible to run the agricultural events. It's an old-fashioned agricultural fair, with rows of jellies, plates of perfect vegetables, and vases of garden flowers hung with blue ribbons. Entertainment is family oriented and fun.

In the center of the fairgrounds is an entire museum building, filled with an impressive display of antiques and old agricultural equipment collected from central Vermont. Amid these fascinating artifacts, craftsmen demonstrate skills that range from rug hooking to violin making. It's worth a trip to the fair just for this museum, which is open only during fair week in mid-September. Demonstrations of cider making and many other rural skills are going on constantly, and most of the performances and grandstand events are free.

Places to Stay in Central Vermont

MARSHFIELD

Hollister Hill Farm B&B
2193 Hollister Hill Rd.
(802) 454-7725
hollisterhillfarm.com
Moderate
A B&B in a 19th-century farmhouse on a working farm.

MONTPELIER

Betsy's Bed & Breakfast
74 E. State St.
(802) 229-0466
betsysbnb.com
Inexpensive to moderate
Winner of the Montpelier Historical Society's award for best commercial renovation, this property consists of 2 restored Victorian homes that offer 12 total guest rooms. All rooms have cable TV, telephones, data ports, and private baths. The plentiful and delicious breakfasts feature cereal, compote, blueberry pancakes, and omelets.

WAITSFIELD

Lareau Farm Inn
48 Lareau Rd.
(802) 496-4949
lareaufarminn.com
Inexpensive to moderate
Has 13 homey rooms with private or shared baths in a rambling farmhouse.

WARREN

The Pitcher Inn
275 Main St.
(802) 496-6350
pitcherinn.com
Expensive
Offers 9 individually decorated guest rooms in the main house and 2 more in a beautifully restored barn. Some rooms have balconies, some have wood-burning fireplaces, and all have private baths, some with Jacuzzi tubs. Open year-round. Voted one of Condé Nast *Traveler*'s best places to stay in the world in 2013.

West Hill House B&B
1496 W. Hill Rd.
(802) 496-7162
westhillbb.com
Moderate to expensive

TO LEARN MORE IN CENTRAL VERMONT

Central Vermont Chamber of Commerce
PO Box 336
Barre 05641
(802) 229-5711
central-vt.com.

Mad River Valley Chamber of Commerce
4061 Main St.
Waitsfield
(800) 828-4748 or (802) 496-3409
madrivervalley.com

Randolph Area Chamber of Commerce
31 Rte. 66
Randolph
(802) 728-9027
randolph-chamber.com

A 9-room B&B located close to Sugarbush Ski Area. All rooms are individually decorated and have a full bath with Jacuzzi tub or steam shower. Full breakfast is included in the rates.

Places to Eat in Central Vermont

BARNARD

Barnard Inn
5518 Old Rte. 12
(802) 234-9961
barnardinn.com
Moderate to expensive
Fine dining (by reservation) or informal bistro-style menu in the pub, with good American dishes, such as bowls of plump mussels. Open Tues through Thurs 5 to 8:30 p.m., Fri and Sat 5 to 9 p.m.

BARRE

Cornerstone Pub & Kitchen
47 N. Main St.
(802) 476-2121
cornerstonepk.com
Moderate to expensive
A "modern American pub" serving craft beers and comfort pub food. Open Tues through Sat 11:30 a.m. to 9 p.m.

BROOKFIELD

Ariel's Restaurant
29 Stone Rd.
(802) 276-3939
arielsrestaurant.com
Moderate to expensive
Fine dining in a 19th-century farmhouse or a bit more casually in the pub. Open May through Oct, Wed through Sun 5:30 to 9:30 p.m.; Dec through Mar, Fri through Sat 5:30 to 9:30 p.m. Closed Nov and Apr.

MONTPELIER

McGillicuddy's Irish Pub
14 Langdon St
(802) 223-2721
mcgillicuddysvt.com
Inexpensive to moderate
Pub fare, with hot and cold sandwiches and a selection of ales. Daily specials, such as buy one appetizer, get one free on Mon, 5 to 11 p.m. Free wings on Fri (4:30 to 6 p.m.). Open Mon through Sun 11 a.m. to 2 p.m.

WAITSFIELD

American Flatbread
Lareau Farm, Route 100
(802) 496-8856
americanflatbread.com
Moderate
Bakes pizzas in a wood-fired oven and serves them in an informal setting 5 to 9:30 p.m. Thurs through Sun.

WARREN

The Common Man Restaurant
3209 German Flats Rd.
(802) 583-2800
commonmanrestaurant.com
Moderate to expensive
Offers an uncommon menu of New American and European dishes, expertly prepared Tues through Sat at 6 p.m. Reservation a good idea.

275 Main at The Pitcher Inn
275 Main St.
(802) 496-6350
pitcherinn.com
Expensive
An incredible dining experience with a menu that changes almost daily. Be sure to call ahead and make reservations.

Tracks at The Pitcher Inn
275 Main St.
(802) 496-6350
pitcherinn.com
Moderate to expensive
The less formal of dining options at The Pitcher Inn, this is more a pub style, offering delicious pub options and craft beers.

CONNECTICUT RIVER VALLEY

→

The Connecticut River cuts a wide swath between Vermont and New Hampshire—at least in this area—as though underscoring the differences between the two states. Beside it, and in sight of it for much of its route, runs I-91, high along a shoulder of the hills that rise on the river's western bank. The views are of rich fertile farmlands, the wide winding river with its oxbows and tributary streams, and the hills and mountains of New Hampshire across the river. It's New England scenery at its best at any time of year, and a spectacular panorama in the fall.

Route 5 also parallels the river, often weaving back and forth across the straighter interstate, and passing through some of the most fertile farmland in New England as it strings together the towns from Brattleboro to Newbury—and beyond to the Northeast Kingdom.

Early settlers homesteaded along the river so that they could easily receive supplies from their previous homes in Connecticut and Massachusetts. They weren't dissuaded by the countless bends in the river that are especially common between Thetford and Newbury. In fact, Bradford's high school is called Oxbow.

CONNECTICUT RIVER VALLEY

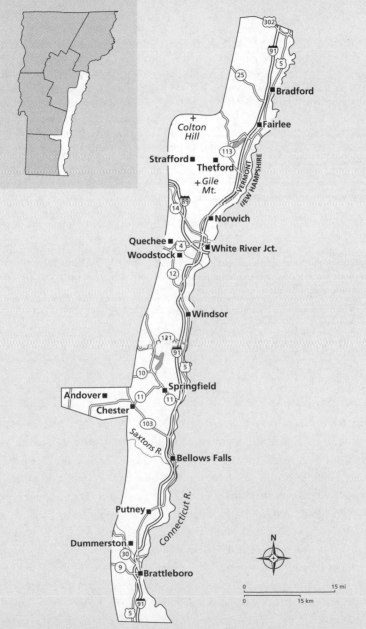

Humble Beginnings

Boston University alumni may be surprised to learn that their alma mater began just north of Bradford, in the tiny town of Newbury. Originating in 1836 as a school for the classical education of Methodist clergy, the Newbury Biblical Institute (as it was first called) was in a four-story brick building overlooking Newbury's common, next to the white Methodist Church, which was also part of the school. In 1846 the institute moved to Concord, New Hampshire, then to Boston in 1849, when it was renamed Boston University. A 1913 fire destroyed the original brick building, but the white *Old Village Church* still stands, restored and cared for by the Newbury Women's Club.

In some towns in the Upper Valley—the towns that fall between Springfield and Newbury—the line between Vermont and New Hampshire across the river begins to blur. A phone call from Norwich to Hanover, even though it's from Vermont to New Hampshire, is not a toll call; there are ample bridges for residents to travel from one state to the other. Since the area is touted as a region and not two different states, the line gets even fuzzier. In fact, the Norwich/Hanover school district is the only multistate local school district in the country. Let's go explore!

White River Junction

White River Junction, in the center of the valley and part of Hartford, Vermont, is an old railroad town that, like many others, had its heyday when the trains made the air thick with smoke. Today the town is still a stop for Amtrak. The Vermonter travels through the state and stops at the *White River Junction station* (102 Railroad Row), which is also used by the Green Mountain Railroad for scenic trips throughout the region. At this same station you will find another piece of history. A historic steam locomotive from the Boston and Maine Railroad. *Engine 494,* with its tender and caboose, stands as a reminder of the days when as many as 50 trains a day brought passengers to and from the depot here. But Engine 494 is not just any old steam locomotive; it has a unique history of its own. Built in Manchester, New Hampshire, in 1892, Engine 494 hauled passengers on the company's Eastern Line, then was used on the uphill run from Fabyan

Station to Marshfield Station, 2,700 feet up the side of New Hampshire's Mount Washington. It hauled coal to fuel the Cog Railway, which ran from Marshfield to the summit. Over its lifetime, many improvements were made in train construction, and with each, Engine 494 was modernized to keep up with the times. It was retired in 1938.

But not quite. In 1939 Engine 494 was chosen to represent Boston & Maine at the New York World's Fair, and it was unmodernized, its steel cab replaced with wood, its electric headlamp replaced with an oil light. After the fair it was stored and almost scrapped, but a group called the Railroad Enthusiasts was unwilling to see this unique example of a restored 19th-century locomotive die, and a new home was found for it in White River Junction.

Within sight of Engine 494 is ***Vermont Salvage Exchange*** (4 Gates St.; 802-295-7616; vermontsalvage.com), a used-house-parts store, both funky and utilitarian, where you can find everything from stained-glass windows to doors, wainscoting, and heating grilles, all in one place.

Amid the three floors of boxes of doorknobs, light fixtures, and gargoyles are treasures you'll have to use your imagination to utilize. Everything deserves a second chance; perhaps you will create something magical from some of these pieces and bring them back to their former glory. Take your time browsing through everything. While some of the prices can be on the high side, they are most likely lower than if you bought new, and you'll have something original and one-of-a-kind. Open Mon through Fri from 9 a.m. to 4:30 p.m., Sat 9 a.m. to 3 p.m., and Sun 10 a.m. to 2 p.m.

If you have time to take in a show, plan a stop at the ***Briggs Opera House*** (5 S. Main St.; 802-291-9009; northernstage.org). Home to Northern

BEST ATTRACTIONS IN THE CONNECTICUT RIVER VALLEY

The Montshire Museum of Science	Boland Balloon
Chester	Vermont Salvage Exchange
Justin Smith Morrill Homestead	

Stage theater company, the Briggs Opera House has had quite a history. Built in 1890, the building has served as a town meeting place, exhibition hall, theater, sports venue, shelter for WWII service members, department store, and eventually the opera and theater house it is today. It has been through many changes, years of neglect, and subsequent rehabilitation. Today Northern Stage is bringing the opera house alive again. Tickets are reasonable and the shows varied. Visit their website for more details and information on special events.

North of White River, off Route 5, the town of Hartford has established the *Hurricane Forest Wildlife Refuge* (270 Wright Reservoir Rd.; 802-295-5036; artford-vt.org/content/parks), thanks to a gift from Windsor and Bertha Brown. The entrance to the 142-acre tract is off of Old King's Highway. Four trails are from 2/10 mile (Pond Loop) to 8/10 mile (Beacon Hill Loop) in length. Benches are placed at strategic points for resting or observing nature. Look for the turn on the left, close to the I-89 underpass on Route 5. The park is open daily Apr through Oct, sunrise to 9 p.m.

Norwich–Strafford

Norwich is home to hundreds of Dartmouth College employees, professors, and students, as well as a number of multi-generation Norwichers. The town has a countrified, genteel air, from the Montessori school to the green that serves as playground for the town's elementary school. Norwich is a curious blend of culture and country.

Located right on the banks of the Connecticut River, the *Montshire Museum of Science* (1 Montshire Rd.; 802-649-2200; montshire.org) is a place where both adults and children can act like children.

The first Montshire opened in Hanover, New Hampshire, in January 1976 in an abandoned bowling alley as a community museum for the public—which was a novel idea at the time. From the beginning it was operated as a learning center instead of a museum. Montshire moved across the river to a new facility in Norwich in November 1989 and was designed top to bottom to be a hands-on science museum, from the color-coded

vermonttrivia

"Montshire" is an amalgam of Vermont and New Hampshire.

ventilation systems to the exposed trusses. They must have done something right; *Yankee Magazine* voted them Editor's Choice in 2013. They also received the 2012 and 2013 Certificate of Excellence from TripAdvisor.

When you enter, kids may take a few minutes to make the transition from a world of "Don't Touch" to the freedom of the Montshire, where even adults feel as if they're getting away with something. You can play with light switches, shoot baskets, blow bubbles, and splash around in soapy water.

Upstairs are a variety of beetles (dead ones) and boa constrictors (live ones). There's also a dinosaur-size ant colony with hundreds of thousands of ants climbing through 11 Plexiglas chambers. Even if you had an ant colony as a kid, the Leafcutter Ant Colony will make your skin crawl. The Montshire also hosts a number of traveling exhibits—one year it was a collection of dinosaur eggs—so you'll never know what you'll find when you visit. If everyone is not too tired after visiting *inside,* there are 100 acres of trails and outdoor exhibits to explore, including a warm-weather water park.

The Montshire is open from 10 a.m. to 5 p.m. 7 days a week. It's closed on New Year's Day, Thanksgiving, and Christmas. Admission is charged.

On Route 5, just south of the I-91 exit, is a mecca for home bread bakers. **The Baker's Store** (135 Rte. 5 South; 802-649-3361; kingarthurflour .com) is the real-life version of the King Arthur Flour catalog, which supplies bakers all over the country with everything from the right pan to the right type of yeast and plump dried currants for real scones. Here you can see it all and taste the breads that the catalog only gives you the recipes for (we wonder if they've thought of a scratch-and-sniff patch so readers will have the aroma of fresh-baked bread to inspire them). The store would inspire anyone to get elbow-deep in bread dough, and it offers some specialty items not shown in the catalog. You'll never again think of King Arthur as just flour. Recently the

hailtheking!

In the 1920s, when barrels of King Arthur Flour were delivered throughout New England by truck, the company's advertising consisted of a white truck with a life-size wooden statue of King Arthur on his horse. It was a three-dimensional version of the logo used today, complete with standard flying over his head. Just in case no one noticed this king and his horse hitching a ride through town, the white truck was equipped with a calliope to draw attention to the royal visit.

ANNUAL EVENTS IN THE CONNECTICUT RIVER VALLEY

FEBRUARY

Brattleboro Winter Carnival

Various venues
Brattleboro
(802) 348-1956
brattleborowintercarnival.org
Held in mid- to late February, this is one of New England's oldest winter carnivals. Features events for all ages, including the lighting of the torches, an ice-fishing derby, outdoor carnival, snowmobile rides, dogsled demonstrations, ice skating, skiing, the requisite sugar-on-snow, sleigh rides, a petting zoo, and more.

MAY

Open Fields Medieval Festival

Thetford Green
Thetford Hill
(802) 785-2077
vtmedfest.com
Family-friendly celebration held in late May every *other* year on odd years. The town is transformed into a medieval village with music, storytelling, costumes, dancing, games, food, a parade, and demonstrations of falconry.

JUNE

Strolling of the Heifers Parade & Festival

Main Street
Brattleboro
strollingoftheheifers.com
Held during the first week in June, this parade kicks off National Dairy Month as salute to family farms and their contributions to Vermont's agricultural heritage. Don't be fooled, this event is huge and tens of thousands of spectators turn out every year for it.

Yellow Barn's Summer Season

The Big Barn
63 Main St. (between the co-op and library)
Putney
(802) 387-6637
yellowbarn.org
From late June through early Aug, the Yellow Barn presents a series of concerts by well-known musicians. Pre-concert discussions are often held at the public library.

JULY

Cow Appreciation Day

Billings Farm Museum
69 Old River Rd.
Woodstock
(802) 457-2355
billingsfarm.org/programs-events/special_events/cow_day.html
A celebration where you can try your hand at milking and enjoy freshly churned butter and hand-cranked ice cream. Admission includes all programs and activities, plus a tour of the museum and farm.

Marlboro College Music Festival

Marlboro College Campus
Marlboro
(802) 254-2394
marlboromusic.org/summer-concerts/overview

On Saturday evenings and Sunday afternoons from mid-July to mid-Aug, music students and professionals share their music with audiences. Ticket information and schedules are available on the website.

Stoweflake Hot Air Balloon Festival
Stoweflake Mountain Resort & Spa
(800) 253-2232
stoweflake.com/activities_balloon_festival.aspx
This mid-July festival featuring balloon launches 3 times a day is one of the state's more popular events. Also offers live music, wonderful food, beer, and wine.

AUGUST

Annual pilgrimage to Rockingham Meeting House
Meeting House Road
(802) 463-3941, ext. 100
Rockingham
For more than a century, the Rockingham Meeting House has been commemorated with music and historical programs on the first Sun in Aug.

Quechee Scottish Festival and Celtic Fair
Quechee Polo Field
Quechee
quecheescottishfestival.com
(800) 295-5351
Features bagpipes, dancing, foods, rugby, sheepdogs, and massed bands in late Aug. Admission for those older than 5.

SEPTEMBER

Woodstock Art & Wine Festival
Village Green
Woodstock
(802) 457-3555
Local crafters set up tents and booths on the town green. You'll find hand-blown glass, paintings, pottery, and food booths that offer great food paired with Vermont wine.

Vermont Find Furniture and Woodworking Festival
496 Rte. 4
Woodstock
(802) 747-7900
vermontwoodfestival.org
This annual event in late Sept celebrates Vermont's woodworking heritage. Learn how generations of New Englanders used wood for a variety of products. Music, demonstrations, and products are available.

OCTOBER

Dummerston Apple Pie Festival
Various locations
Dummerston
(802) 257-9158
Held on the Sunday of Columbus Day weekend for more than 40 years, this free annual festival offers all things apple, including more than 1,000 pies for sale. Oh, and there's homemade ice cream, cheese, cider, coffee, crafts, and donuts, too.

Heritage Festival
Route 30
Newfane
(802) 365-4079
newfaneheritagefestival.blogspot.com
A Columbus Day weekend festival featuring juried arts, crafts, Vermont products, a flea market, and entertainment on the common.

Harvest Celebration
Billings Farm Museum
5302 River Rd.
Woodstock
(802) 457-2355
billingsfarm.org
Held in mid-Oct when the fall activities of a 19th-century farm are demonstrated and celebrated: cider pressing, the pumpkin harvest, a husking bee, preserving, and more.

DECEMBER

Woodstock's Winter Wassail Weekend
various venues
Woodstock
(802) 457-3555 or (888) 496-6378
woodstockvt.com/wassail.php
Vermont claims that their Wassail Weekend, held in early Dec, is "Woodstock's gift to Vermont." This festival offers a parade of holiday-outfitted horses and riders, an appearance of Santa, performances of local theater groups, shopping, and sleigh rides at Billings Farm & Museum.

company started offering classes in all levels of baking, from basic demonstrations to in-depth weeklong courses for the more serious baker. We have heard nothing but positive reviews on these classes. Information is listed on their website. The store is open from 7:30 a.m. to 6 p.m. daily.

On your left just past the three-way stop in the village is **Dan & Whit's** (319 Main St.; 802-649-1602; danandwhits.com), a country store that's unusual even by Vermont standards. Whenever anyone in Norwich gives out directions, the inevitable benchmark is: "Oh, go a mile past Dan & Whit's, turn left onto Turnpike Road, and keep going."

Dan Fraser and Whit Hicks purchased the business in 1955. Two years later they purchased the building and retained a partnership until 1972, having their wives, Bunny and Grace, respectively, join in and help. Eventually the kids joined the operation as well. The store did well and the business prospered. Whit Hicks died at the age of 80 in 1987 and the Fraser family continued with the business, and they still do today. While Dan and Bunny retired in 1992, their sons (George and Jack) carry on the family tradition.

The immense outdoor bulletin board on the front of the building serves as the contemporary version of a town crier. Notices about everything from rooms for rent to goat's milk for sale to pancake suppers are posted here. Inside, Dan & Whit's is the antithesis of the modern-day supermarket. No scanners here, just shelves with loaves of locally baked bread next to boxes of doodads. Wander around the aisles up front, but the real treasure is through the door next to the meat counter, a door that looks like it should have an employees only sign hanging over it. The hardware department is in here. Stovepipes, birdseed, shovels, sleds, and inner tubes compete for space and more often than not haphazardly spill onto the cement floor. We wouldn't want it any other way. Dan & Whit's is open daily 7 a.m. to 9 p.m.

If you continue on Main Street heading west, the road ascends, climbing up into the mountains from the Connecticut River basin, winding past working farms. Some 5.5 miles from Dan & Whit's, the road forks. Bear left onto Route 132 and about 8 miles from the fork take a sharp right. You'll be in the village of South Strafford.

If instead of continuing west on Route 132, you bear right at the T on the Justin Smith Morrill Highway and drive 2 miles, you'll be in the Strafford town center. Justin Morrill served Vermont in the US House of Representatives from 1855 to 1867 and in the US Senate from 1867 to 1898. He is remembered for the Morrill Act of 1862, which provided land grants to help found state colleges to promote agricultural, mechanical, science, and classical studies. He is often called "the Father of the Agricultural Colleges." It's hard to miss his home, now a museum dedicated to his memory. The ***Justin Smith Morrill Homestead*** (214 Justin Morrill Memorial Hwy.; 802-828-3051; morrillhomestead.org) is a large, peach-colored Victorian fantasy with steep gables and generous gingerbread trim, sitting on a hillside along the road in the center of town. The 17-room mansion was built in the Gothic revival style and remains as it was designed, complete with original furnishings, gardens, outbuildings, and an exquisite hand-painted window in the ceiling of the library. Although posted hours are 11 a.m. to 5 p.m. Wed through Sun from Memorial Day through Columbus Day, it's requested that you call ahead to be sure someone is there to greet you.

OTHER ATTRACTIONS WORTH SEEING IN THE CONNECTICUT RIVER VALLEY

Basketville
8 Bellows Falls Rd. (Route 5)
Putney
(800) 258-4553 or (802) 387-5509
basketville.com
Famous Vermont basket maker store, but they don't just carry baskets anymore. Open daily year-round.

Green Mountain Flyer Scenic Train Ride
54 Depot St.
Bellows Falls
(802) 463-4756
rails-vt.com
Scenic train rides throughout the state with various departure sites. Dinner trains, foliage rides, and more.

Rockingham Meeting House
Meeting House Road
Rockingham
(802) 463-3964, ext. 100
One of the oldest public buildings in the state. Built between 1787 and 1801. Open Memorial Day weekend through Columbus Day weekend.

Vermont Institute of Natural Science Nature Center
6565 Rte. 4 (Woodstock Road)
Quechee
(802) 359-5000
vinsweb.org
Visit for live raptor shows, nature displays, and children's activities. Walk or snowshoe these trails to the Quechee Gorge Open daily at 10 a.m. year-round. Closing hours depend on the season. Admission is charged for those older than 3.

Yellow Barn
63 Main St.
Putney
(802) 387-6637
yellowbarn.org
An international center for chamber music offers performances and educational opportunities throughout the year.

Norwich to Fairlee

Route 5 North out of Norwich parallels the Connecticut River and the old Boston & Maine tracks. This is a route that's popular with bicyclists, and on the river you may see the Dartmouth sculling team.

About 10 miles north is Route 113 West. Just north of the turnoff on the right is **Pompanoosuc Mills** (3184 Rte. 5, East Thetford; 802-785-4851 or 800-841-6671; pompy.com), which produces and sells finely designed furniture at its 7 stores located throughout New England. But all the furniture is made here.

Founder Dwight Sargent is a native of the area. He attended Dartmouth both as an undergraduate and as an MBA candidate at Dartmouth's Tuck Business School. While he was at Tuck, he decided that starting up Pompanoosuc Mills was the best way he could apply what he had learned about furniture making from his grandfather.

Dwight proved to be a good student. The East Thetford showroom is spacious and airy and shows off Pompanoosuc's beds, tables, cabinets, and other furniture to their best advantage via decor suggestions and floor layouts. Each piece of furniture is available in cherry, oak, maple, birch, walnut, and occasionally bird's-eye.

Head upstairs to another showroom and a picture window that looks out onto the mill floor, where you can see workers sanding, shaping, and creating the furniture. Several times a year Pompanoosuc Mills conducts tours of the mill for the public. Call for the dates of its next tour or check the website.

Open Mon through Fri from 9 a.m. to 6 p.m., Sat 9 a.m. to 5 p.m., and Sun from 11 a.m. to 5 p.m.

Route 113 heads west, through several of the villages of Thetford. At Thetford Center you'll see a cluster of nice brick homes, and if you turn left there, you'll drop into a little hollow with a covered bridge, waterfall, and old mill foundations. Farther along Route 113 is Post Mills Airport, where **Boland Balloon** (802-333-9254 or 800-666-1946) offers scenic balloon rides over the Connecticut Valley from May through Oct. You might see the brightly colored balloons drifting above the treetops as you

Got Milk?

The old joke about Vermont having more cows than people, although once true, has gone the way of the family farm. Over the past decades, Vermont has been losing dairy farms at a rate of about 4 percent a year. But the trend seems to have slowed, then reversed. Not that you can expect to find an overflow of cows grazing on the statehouse lawn in Montpelier—the increase amounts to fewer than a dozen new farms a year. But it's progress in keeping the dairy farmer from joining the piping plover on the endangered species list.

drive along the interstate. Owner, retired teacher, and very experienced balloonist Brian Boland usually offers rides for early morning or early evening. Boland has flown all over the world and has been ballooning for more than 40 years. Over those years, he has collected lots of flying memorabilia and now showcases it in his **Balloon Museum,** housed at the airport. Here you will find more than 100 flying ships of varying shapes and sizes and other very cool stuff. Admission is free and open during ballooning season.

If you do get a chance to visit the area and happen to drive by Boland's place, don't be alarmed when you see the dinosaur. Yep, we said dinosaur—well, **Vermontasaurus,** to be exact. Boland and a group of volunteers constructed the 122-foot-long structure in 2010 with wood from a collapsed portion of a barn on his property. It wasn't long before the Vermontasaurus was gaining attention—some good, some bad. As it always seems to go, the government became involved and had to decide what to do with the structure. Was it art? Was it a building? Did Boland need a permit? Most important, was it safe? Meetings were held, support groups were formed, and eventually the State of Vermont approved it and in 2011 Vermontasaurus was granted permission to stay. About three months later, however, the structure succumbed to damage from Hurricane Irene and the odd October snowfall that year. It appeared that the dinosaur's belly hit the ground, but Boland and his supporters were not to be beaten. They rebuilt the structure and added a "babysaurus" to boot. Today the two structures stand side by side, stronger than ever.

From here, Route 113 wanders on to West Fairlee. Less than a mile past the village center, take a left where the sign reads south vershire and straf-ford. This road is known in various parts as Beanville Road, Copper Mine Road, and farther west, Algerin Road. The road parallels Copper Creek on the left and follows several of the river's twists and turns. Stay on this road, and 3/10 mile from Route 113 you'll see copper-colored rocks on the left in the creek. Just 1/10 mile later is a reddish parking area on the right that is the entrance to what used to be the **Vermont Copper Mining Company.** Pull in here and walk in at the gate to see the rusting and crumbling remains of the old copper mine.

The town of Vershire was first known as Ely, and this area was called Copperfield. This road used to see a lot of traffic. At its height in 1880, 600 miners and 225 horses worked here at the mine, which produced more than 60 percent of the copper in the US.

Vegetation grows to the left of the road, but other sections remain spookily barren. The fumes and smoke from the copper smelter and the roasting beds up ahead killed off most of the area's vegetation by 1875, after only 20 years of operation. No vegetation meant that the thin layer of topsoil was easily washed away, and the land is still recovering.

Scraps of iron and slag are scattered throughout the old roasting beds. Straight ahead 100 yards or so is the path the old tramway took to bring the copper ore down from the mines. There's an old cellar hole, quite elaborate, that, judging from old maps, photographs, and descriptions, was the smelter. Parts of the wall still stand, and where the bricks lie used to be the furnace. If you go back a little farther, about 50 feet or so, you'll see what looks like a heap of copper-colored dirt with large spidery cables sticking out of it. A couple of huge rusted bolts and nuts also stick up out of the concrete walls.

There are plenty of trails to explore at the mine, summer or winter. In fact, local snowmobile clubs and cross-country skiers use the trails in the winter.

Fairlee, on Route 5, is blessed with two sizable lakes that have attracted summer visitors for almost as long as Vermont has been a state. Fairlee can become quite congested during July and August, but at any time of year it's a pretty detour from Route 5 to drive around the wooded shore of *Lake*

Wouldn't That Steam You?

Originally from Orford, across the river in New Hampshire, *Samuel Morey* invented a steam engine and used it in a tiny skiff that he operated on the Connecticut River on a quiet Sunday morning in the early spring of 1793. Morey later moved to Fairlee, Vermont, and worked on his invention while plying the waters of the nearby lake that bears his name. There is a strong tradition that says that somewhere on the bottom of Lake Morey are the remains of the very first steamboat, and it wasn't invented by Robert Fulton. Robert Fulton reportedly visited with Morey in New York and at Orford, and with another Rhode Island steamboat inventor, years before he built his own steamboat and claimed the patent on steam navigation, denying Morey recognition as the inventor of steam propulsion for boats and ships.

Morey (lakemorey.org). The lake is named after Samuel Morey, who was a pioneer in the invention of the steam engine. It covers more than 540 acres and lays claim, when the weather cooperates, to the country's longest groomed ice skating trail. Check out our Annual Events listing for information on the Lake Morey Winterfest, too.

Fairlee's other lake, *Lake Fairlee* (of course), is facing some difficulties. For the past 200 years or so, Lake Fairlee has been held back by a dam that was originally constructed to supply water to nearby mills. While the state of Vermont owns the lake itself, the dam, which is in need of substantial repairs, is privately owned. Its water level has been steadily declining and surrounding businesses and residents are concerned. The Lake Fairlee Association (lakefairlee.org) has been formed to help find a solution and to protect the lake for future generations. Studies continue to be done and options considered.

You can't visit Fairlee in the warm weather months and fall without a visit to *Whippi Dip* (158 Main St.; 802-333-3730). They serve all the typical diner food and then some. Choose from overstuffed lobster rolls, sweet potato fries, beef brisket sandwiches, or the classic, perfectly cooked cheeseburger. If you have room, finish with a scoop of delicious ice cream, or sundae smothered in hot fudge or melted butterscotch. Be aware, they don't scrimp on the servings. Open Mon through Fri 6 a.m. to 8 p.m., Fri until 9 p.m., Sat 7 a.m. to 9 p.m., and Sun to 8 p.m. Their season is not written in stone, but generally runs mid-May through mid-Oct.

Vermont is beautiful, we all know that, but what better way to experience its beauty than from astride a horse? *Open Acre Ranch* (1478 Blood Brook Rd.; 802-333-9196 or 802-272-9045; openacreranch.com) offers the opportunity to do just that. Ranch owner and operator Rebecca Guillette welcomes riders of all skill levels to come and enjoy her 400-acre horse farm. She offers 1- and 2-hour trail rides, private and group lessons, and a longer (2- to 4- hour) trail ride that includes a picnic lunch. While Open Acre Ranch has many horses of their own, and many will suit riders from young to old, Rebecca invites you to bring your own horse if you wish; just be sure to call ahead to make arrangements.

If you have had your fill of country general stores (again, is that even possible?), then keep driving. If you love quaint pieces of yesteryear (umm, who doesn't?), then don't miss *Chapman's Country Store* (491 Main St.;

He Sure Pulled the Wool Over Their Eyes

Vermont is full of memorable characters. One of the better-known residents of the town of Corinth, west of Bradford, was *Horace McDuffee,* who lived here in the late 1800s. He had a graduate degree in engineering from Dartmouth and compensated for his small stature by wearing many layers of overalls. Another Corinthian was *Daniel Flagg,* who loved animals so much that he didn't wear shoes because they were made out of leather; he wouldn't ride a horse; and he invented the cowcatcher because he felt sorry for the cows that were speared when trains came roaring through the valley. And *Orson Clement,* still another Corinth native, raised sheep to such an extent that he stored the wool anywhere he could on his 600-acre farm: in the barn, the house, the granary basement, the stables. Clement was the equivalent of the man who saved every piece of string to make into a big ball. He never sold any of his wool until he was forced to do so by the federal government, which needed wool for uniforms during World War I. Even then, Clement managed to keep a sizable cache for himself that wasn't discovered until his death.

802-333-9709; chapmansstore.com). Since 1897 Chapman's has been providing quality necessities and kitsch to travelers and residents alike. You'll find toys, fishing supplies (including live bait), jewelry, maps, books, the requisite Vermont products, a great cup of coffee, and a surprising selection of wine and craft beers. They also offer paddleboats for rent. Open Mon through Thurs 8 a.m. to 6 p.m., Fri 8 a.m. to 7 p.m., Sat and Sun 8 a.m. to 5 p.m. Oh, and don't be alarmed by the cat lounging on the counter. We're pretty sure he was breathing.

If Fairlee is known for the first steamboat, then *Bradford,* the next town north of Fairlee, is known for James Wilson, who created the first geographic globes sold in the US in the early part of the 19th century.

Bradford is also an important early mill town. Lots of the old mill buildings have been converted for new businesses and residential use. But there's no mistaking them.

At *Colatina Exit* (164 Main St.; 802-222-9008; colatinaexit.com) you can enjoy Italian veal, chicken, and seafood entrees and your choice of spaghetti, linguine, or fettuccine heaped with a thick tomato sauce that's made fresh every day. Antipasto and good, hearty soups such as an Italian white-bean-and-sausage soup with a touch of tarragon are among Colatina's appetizers.

But most people come here for the pizza, available in four sizes with every topping imaginable and even some you never thought of before. Chopped onions are free. The one room holds 20 tables, but if you want to hear quiet local music while dining on pizza and sandwiches, Colatina has a bar upstairs that's open till late. Colatina's main dining room is open from 11 a.m. to about 9 p.m. 7 days a week. They have open-mic nights on Tues and great coupons on their website.

The Southern Connecticut River Valley

I-91 roughly parallels the Connecticut River until just south of St. Johnsbury, providing elevated river and valley views that the slower, lower Route 5 can't match. But Route 5 winds through a series of very interesting towns that I-91 travelers will miss. Other numbered routes branch off from Route 5, most heading northwest—Route 30 in Brattleboro, Route 103 in Rockingham, Route 108 in Springfield, Route 12 in Hartland, and Route 14 in White River Junction. Routes 9, 11, 131, and 4 head west, connecting Route 5 to Route 100, which runs up the center of the state.

Each of these roads leads through small towns and long stretches of rural landscapes marked by mountains and narrow valleys. Take any of these, and wander deeper into rural Vermont on the unnumbered roads that branch off of them. Don't worry (except in mud season) about leaving the pavement behind. Vermont has many unpaved roads, a wise decision in a climate where frost makes smaller paved roads look like fruitcake with all the nuts pulled out. These unpaved roads are usually smooth to travel and are easy to repair in the spring by simply running a road grader over them.

Quechee and Woodstock

Route 4 crosses over the deep and dramatic **Quechee Gorge** in the town of Quechee, well worth a stop to walk along the rim and down to the base on the southern side of the road. The village of Quechee is heavily developed, but if you pass through the covered bridge and turn right, you'll soon be out of it and find the peaceful setting of the **Quechee Inn at Marshland Farm** (1119 Main St.; 802-295-3133 or 800-235-3133; quecheeinn.com).

Once the home of Colonel Joseph Marsh, Vermont's first lieutenant governor, the 1793 home has been lovingly restored into a family-friendly and comfortably warm and casual country inn with 22 nicely decorated guest rooms, with pieced quilts, wide-board floors (some as wide as 24 inches), and views of the pond, the river, and the woodlands that surround the property.

Rates include a substantial buffet breakfast. Children are more than welcome and a family suite is located on the lower floor with no surrounding guest rooms, perfect for parents who worry that other guests may not enjoy their children's enthusiasm.

The inn also boasts one of the state's finest dining options, **Quechee Inn Restaurant,** where you can find creations such as sage-rubbed pork tenderloin seared and sliced over apricot-brandied butternut leeks with cheddar potato croquettes and a port wine peppercorn reduction. If you're driving through, the luncheon is delectable with offerings such as a fresh sandwich buffet and a choice of two salads, or marinated beef tips with sautéed wild mushrooms, onions, and egg noodles. There is a comprehensive wine list and a range of decadent desserts. The talented chefs here are passionate about using locally grown and produced ingredients whenever they can, and they combine them brilliantly. This is a restaurant to travel far for. Reservations are suggested.

If it's the outdoors you crave, check out Quechee Inn's wide range of outdoor sports for all age groups in their **Wilderness Trails** program, among them: flat-water and whitewater paddling through the waters of the neighboring wildlife sanctuary, a fly-fishing school, mountain bikes, cross-country ski trails alongside Quechee Gorge, ice skating, tubing, and snowshoeing, all with or without guides, instruction, and equipment—even ice-skate rentals. Wilderness Trails has 18 kilometers of groomed cross-country ski trails, over rolling terrain and past beaver lodges, waterfalls, and the fields and woods of Marshland Farm. Four kilometers of the trails are suitable for ski skating.

Nearby **Woodstock** is unquestionably pretty, especially around its town green, from which a covered bridge is visible. It is also well aware of its own charms, and is perhaps the state's most pernicious speed trap. That said, there is a lot to see and do here, and tourism has been a part of the town's history for at least the past century, so the tourists who fill the little boutiques are authentic, too.

Woodstock can thank the late Laurance Rockefeller for a great many things, not the least of which is preserving its early village landscape by burying telephone and electric lines. Woodstock's history as a retreat for the wealthy has left it a legacy of fine homes and estates, one of which has become the nucleus for an unusual national park.

In addition to its great wealth, the Rockefeller family is well known for its deep commitment to conservation, an interest that first took shape in Woodstock. At the ***Marsh-Billings-Rockefeller National Historic Park*** (54 Elm St.; 802-457-3368), visitors can discover how the ideas of the first American conservationist, George Perkins Marsh, were put into action, first by rail king Frederick Billings and later by the Rockefellers. This is the only national park to concentrate on land stewardship and its evolution in America. The park's visitor center is located in an 1895 carriage barn, and provides self-guided maps and information on what there is to see here. There are approximately 20 miles of carriage roads and trails to explore. In fact, part of this network of trails leads to the ***Precipice Trail***, which in turn leads to the summit of Mount Tom. It's about 2.5 miles round-trip, but the views are worth it.

Atop a wooded hill sits ***Marsh-Billings-Rockefeller Mansion and Gardens.*** Originally a brick federal-style home, this mansion is part of the park and has been transformed in several stages into a stylish Victorian, with windows, fabrics, and wallpapers by the Tiffany studio. Like the house, the gardens were updated and expanded in stages, each time by a foremost landscape architect. Ranger-led tours, the only way to see the house and gardens, are offered while the park is open, 10 a.m. to 5 p.m. every day from Memorial Day through Oct. Reservations for the tours are a good idea. Admission is charged.

Adjacent to the park you will find the ***Billings Farm & Museum*** (69 Old River Rd.; 802-457-2355; billingsfarm.org), a working farm and a museum of New England farm and rural life. Your visit here will include visiting the Jersey cows in the dairy barn, meeting the other livestock that live here, and exploring the 1890 farmhouse, creamery, and dairy.

Open daily late Apr through Oct, 10 a.m. to 5 p.m. Open weekends only Nov through Feb and school vacations from 10 a.m. to 3:30 p.m. Admission is charged.

Love Those Cows

Test your bovine IQ at the "Cowlege Bowl" competition for families and sample Vermont dairy products, from freshly churned butter to hand-cranked ice cream. Billings Farm & Museum makes learning about its resident Jersey cows fun for the whole family at the Annual Cow Appreciation Day in late July.

In 2003 Woodstock became the home of the National Park Service's first interpretive program devoted to understanding the Civil War from a civilian perspective. Park historians schedule and lead the *Civil War Home Front Walking Tour* of sites in Woodstock that were significant in Vermont's considerable war effort. The 2-hour tour documents the war's impact on small towns in Vermont, examining its effects on places far from the battlefields. Sites on the tours—which you can also visit on your own—include the Woodstock First Congregational Church, where abolitionists met long before the war itself; River Street Cemetery, burial site of black Civil War veterans from Woodstock's free African-American community; the home of Senator Jacob Collamer, fighter for equal rights and Lincoln supporter, the "Pentagon of Vermont," and office of Adjutant General Peter Washburn; and the Marsh-Billings-Rockefeller National Historical Park. The tours are free, but reservations are essential: (802) 457-3368, ext. 22. And yes, there's an app for that. Check for links on the National Park Service's website (nps.gov/mabi/planyourvisit/civil-war-home-front-walking-tour.htm).

Woodstock is unique in many ways, not the least of which is that it is home to more Paul Revere foundry bells than any other town in the US—a total of five. The earliest, dating to 1818, resides on the porch of the Congregational church. Another is on a plinth behind the Woodstock Inn, one is at the Masonic Temple, and the remaining two are at the Universalist and Episcopal churches.

The *Appalachian Trail* crosses Route 12 just north of Woodstock, and you can easily hike a section as a day hike, or begin a more extended trip there. This part of the trail covers fairly gentle terrain, through hillside forests and lowland meadows. Bordered by a strip of public land, this narrow ribbon is home to rare and endangered plants. It also provides a valuable habitat for wildlife, and traverses the headwaters of the White and Ottauquechee Rivers. Volunteers from the Green Mountain Club and the Dartmouth College Outing Club maintain this part of the famous trail, which crosses Vermont on its way from Maine to Georgia.

A few miles west of Woodstock is *Jackson House Inn* (43 Senior Ln.; 802-457-2065 or 800-448-1890; jacksonhouse.com), with 11 richly appointed guest rooms and suites, which all received an updating when new innkeepers Rick and Kathy Terwelp purchased the property in 2010. Each room is designed in a different style, ranging from the floral Victorian air of the Mary Todd Lincoln Room to Clara's Corner, which features crisp geometric lines, beiges, and leather with crimson accents. Rooms feature massage tubs, individual climate control, sitting areas, gas fireplaces, and other amenities.

There are extensive gardens behind the inn, and the dining room overlooks these through a wall of windows. Room rates include breakfast. Check the website regularly for specials and packages offered throughout the year.

Heading south on Senior Lane, then turning right onto Route 4 will bring you to Bridges Road (a right off Route 4 about 1/10 mile after Westerdale Road). Here you will find *Lincoln Bridge,* which used to be in the middle of Woodstock, where the Billings Bridge is now. But in an 1869 flood, the entire structure was washed some distance downstream, where it came to rest, intact, on an island. Charles Lincoln's bridge had also been washed away by the flood, but it was completely destroyed. Lincoln waited for a heavy winter with a hard freeze and plenty of snow, and hauled his newfound bridge up Route 4 on a sled. It has been at its present location, through hail and high water, since 1877.

Its ability to withstand being ripped from its moorings and carried by floodwaters is a testimony to its design, patented by T. W. Pratt in 1844. Its vertical posts and crossed iron rods were to become the prototype for hundreds of steel railroad bridges built with the growth of the railroads, but this one is the only remaining original covered bridge of this design.

A few miles south of Woodstock is *Kedron Valley Inn* (10671 South Rd.; 802-457-1473; kedronvalleyinn.com), which has an excellent restaurant with a talented culinary team. The menu changes seasonally, and may include an herbed Misty Knoll turkey burger with cranberry sage mayo

A Stop for Freedom

The *Kedron Valley Inn* has an interesting history and is one of only a handful of places in the state that can be documented as a stop on the Underground Railroad. The nature of the endeavor—which was illegal—made it important not to keep any written records, so although many homes are thought to have been involved, only a few can be identified for certain. The building, which sits in front of the main inn and is now an annex with more guest rooms, was once a general store, and its owner was very active in helping escaping slaves. One of the guest rooms occupies two floors, and the stairway between the two was once concealed in a closet. The room above was completely out of sight, an excellent hiding place. General stores made good stations in the Underground Railroad because no one took any special notice when large boxes were loaded and unloaded there.

and sweet potato steak fries, or a filet of beef with a Madeira mushroom demi, parsley oil, Vermont blue cheese mashed potatoes, and seasonal vegetables.

If you opt to stay at the inn, you'll have 25 rooms from which to choose, all with private baths. The inn also has its own private swimming pond with a sandy beach and comfortable waterside chairs. Oh, and if the inn looks somehow familiar to you and you're not sure why, think back to those classic Budweiser commercials, the ones with the beautiful Clydesdales prancing through the snow past a gorgeous New England–style inn. Remember now? Yep, that's Kedron Valley Inn in the background. Cool.

Suicide Six ski area (Stagecoach Road, South Pomfret; 802-457-6661 or 800-448-7900, snow conditions (802) 457-6666; suicide6.com) sounds fiercer than it is. One of the smaller of the state's ski areas, it is well designed for families and offers adult-and-child ski clinics on weekends, when parents can learn to help their children become better skiers, as well as pick up a few tips themselves. Although the elevation is not as high as many other areas, Suicide Six has an evenly divided mix of beginner, intermediate, and expert terrain. It is under the same ownership as the Woodstock Inn, and the inn offers a number of attractive packages that combine lodging and lift tickets.

Hartland–Windsor

On Route 5 south out of White River Junction, you'll find a relatively large amount of industry in the form of farms, factories, computer-consulting companies, and other businesses. This part of the road is relatively industrial, but farms suddenly appear, along with a sprinkling of motels, campgrounds, and private homes. This state highway is a winding, downhill road that plays tag with parallel I-91, weaving over and under it at various points. As you drive into Hartland proper, Routes 5 and 12 merge. Head north on Route 12 for 2 miles; you'll come into Hartland Four Corners and *Skunk Hollow Tavern* (12 Brownsville Rd.; 802-436-2139; skunkhollowtavern.com), a neighborhood pub and restaurant that was voted *Yankee Magazine's* "Best Locals Tavern" in Vermont in 2011. Good prices and good food are on tap here, the menu is written on a large slate, and darts fly on Fri nights.

The second floor at Skunk Hollow is more formally decorated, but the same menu is served. Reservations are strongly suggested since the downstairs pub, a favorite local hangout, fills up most weekends by 6 p.m.

Open Wed through Sun 5 p.m. to close. Wed is open-mic night and live bands play on Fri.

that'salotof baaaaaaa

In 1838 a herd of 18,000 sheep passed over the *Cornish Windsor Covered Bridge,* a predecessor of the one that spans the Connecticut River between the two towns today. Three presidents—Hayes, Wilson, and Theodore Roosevelt—have crossed the present bridge, which was built in 1866 after the earlier bridge was swept away in a flood. No one has recorded just how many sheep fit onto the bridge at one time, or what it sounded like in there as they crossed.

A few miles south on Route 5 is *Windsor.* A short distance north of town is *Artisan's Park.* It's not a park but more a grouping of incredibly down-to-earth hidden gems. Within this "park" you will find a brewery, a distillery, a cheese shop, a sculpture garden, glass factory and pottery, and an outdoor outfitter. Huh—who knew? Here's a little more about all of them:

Harpoon Brewery (336 Ruth Carney Dr.; 802-674-5491; harpoonbrewery.com) offers tastings and tours, the latter every hour from 5 to 7 p.m. Fri, 11 a.m. to 5 p.m. Sat, and noon to 4 p.m. Sun. Sister brewery to the Boston Harpoon Brewery, this one is housed in the former Catamount Brewery building. They expanded to keep up with demand. Lunch is served in the brewery or in the Riverbend Taps and Beer Garden. You can get samplers of their ales to taste with your grilled panini sandwiches. Open Sun through Wed 10 a.m. to 6 p.m. and until 9 p.m. Thurs through Sat.

The Brewery has also teamed up with the **Sustainable Farmer** (Artisans Way; 802-674-4260; mysustainablefarmer.com) to sponsor a free summer music series on the pavilion in front of the brewery. Every weekend from 2 to 8 p.m. beginning in June, a selection of bands will play under the stars. The brewery promises to have its outdoor taps flowing and pizza ovens hot.

Not a beer and pizza kind of person? (Um, we just can't call you "friend," then.) Head over to the Sustainable Farmer for an incredible array of Vermont cheeses, maple products, sustainable honey products, and other Vermont-made goodies. Everything is from local farms that embrace sustainable agriculture. Free tastings abound. Many of their products are also offered at their website, and classes are offered year-round. Open daily 11 a.m. to 5 p.m.

Okay, now that you have your food, walk a ways to the **SILO/American Crafted Spirits** (3 Artisans Way; 802-674-4220; silovodka.com) for your libations. You can also take a tour of this new distillery and enjoy a sampling of their very own SILO Vodka. Open Thurs through Mon 11 a.m. to 5 p.m.

Don't leave Artisan's Park without visiting **Simon Pearce's** glass factory and pottery (109 Park Rd.; 802-674-6280; simonpearce.com). Take a self-guided tour through this glass master's creations. The store and glass factory are open daily 10 a.m. to 5 p.m., and the pottery is open 10 a.m. to 3 p.m. on the weekends.

What would you do if you found yourself with a 14-acre field along the Connecticut River in the middle of Vermont? Build a garden, of course. At least that's what you do when you are Terry McDonnell (owner of the Sustainable Farmer) and have no formal landscaping training whatsoever. No, really, we're not joking. He did just that. In 1997 Terry started working on the **Path of Life Garden** (36 Park Rd; 802-674-9933; pathoflifegarden.com), which now features 18 works of art that symbolize one's journey through life. Also a part of Artisan's Park, this garden can be enjoyed by people of all ages and includes a maze, an amphitheater, a tunnel, and other structures that tell a story and just might prompt you to ponder where *your* journey is going. There are also hiking trails to be explored, both in warm weather and on skis in the snow months. Path of Life Garden is open year-round dawn to dusk. Admission is charged.

Great River Outfitters (same contact information as Path of Life) is a great organization to use for your outdoor needs. They operate year-round and offer just about everything outdoorsy—canoeing, kayaking, rafting, tubing, camping, snowshoeing, yoga, and more. They can guide you on a trip and/or give you lessons. Large and small groups can be accommodated. Check out the website for all their offerings.

They also offer ***dogsledding trips*** through the Path of Life Garden. The trips take about an hour and you have the opportunity to meet the dogs, ask questions, and take pictures. About four adults can fit on the sled, but two more small children may be able to be accommodated if they can fit on your lap. There is a strict 400-pound limit for the safety of the dogs and riders. It's always best to call ahead to make sure there's enough snow and that your needs can be accommodated.

Back on Route 5, which is also the main street of Windsor, and you'll pass between rows of well-kept brick houses and distinguished business blocks, built when Windsor was a major player in the precision tool industry.

Just south of the intersection with Route 44 is a huge brick building, the ***American Precision Museum*** (196 S. Main St.; 802-674-5781; american precision.org) on Route 5. The museum is a tribute to a bygone era when automated machines were a wonder to behold. Huge milling machines, lathes, steam engines, and generators fill an entire room, looking every bit the dinosaurs they are today.

Many of the machines here were invented by Vermonters who, far too stubborn to ask for help from the outside world, had to find a way to perform the tasks themselves. It seems strange to see all these machines placed together like some Industrial Revolution graveyard. Glass showcases contain salesman's samples, planes, and levels, some with the original instruction booklets. Other display cases hold the modern calculator of 1903, a cylindrical slide rule, plastic toy molds, and early-model pencil sharpeners.

Cases display miniature models of lathes, presses, band saws, and shapers, scaled to 1/16 of their true size. They actually run—press a button and the gears spin, just like the real thing. They're built by John Aschauer, a former toolmaker who spent 27 years making these miniature machines. He used his memory to re-create them. The museum is open daily from late May through Oct, 10 a.m. to 5 p.m. Children under 6 are admitted free.

High on a hill overlooking the town stands a mansion built in 1901 during Windsor's glory days, which has been restored as *Juniper Hill Inn* (153 Pembroke Rd.; 802-674-5273; juniperhillinn.com). Listed on the National Register of Historic Places, this inn does it right. It is also a 2013 recipient of TripAdvisor's Certificate of Excellence. In the summer its gardens are lovely, and you can enjoy them from a terrace with valley views for a backdrop. Fine paneling gives the large public rooms elegance, but they are still very comfortable, with big windows and well-chosen antiques. Its 16 guest rooms are bright and large, some with fireplaces, all with private baths. Breakfast is included in your rate and can be served in your room if you ask.

If you choose to venture out to *Madelyn's Dining Room at Juniper Hill Inn* you can have breakfast there, but only if you're a guest. Dinner, however, is open to the public and both are scrumptious affairs with farm-to-table offerings prepared by the inn's executive chef. You have your choice of dining areas: If you want formal, eat inside in the candlelit dining room. If al fresco is in order, the terrace overlooking the gardens is the perfect place to enjoy the delicious cauliflower and cheddar soup, maybe followed by a maple-glazed roasted chicken with bread and apple pudding. For very special occasions, plan an intimate dinner for two to a party of eight under the inn's tent on their grounds or maybe dine beneath their grape arbor and enjoy the sounds of a country evening. Whatever you desire, call ahead for reservations so your every need can be met. The restaurant is open daily for dinner starting at 6 p.m.

So if you've stuffed yourself at the inn and want to walk off some calories, head across the street to *Paradise Park* (Paradise Park Road), where you will find 5.5 miles of trails through Windsor Town Forest to explore. The bird watching here is wonderful.

South of Windsor is Mount Ascutney, a lone mountain (known as a monadnock) with an elevation of 3,130 feet. Vermont Routes 131, 44, and 44A travel up the sides of the mountain and afford great views, as do a number of New Hampshire roads and I-91. The name is probably better known to some because of the major ski area that graced the mountain. The ski area has recently seen some financial difficulties and is not operating as of press time. The resort at the base of the mountain, the Holiday Inn Club Vacations at Ascutney Mountain Resort, is still in operation as both a hotel and a time share, however, and has no ties with the ski area at this time. Time will tell what happens with the ski area; we can only hope it will be revived once again.

But if you've been reading this book, you know that Vermont mountains are not only good for their skiing. Mount Ascutney is no exception. Just ask the members of the **Vermont Hang Gliding Association** (vhga.aero). Ascutney's solid granite outcroppings serve as a perfect departure point for these winged aeronauts. On nice days three seasons of the year, as many as 30 hang gliders launch from the 2 mountaintop sites. They're fun to watch, and if you're there when the last pilot lifts off, you may be asked to assist in the launch. The most successful flights can last 90 miles to the New Hampshire shore. The current record, set in 2002, is held by Curt Warren, who traveled 131.6 miles to Connecticut!

There are also plenty of hiking trails on the mountain and camping is available at the 2,000-acre **Mt. Ascutney State Park** (1826 Back Mountain Rd.; 802-674-2060; vtstateparks.com/htm/ascutney.htm). There are 39 tent and trailer sites and 10 lean-tos available. There are 2 bath buildings with hot paid showers. While you can hike the miles of trails, you can also travel to the top of the mountain by car. The summit road through the park winds through mixed hardwood forests to a parking area at about 2,800 feet. You can walk from here another 344 steep feet to the actual summit, where you can climb a former fire tower for outstanding views on a clear day. The park is open late May through mid-Oct., 10 a.m. to sunset. The summit road may occasionally be closed due to park events.

Springfield–Chester

Route 5 heading south from Windsor into Springfield is a winding road with more farms, where in some spots the forest is so thick, it almost forms a canopy that blots out the summer sun. Just past Wilgus State Park about a mile south of Route 131 in Windsor, rows and rows of corn line both sides of the road from late spring into September. Between Windsor and Springfield lies the town of Weathersfield. As you pass through Weathersfield Bow, where the peninsula juts out sharply to the left, the identity of the land seems to meld with that of New Hampshire, which is visible most of the time from Route 5. Sometimes it seems as if you can wade across the river.

On a blustery winter night, few sights in Vermont are as welcome as that of the ***Inn at Weathersfield*** (1342 Rte. 106, Perkinsville; 802-263-9217; weathersfieldinn.com), its white clapboard facade aglow across the snow-covered front yard. Well, okay, it's beautiful in the summer, too. Each of the 12 rooms is individually decorated, and since the inn's 2 buildings date from 1792 and 1890, respectively, you know that each will be shaped differently. Taking advantage of the vagaries of historic buildings, rooms are tucked under the eaves (often with skylights) and even on the top floor, where a charming aerie offers a whirlpool tub, fireplace, sitting room, and a private rooftop deck. New innkeepers Richard and Marilee Spanjan are Tennessee transplants and some scoffed at their decision to make such a drastic change in their lives. They seem to be doing just fine, though. The inn has recently been named to the governor's list of Green Hotels and they work hard to reduce their carbon footprint. They are also incorporating plans for a cooking school that will offer classes to nonprofessional chefs of all skill levels. They certainly have the basis for this.

Inn Chef Jason Tostrup believes strongly in local agriculture, and works with local farms to keep his menu filled with Vermont-raised ingredients, from the syrup on the breakfast pancakes (even the eggs they are made with) to the tangy-sweet raspberries that garnish dessert. Meals at the inn are incredible and award-winning.

Route 11 leads from Route 5 to ***Springfield,*** an old mill town with more than its fair share of ups and downs, but currently well on the up side. There are many towns in the US named Springfield. All of them were named after Springfield, Massachusetts, and the Springfield in Vermont holds the distinction of being the first.

The ***Eureka Schoolhouse*** (470 Charlestown Rd; 802-828-3051), located on Route 11 just west of I-91, is the oldest schoolhouse still standing in Vermont. It was used continually from 1785 until 1900 and was

vermonttrivia

In 2008 Springfield also was declared home of television's *The Simpsons,* winning a nationwide contest with the other 12 Springfields that submitted three- to five-minute videos.

reconstructed in 1968 on its current spot. It is currently in use as a tourist information center.

Inside, the schoolhouse is still set up as though a group of children will walk through at any minute, with desks and slates and quill pens and inkwells. But in a nod to current realities, such modern amenities as a fire extinguisher, telephone, and space heater are inside, too. Each of the old wooden shakes on the roof seems to have a personality of its own, as no two adjacent shakes point in the same direction. Open Wed through Mon, Memorial Day to Columbus Day, 10 a.m. to 4 p.m.

To the left of the schoolhouse is the 37-foot-long **Baltimore Covered Bridge.** It's the last covered bridge in existence in the town of Springfield. It, too, was moved from its original spot over Great Brook in North Springfield, where it had stood since it was built in 1870 and was reassembled on this site in 1970. It is dedicated to Senator Ralph E. Flanders, who was active in its preservation.

The **Springfield Art and Historical Society** (9 Elm St.; 802-885-2415; springfieldartandhistoricalsociety.org) maintains memorabilia of early Springfield, and its Miller Art Center houses a collection of dolls and information on Joel Ellis, America's first doll manufacturer. Born in Barnard, Vermont, in 1830, he was an inventor and manufacturer who started out making baby buggies and tops, and at the age of 28 started a factory for the manufacture of wooden dolls. He took out a patent on his system for the assembly of movable joints. They also have a collection of Bennington Pottery, railroad artifacts, old photographs and postcards, World War II memorabilia, and other items. The Miller Center is free and open Sat only, from 11 a.m. to 4 p.m., June through Aug. While they don't answer their phones during their off-season, you can usually reach someone via e-mail through the website.

For a feeling of upper-crust and intellectual Vermont of the 19th century, stay at **Hartness House** (30 Orchard St.; 802-885-2115; hartness house.com). Listed on the National Register of Historic Places, this house was the home of James Hartness, whose fortune was based upon his invention of the turret lathe, and the

vermonttrivia

Springfield became such a major manufacturing force in the machine tool industry that it gained the attention of Hitler during World War II—it was on his top-10 list of targets.

more than 120 other patents he held. The inn today holds many pieces of memorabilia from Hartness's life, including pages from his granddaughter Mary Fenn that give a glimpse into the family's daily life. Be prepared if you stay here, though; the house is old and as such has character (and is rumored to have a ghost as well). Each of the rooms is displayed on the inn's website so you can have an idea of what you would like to book.

When you enter the inn, you may be surprised by a strange-looking object on the lawn. Not to worry, this object is Hartness's 1910 Equalatoral Turret Telescope, and one of the first tracking telescopes in the US. You can learn more about this telescope and its unique, talented inventor in the underground museum at the inn, the very same room where Hartness designed many of his tools. Yes, we said "underground." How cool is that?

Springfield is also home to **Wellwood Orchards** (529 Wellwood Orchard Rd.; 802-263-5200; wellwoodorchards.net), where from mid-June you can pick your own strawberries, raspberries, and blueberries. In early September to November you can either pick your own apples or buy them from the stand. Tour the orchards on a wagon ride, and before picking, let the kids enjoy the petting zoo. Among the apple varieties are Macoun, McIntosh, Empire, Cortland, and Red Delicious; there are also a few old-fashioned varieties. The shop has pies, cider, maple syrup and candies, pumpkins, and squash.

Route 11 leads to Chester, 8 miles to the west. Beautifully restored Victorian houses line both sides of the narrow green. Look for School Street, a block off the green, and **Rose Arbour Tea Room & Gift Shop** (55 School St.; 802-875-4767; rosearbour.com). This is an old-fashioned kind of tea shop—you thought nobody made finger sandwiches and served fresh berries with clotted cream anymore?—that takes its tea seriously. While cream teas with scones are available anytime, for the full traditional afternoon tea, you'll need to give the owner 48 hours' notice, so she can prepare the special treats that bring her customers from all over southern Vermont.

Classical music plays throughout lunch, which may include real English scones, a light herbal chicken salad, or an authentic ploughman's plate, with hearty cheddar, homemade bread, and an apple.

The tearoom is open from 11 a.m. to 5 p.m. Wed through Sat, Nov through June and every day July through Oct.

Upstairs at Rose Arbour are 3 well-appointed rooms with four-poster beds, old samplers, and feather duvets. When you're not sleeping upstairs or relaxing on the screened second-floor porch, you can play croquet or admire the herb gardens out back.

Fine homes, mostly Victorian, line the main street of Chester, which is also Route 11. Just out of the village in Proctorsville is **Baba-à-Louis Bakery** (92 Route 11; 802-875-4666; babalouisbakery.com), best known outside the area for the popular cookbook *Baba à Louis Bread Book,* featuring Chef John McLure's best bread and pastry recipes. Breads and cookies are for sale, along with light lunches, in this glistening, high-ceilinged bakeshop, where you can buy the book, meet the author, and even get his floury autograph. Bread is not the only thing John McLure designs, however; he also designed the unique building as well. Open Wed noon to 6 p.m., Thurs 7 a.m. to 6 p.m., Fri 7 a.m. to 7 p.m., Sat 7 a.m. to 6 p.m., and Sun 9 a.m. to 5 p.m. Buffet lunch is served Thurs through Sat, with brunch being served on Sun. If you're lucky, you'll happen onto one of their "Leftovers" sales that sometimes happen on Monday; call to check.

If you leave Chester on Route 103 to head back to Route 5 and the Connecticut River, you'll see **Curtis' All American Restaurant** (908 Rte. 103 South; 802-875-6999) on the right, just outside of town. Co-owner Sarah Tuff is daughter of Curtis Tuff, whose outdoor barbecue has been an institution in Putney since 1968 (curtisbbqvt.com). Sarah and her husband, Christopher Parker, apprenticed under the tutelage of Curtis, the master, for several years

Mountain Lions in Vermont?

Catamount is the name given to the eastern native puma by Vermonters. Also known as the mountain lion, this cat is capable of 40-foot leaps and incredible speeds over short distances. The animals were thought to be extinct in Vermont since early in the 20th century, victims of a bounty imposed to protect domestic sheep and cattle.

Recently residents have reported sightings that have raised hopes that there is still a viable population. If you happen to see a big, golden-brownish cat, 4 to 6 feet long with a 4-foot tail, above all, keep a safe distance. But if you can, take a picture of it, then call Vermont Fish and Game. They'll probably tell you it's a bobcat, but you'll have your picture.

Say "Cheese!"

As interest in cooking and fine dining has blossomed, so has interest in Vermont's fine farm-made cheeses. Sometimes referred to as farmhouse cheeses, these excellent specialty cheeses are made in small lots. One producer is Vermont Shepherd, founded by sheep farmers in 1990 who had to deal with an excess of ewe's milk after spring lambing. When demand exceeded their production capacity, they enlisted other sheep farmers, who now make cheese that is aged in the Vermont Shepherd caves. Other farms to look for are Vermont Butter and Cheese Creamery, Orb Weaver Farm, Shelburne Farms, and Grafton Village Cheese. The Vermont Cheese Council website features a virtual tour of the cheese farms; vtcheese.com.

before starting out on their own—and they seem to have gotten things just about right. They serve the same succulent ribs and chicken available in Putney, as well as smoked beef brisket, chopped barbecue chicken and pork (to eat in their spacious restaurant or to go, by the pint), nachos, and quesadillas. All meat is served with a wide choice of sides, including baked beans, coleslaw, corn bread, collard greens, potato salad, and corn on the cob. Open 11 a.m. to 11 p.m. Wed, 11 a.m. to 9 p.m. Thurs through Sat, and 11 a.m. to 8 p.m. Sun.

If you head out of Chester on Route 35 South, you'll soon enter the village of Grafton, a very tourist-oriented town. Here you will find *The Grafton Inn* (92 Main St.; 800-843-1801; graftoninnvermont.com), a historic inn offering a page of yesteryear. With a 200-year history, this inn's hand-hewn beams and antique furnishings will make you feel as if you stepped back in time. But that doesn't mean you have to make do without modern amenities. Oh, no, this inn offers many, including private baths, Wi-Fi, and fitness center. One of the best amenities, however, is access to *Grafton Ponds Outdoor Center,* the inn's year-round recreation center that offers Nordic skiing, snowshoeing, and snow tubing in the winter and mountain biking, hiking, canoeing, Frisbee golf, and swimming in the swim pond. Check for details at the inn or on the inn's website.

Before leaving town, stop at *Grafton Village Cheese* (56 Townshend Rd.; 802-843-2221 or 800-472-3866; graftonvillagecheese.com), where you'll find a large artisanal cheese selection (more than 80 varieties), wines, microbrews, Vermont products, and gifts. There are plenty of samples available to help you make your decision. Be sure to check out the new Grafton Cave Aged line, introduced in 2011 and sending the company in a new direction, away from their traditional cheddar cheese. You can see parts of the cheese-making process at their production facility at 533 Townshend Rd., but only on select days. Call ahead or check at the shop to see which ones. They also have a shop in Brattleboro.

vermonttrivia

Some states have wine trails, some states have historic walks—well, Vermont has a Cheese Trail (really, what did you expect?). There are more than 40 stops on the trail and they are detailed on the Vermont Cheese Council's website (vtcheese.com).

Route 35 continues south through the town of Athens. As with Route 121 in Grafton, it's common in Vermont to have numbered main state roads turn to dirt in certain areas. Route 35 is dirt for a few miles, then turns back to blacktop.

In summertime pick-your-own and porch-side farm stands abound throughout the state. There's usually at least one in each town. Also keep a lookout for the ingenious scarecrows people construct to fend off intruders.

Route 35 meets up with Route 30 in Townshend, sitting around its postcard-picture common. North on Route 30 is the **Townshend Lake Dam** over the West River, operated by the US Army Corps of Engineers. The dam was built between 1958 and 1961 to better control flooding of the West River. The dam is 1,000 feet long and 133 feet tall and has a capacity of almost 11 billion gallons of water.

If you drive across the top of the dam, you'll get a strange, vertiginous feeling. There are lots of paths to explore. On weekends the parking lot to the Townshend Dam Recreation Area may be almost full with mostly Vermont plates, but it is usually relatively quiet: no loud radios and just the clink of horseshoes and the sound of people's voices.

The recreational facilities at the dam include picnic tables, horseshoes, boating and swimming areas, volleyball, and several trails, all with a view of the dam.

On the other side of the dam is **Townshend State Park** (2755 State Forest Rd.; 802-365-7500; vtstateparks.com/htm/townshend.htm), which sits at the base of Bald Mountain (elevation: 1,680 feet). The land on which the park sits was originally purchased to be preserved as a state forest. The state park was later built by the Civilian Conservation Corps. Their work can be seen in the park office and tent platforms. The forest has a total of 856 acres and the park offers 34 camping sites on its 41 acres. There are bathrooms and paid showers. The swimming, boating, and fishing in the 95-acre Townshend Lake is great, too. Hiking trails up Bald Mountain lead to amazing views to the north, south, and east, but the 1.7-mile vertical hike up 1,100 feet can be a bit difficult, so be prepared. The park is open Memorial Day to Labor Day.

Scott Covered Bridge, which you can see from Route 30, not far from the dam, is the longest wooden span in Vermont. (Remember the one in Windsor is not completely in Vermont.) Built in 1870 by Harrison Chamberlain, the bridge's 277-foot length consists of three spans: one town lattice truss and two king post trusses. Attempts to secure and support the bridge have met with limited success throughout the years. In February 2012 the state transportation agency deemed it unsafe and closed it to foot traffic. While the bridge survived extensive flooding from Hurricane Irene, officials feared it wouldn't take much to cause a collapse. So, please view the bridge from a safe distance while preservation agencies work to find a way to save it.

Bellows Falls–Putney

As you travel south on Route 5, Springfield melds into Rockingham and the town of *Bellows Falls,* which is actually a village within the town of Rockingham—as is Saxtons River, farther west. Perhaps this habit of having what seems like towns inside of other towns is the most puzzling of all New England's idiosyncrasies.

On Route 5 in Rockingham you'll spot *Leslie's Tavern* (660 Rockingham Rd.; 802-463-4929; lesliestavern.com), an informal restaurant located in an 18th-century farmhouse. Husband-and-wife team John and Leslie Marston offer what they call "local-world cuisine" based on fresh produce from their own extensive gardens. Many of the dishes are low-fat and heart-healthy as well as delicious and unique—oh, and always changing. The setting is beautiful and the couple invite you to stroll through their gardens when the weather warrants it or sit by one of the inn's 7 fireplaces if your toes need warming. Alfresco dining on the deck is available in the warmer months and cooking classes are offered throughout the year. Leslie's is open Wed through Sun; dinner is served beginning at 5 p.m. Reservations can be made by phone or at their website.

Bear left as you head south on Route 5 to enter Bellows Falls for a cross-section of modern-day Vermont history: the *Miss Bellows Falls Diner* (90 Rockingham St.; 802-463-3700). Housed in one of the original Worcester dining cars from the 1920s and 1930s, which was moved from a former location in Lowell, Massachusetts, in 1942, this is Vermont's only surviving barrel-roofed diner. Miss Bellows Falls Diner has retained the original paneling, counter, stools, and many of the other pieces. You really will feel as if you've stepped back into history. Sit back and enjoy the banter between the many locals who visit the well-liked staff here.

It would be a shame to pass through here without seeing *Bellows Falls* (the actual falls for which the village was named), just to your left at the square and visible from the tall stone bridge that leads to New Hampshire. Upstream are the dammed falls and another iron bridge, but the best views are of this lower section. These are a raging torrent of froth in the spring, but impressive anytime, not so much for their height as for the depth of the gorge and the amount of water compressed between the narrow rock walls. In case you're interested in geology, this is about the only place where you can actually see the seam in the rocks where the two tectonic plates meet—New Hampshire is actually a piece of Africa left off when that plate moved away. If that continent had taken all of itself, you'd be standing on the Atlantic shore here, and Vermont wouldn't be the only New England state without a coastline.

fallsfirsts

The first bridge to span the Connecticut River was built from Bellows Falls across to Walpole, New Hampshire. Built in 1785 by Colonel Enoch Hale, the bridge was replaced by a toll bridge in 1840.

The falls claims to be the site of the first canal built in the country, completed in 1802, but the definition of "canal" varies and many places claim to be the first. Regardless, this one was at the very beginning.

While in Bellows Falls, take a walk to *The Square,* the area of town at the intersection of Westminster, Bridge, Rockingham, and Canal Streets. This is where a lot of the action is. Read on for more information.

Exner Block (7 Canal St.; 802-463-3252; ramp-vt.org) is a historic building beautifully restored to serve as a live/work setting for emerging artists.
The structure is charming, with wainscoting, pressed tin ceilings, and traditional hardware. The storefronts are eclectic and interesting.

Check out Bellows Falls' growing art scene the third Friday of each
month when the village opens its doors and hosts special events throughout.
Known as ***BF3F*** (The Square; 802-463-9404; bf3f.org), third Fridays feature
art, music, food, shopping, and fun from 5 to 8 p.m. Many businesses
participate.

The ***Bellows Falls Farmers' Market*** (bffarmersmarket.com) has
recently jumped into the BF3F action and has plans to extend their seasonal
market into the colder months in conjunction with the third Friday happen-
ings. They offer a wide variety of fresh fruit, vegetables, and baked goods
sold by local producers, as well as several takeout stalls featuring Thai,
Indian, and down-home goodies. A list of participating vendors and their
history is located on the website. Look for the market to be open from 4 to
6:30 or 7 p.m. depending on weather. Their regular season is from mid-May
to mid-Oct; after that they will be open on third Fridays only.

You're likely to see products from some of these very farms on the
menu at ***Popolo*** (36 The Square; 802 460 7676; popolo.us), which opened
in May 2012. Housed in the Wyndham Hotel building, Popolo uses locally
sourced products whenever possible in their panini sandwiches and salads, and on their pizzas. There is an extensive local beer list and the wine
choices are great as well. Open for lunch (11:30 a.m. to 2:30 p.m.), light fare
(2:30 to 5 p.m.), and dinner (5 to 9:30 p.m.) Tues through Sat and for brunch
on Sun (10 a.m. to 2 p.m.), with the bar remaining open later. Reservations
are suggested and recommended, but they will try to accommodate walk-ins
if they can. If you're a fan of Italian-inspired farm-to-table cuisine, Popolo
is the place to be.

Once you're stuffed, take a walk next door to see the huge (32-by-
40-foot) ***wall mural*** (52 The Square), painted by local artists Bonnie Turner
and Cliff Clear. It depicts the town square at the turn of the 19th century.
Many of the same buildings are still there.

In its long history, the town of ***Westminster,*** south of Bellows Falls,
has been variously part of New Hampshire, Massachusetts, New York, and
Vermont.

Waste Not, Want Not to the End

Bellows Falls resident Hetty Green, popularly known as "the Witch of Wall Street," was born in New Bedford, Massachusetts, in 1834. She was regarded as the richest woman in America and probably the cheapest, too.

As a young woman and heir to a New Bedford whaling fortune, Hetty Howland Robinson had flirted with New York society and danced with the Prince of Wales. She then multiplied her net worth by acquiring her aunt's sizable fortune as well, and by marrying Edward Green, a wealthy silk and tea trader who grew up in Bellows Falls. She threw him out after he failed to take her advice in business. Her son lost a leg because she was too stingy to take him to a doctor for a kneecap injury; when she finally did, a year later, it was under an assumed name so she could put him in the hospital's charity ward. By the time of her death in 1916, she had amassed a total of about $100 million, but when she had to travel to New York on business, she still stayed in a dollar-a-night rooming house in Brooklyn.

The town was first granted as part of Massachusetts and was known as Number One in 1735. The main village of Westminster lies on Route 5, which was originally constructed as the King's Highway and was built wide to allow for military training sessions by pre–Revolutionary War soldiers.

Westminster was in flux for the 12 years between 1740 and 1752, when the northern boundary of Massachusetts was determined to be farther south, and New Hampshire governor Benning Wentworth regranted the land to New Hampshirites. In 1772, however, New York got into the act by locating a county courthouse in the town. Westminster officially became part of Vermont along with the rest of the state in 1777, when the Vermont government proclaimed itself a free and independent republic.

On Route 5 in Westminster you'll see **_Harlow's Farm Stand_** (6365 Rte. 5; 802-722-3515; harlowfarm.com). After four generations in the same location—and beginning as a small roadside shack—Harlow's has grown to become a handsome, modern store, and recognized as one of the earliest organic farms in southern Vermont. It includes a wide assortment of organic vegetables, bedding plants, and a profusion of hanging baskets. Stop in for breakfast or lunch and select a table outside, where you can watch the cows graze in the back fields. Open 9 a.m. to 6 p.m. daily, May through Nov.

Going south on Route 5 for another 7 miles or so will take you straight into *Putney* and a slice of life almost frozen in time from the 1960s, when Putney was hippie heaven. As you roam its back roads, you'll still see, mixed in with the trust-fund farms, metamorphosed homes that grew out of the back-to-the-land homesteads of escapees from the draft and the modern world itself. Communes thrived, and while those days have gone, they have left Putney a nice, mellow place to spend time, a haven for artists and craftspeople.

In the center of town—the very center of town—you will find *The Gleanery* (133 Main St.; 802-387-3052; thegleanery.com). This BYOB cafe considers itself a gathering place for area artists, farmers, diners, chefs, and anyone else who wishes to drop in. They take a unique approach to community, and invite all to join them in their sleek and modern cafe where they serve fresh-baked goods, super fresh salads, burgers, chicken dishes, crepes, and soups. They also offer made-to-order French pressed coffee, loose-leaf teas, and more. Open Wed through Sat, 11:30 a.m. to 9 p.m., and 11:30 a.m. to 8 p.m. Sun. They also offer an array of locally jarred pickles, preserves, and dressings on their "jar wall." Their menu and offerings change with the seasons (sometimes daily) based on availability, so if you see something you want, take the chance to grab it. If it's a nice night, take your iced tea and sit on the front porch as the sun fades.

As the heart of Vermont's back-to-the-land movement, Putney is an appropriate home for an outstanding natural-fiber spinning mill. *Green Mountain Spinnery* (7 Brickyard Ln.; 802-387-4528; spinnery.com) processes local wool into knitting and weaving yarns, which you can purchase at their shop. The mill shop is open Mon through Fri 9 a.m. to 5:30 p.m., Sat 10 a.m. to 5:30 p.m., and Sun noon to 4 p.m.

Another great fit for Vermont ingenuity is the *Putney Mountain Winery* (8 Bellows Falls Rd.; 802-387-5925; putneywine.com), started in the 1990s by Charles and Kate Dodge. Charles, a music professor at Dartmouth College, was amused by his students' stories of home beer brewing. He considered trying it himself, but then inspiration struck and he decided that home winemaking was more his style. Today the winery has moved out of the Dodges' basement and into the Basketville building. They are open daily from 11 a.m. to 5 p.m. and invite you to visit to see the winemaking process and to taste their creations. If you can't make it to the area, Putney

Bogey in a Blizzard

Rudyard Kipling liked Vermont best in the winter, possibly because fewer people tried his patience then by invading his treasured privacy. Sir Arthur Conan Doyle, a frequent guest at Naulakha, gave Kipling a pair of skis, on which he loved to tour the 11-acre property. He was an early golf enthusiast and is credited by the US Golf Association with inventing winter golf. He painted golf balls red and created holes by sinking tin cans into the snow.

Mountain wines are available throughout the state. They are also a presence at numerous Vermont festivals and farmers' markets.

What better place to enjoy a bottle of Putney Mountain Wine than at the summit of **Putney Mountain?** The 1,600-foot elevation that rises west of town has a 360-degree unobstructed view of the valley, the river, and the surrounding hills and mountains. It's an easy walk via a trail that begins in Putney. From the winery, head southwest on Route 5 (Bellows Falls Road). Take your first right onto Kimball, which turns into Westminster Road. Travel about .08 mile and then take a left onto West Hill Road. In about 2.4 miles, you will reach unpaved Putney Mountain Road on your right. Watch for the parking area on the right. Park your car and follow the woods road to the summit, where you can sit, enjoy your wine, and watch hawks soaring on the thermals.

You might expect that Rudyard Kipling wrote *The Jungle Book* during languid and steamy afternoons of the Raj, somewhere in the India it portrayed, but it was actually written in Vermont in the town of **Dummerston**. So were *Captains Courageous* and some of the *Just So Stories*. Now you can relive Kipling's experience by staying at his house, **Naulakha** (481 Kipling Rd; 802-254-5135). Owned by the Landmark Trust USA (707 Kipling Rd.; 802-254-6868; landmarktrustusa.org), the house has been carefully restored, even to the shingled roof, just as Kipling had it built. Inside, the home gleams with polished wood; many of the furnishings belonged to the Kiplings. Available by advance reservation only, the house is entirely self-catering and is big enough for eight people. You'll need to stay for a three-night minimum.

Brattleboro

Brattleboro is a large, bustling town that incorporates the best of urban, rural, and even suburban characteristics. It is influenced by the presence both of the Brattleboro Retreat, a highly respected drug-and-alcohol rehabilitation center and one of the largest employers in town, and of the SIT Graduate Institute, formerly known as the School for International Training. With students and faculty from more than 30 nations, SIT prepares students to address the world's critical challenges.

Many of the men and women who came to Vermont in the 1960s to live in communes ended their journey as soon as they crossed the Massachusetts border into Vermont, so this town still has a New Age flavor, as evidenced by the posters on telephone poles that advertise shiatsu, peace meetings, and Brazilian dance lessons.

Downtown Brattleboro—or "Brat," as locals refer to it—is the old section, with relics of factories and hotels from the booming railroad days. Restaurants, shops, and cultural events abound here. The city's reputation as a top destination for art lovers can be seen in full swing on the first Friday of each month during *Gallery Walk* (gallerywalk.org). From 5:30 to 8:30 p.m., many studios are open, and artists are in a chatting mood, happy to join you in a glass of wine. There are more than 50 exhibitions to see. It's a great time to stroll around town, enjoy some live music, sample the refreshments, and then have dinner at one of the local restaurants. Gallery guides are available in numerous locales around town.

The *Brattleboro Museum and Art Center* (10 Vernon St.; 802-257-0124; brattleboromuseum.org) is housed in a charming former train station. The 1915 Union Station with its intact ticket windows and marble steps is the perfect backdrop for the compelling exhibits by regional internationally acclaimed artists. Open 11 a.m. to 5 p.m. Sun, Mon, Wed, and Thurs; 11 a.m. to 7 p.m. Fri; and 10 a.m. to 5 p.m. Sat.

Drive a few miles out of town. Once you're in the hills you'll feel miles away from Main Street. But when you head west on Route 9 or south on Route 5, all the telltale signs of suburbia are there, from fast-food restaurants to motels and supermarkets.

Brattleboro has no shortage of good places to eat, but for a healthy, delicious lunch at affordable prices, you won't do better than the deli counter and cafe at the *Brattleboro Food Co-op* (2 Main St.; 802-257-0236; brattleborofoodcoop.com), where you may spend more time trying to decide what to order than you will eating it. The choices are mouthwatering and seem endless: custom sandwiches made from nitrite-free meats and artisanal breads, hearty, flavorful soups (they're made from the pick of the co-op's organic fresh produce), salads, and dozens of ready-made dishes, from stuffed grape leaves, curries, and samosas to Thai, Italian, and New England favorites. It's a wonder anyone in Brattleboro cooks for the family with this selection available. Although the deli cafe is probably of more interest to those traveling through, the cheese counter deserves a good look, if for no other reason than to see the diversity of Vermont cheeses. Few places have such a wide and well-chosen variety of small-production farmstead cheeses. Gather your picnic makings and stock up on healthy snacks for the road here, too. Open Mon through Sat 7 a.m. to 9 p.m., Sun 9 a.m. to 9 p.m.

Still on the Asian end of Brattleboro's culinary spectrum, *Anon's Thai Cuisine* (802-257-1376) offers selections from the traditional pad thai and chicken satay to basil calamari and a salad roll with cilantro, Thai noodles, mint, and carrots with a homemade peanut sauce. Watch for them on Saturdays in summer at the Brattleboro Farmers' Market (it's easy to tell which stand is theirs—it's the one with the long line).

Brattleboro is well supplied with restaurants and cafes, including *Peter Haven's* (32 Elliot St.; 802-257-3333; peterhavens.com). There are only 10 tables, so you should make reservations on weekends to sample the deceptively simple-sounding menu. Appetizers include smoked salmon fillet with popover and horseradish dill sauce, while the entrees include fresh sea scallops on a nest of braised spinach with apple brandy and cream sauce, and roast duck with port wine, black currant, and sour cherry sauce. Dinner is served Wed through Sat from 6 p.m.

Farther up Elliot Street is the outstanding but tiny *T.J. Buckley's* (132 Elliot St; 802-257-4922; tjbuckleys.com), with an eclectic menu of only 4 or 5 items, which change constantly depending on what's available locally. Everything is strictly fresh (the chef often shops from local farmers at the biweekly farmers' market) and flawlessly prepared. If it doesn't put too much of a dent in your wallet, it's worth every penny. The restaurant has such a following that you'd better make reservations well in advance if you hope for a table. This is one book you can't judge by its cover—it's located in a 1927 Worcester diner, but diner food it is not.

You can shop from the same local farmers on Sat and Wed at the **Brattleboro Farmers' Market** (Western Avenue; 802-254-8885; brattleboro farmersmarket.com), on Route 9 just west of town. Like so much else in Brattleboro, this is a local institution, where you will find both old-favorite vegetables and the trendiest new varieties. Big truck farms join small homestead farmers here; one stand sells nothing but Asian vegetables and greens. In the spring you can buy plants for your own garden, and all summer you'll find a smattering of handmade crafts and farm-related products, such as herb vinegars, fruit jams, fresh-baked breads, cheese, maple syrup, and organic honey.

Many people go just for lunch and the live music that's often playing on the shaded lawn inside the circle of stands. Several vendors sell only prepared foods, which you can eat at picnic tables or carry off for dinner later. These usually include Japanese *udon* noodles, Lebanese *dolmas* and other dishes, and authentic Mexican and Thai foods. There's a booth with great coffee and tea and freshly baked breakfast goodies and cookies. What you won't find are burgers and fries or hot dogs. At every booth you'll find at least one big smile; it's the friendliest group of people you'll meet anywhere. Open Sat, May through Oct, 9 a.m. to 2 p.m., and Wed 10 a.m. to 2 p.m.

The **Old Creamery Bridge** is close to the Brattleboro Farmers' Market. Named for the Brattleboro Creamery, which once stood on the far side, it was built in 1879 and has ever since provided an easy route from the west end of Brattleboro to downtown. In 1917 a footbridge was added to one side, allowing pedestrians to cross Whetstone Brook without fighting traffic. This is the last of the four covered bridges that once carried traffic in Brattleboro.

Just west of the farmers' market grove on Route 9 is West Brattleboro, an attractive enclave of distinguished old homes and a tiny business center with several places to eat.

Just before this highway heads over Hogback Mountain is the **Chelsea Royal Diner** (487 Marlboro Rd.; 802-254-8399; chelsearoyaldiner.com) in a Worcester dining car from the late 1930s. The menu is a slightly updated version of traditional diner food, self-described as "high-end home style," with liver and onions, macaroni and cheese, and meat loaf along with slightly more sophisticated fare. Tuesday through Saturday evenings you'll find a number of Mexican-style dishes, too. Breakfast is served all day. Be sure to check out the specials board, which may offer an all-you-can-eat catfish fry with hush puppies and other irresistible deals. Open daily 6 a.m. to 9 p.m.

The *Bonnyvale Environmental Education Center* (BEEC; 1221 Bonnyvale Rd.; 802-257-5785; beec.org) sponsors programs in schools and for the public throughout the area. It offers a busy schedule of outdoor activities, usually hikes and walks accompanied by astronomers, geologists, zoologists, botanists, and other experts to examine some phase of the natural world. Most of the trips are free but require advance registration. The Sunday morning A.M. Ambles, also free, don't require registration; just show up at 9 a.m. any Sunday at the appointed place. Past ambles, which last about 2 hours, have explored Putney Mountain, West River, and Hamilton Falls, a rare patch of old-growth forest, and Mount Olga. Call or visit their website for the latest in offerings.

Approaching Brattleboro from the north on Route 5, just after you cross West River at its junction with the Connecticut, you come across *Forty Putney Road Bed & Breakfast* (192 Putney Rd.; 802-254-6268; fortyputneyroad .com), an eye-catching French château. Inside the double-thick brick walls are well-decorated rooms awash with thoughtful amenities. Most rooms have couches or love seats, and all have modern private baths. There's an indoor hot tub with a fireplace. A small private pub downstairs has an extensive beer and wine list for guests, as well as light dishes for those who decide not to sample Brattleboro's ample restaurant offerings. Breakfast is a two-course gourmet affair featuring local ingredients. Eat in a sun-filled dining room or under the awning on the terrace that overlooks a garden with fountains.

vermonttrivia

Don't be confused by the address of this inn. Incongruously, 40 Putney Road Bed & Breakfast is at 192 Putney Road. It *used* to be located at 40, but then the town of Brattleboro changed its street numbers to accommodate 911 identification.

On Memorial Day weekend, do not be alarmed if you see people dancing on nearly every open space in town. The annual *Morris Ale* is held on this weekend at nearby Marlboro College, as it has been since 1976. Morris dancers perform all over the area, with the greatest concentration of them in Brattleboro on

Hey, It's a Live One!

You never know what you'll find happening in Brattleboro. Original *Off the Beaten Path Vermont* author Barbara Radcliffe Rogers tells the story about a trip she and her daughter made to Brattleboro one May. They were driving into town to have lunch, and when they passed the small park at Wells Fountain they noticed a group of young people dressed in white, jingling across the street with bells on their legs. "Morris dancers!" they both said at once.

Barbara quickly found a parking space in front of the library, and they followed the dancers to the park and sat down on the lawn to wait for the fun to begin. The dancers also sat down, in little groups on the granite steps and on the lawn, and quickly became engaged in animated conversations. Assuming that they were waiting for someone or something, Barbara and her daughter waited. And waited. Finally a dancer wandered casually toward them and engaged them in conversation. When he learned that they'd come to watch the dance, he looked startled, then quickly called to the others, "Hey, we've got a real audience!" and they all jumped up and took their places to begin. So, if you find yourself in a similar situation, speak up and let them know you're there!

Saturday. Morris dancing is a type of folk dancing that originated in England. There are teams of these dancers spread throughout the US. Memorial Day weekend is their time to gather and show their craft. Ales are held at different locations throughout the US. Here in Vermont, after individual groups have danced all over town, they come together to perform on Elliot Street at 5 p.m.

Heading west from Brattleboro on Route 9, past West Brattleboro, the road begins to climb . . . and climb. It winds upward through rock-strewn woods, crests momentarily atop a deep ravine, then climbs again to a ridge with views of distant hills.

The final climb takes you to the summit of Hogback Mountain, where the views reach into three states. The fate of Hogback Mountain was in limbo a few years back when the ski area closed. Residents wanted to save their beloved mountain, but how to do it was the question. In 2006 the Hogback Mountain Conservation Association was formed. The intention of this group of local citizens was to raise money to purchase the mountain to create a permanent conservation area open to the public but safe for wildlife. In 2010 the dream was realized. The ***Hogback Mountain Conservation Area*** (hogback.org) is officially owned by the Town of Marlborough and offers

Jumping Off a Mountain

Downhill skiing was still a novelty when Fred Harris started the annual *Harris Hill Ski Jump* (harrishillskijump.com) meet in Brattleboro in 1923. As an under-graduate, he had helped start the annual Winter Carnival at Dartmouth College in Hanover, New Hampshire, in 1911. Some of the world's best ski jumpers have competed here, including Torger Tokle, his brother Art Tokle, Art Devlin, Hugh Barber, and Vladimir Glyvka. The contests take place in three-hour segments on each of two days, and usually include present and future Olympians and World Cup contenders. The date may vary, but the event is usually held on Presidents' Day weekend. It's an exciting show, even for the spectators, who cheer on the contestants by ringing cowbells. If you don't have one to bring, you can buy a bell there. Applauding with mittened hands isn't very effective, hence the bells.

In 2005 the jump was declared unsafe. After competition that year, no events were held until 2009, after $257,000 had been raised by local residents to help pay for essential renovation. In February of that year, world-class competition again came to Harris Hill. "I think my dad would be totally amazed that this is happening again," said Fred's daughter Sandy. "It's a world-class facility that can now be used to train for Olympic events and other tournaments."

nearly 600 acres of exploration. There are miles of hiking trails, some of which connect with neighboring Molly Stark State Park in New Hampshire, that can be explored on foot, ski, or snowshoe. A VAST snowmobile track runs the length of the conservation area. You will pass through hardwood forests that explode with color in the fall. Access to the trails is off Route 9 or through Molly Stark State Park.

If your feet need a break from the trails, stop in at the ***Southern Vermont Natural History Museum*** (7599 Rte. 9; 802-464-0048; vermontmuseum.org). With more than 600 items on display, this little museum has one of the largest collections of native species. You'll find a snake or two at their raptor center, an American bald eagle, a red-tailed hawk, a red-shouldered hawk, American kestrels, screech owls, barred owls, and turtles—and those are just the live ones. The museum also has more than 200 species of native birds and mammals from Luman Ranger Nelson's taxidermy collection on display. There's bound to be something of interest to everyone in your group here. Open daily 10 a.m. to 5 p.m. Memorial Day through Labor Day, and until 4 p.m. the rest of the year.

Places to Stay in the Connecticut River Valley

CHESTER

Inn Victoria
321 Main St.
(802) 875-4288 or
innvictoria.com
Expensive
On the green, a carefully restored Victorian home with 10 guest rooms all named after Queen Victoria's children.

NORWICH

Butternut Lane Bed and Breakfast
32 Butternut Ln.
(802) 649-1549
butternutlanebnb.com
Moderate
Three guest rooms in an 1821 farmhouse. Only 3 miles from Dartmouth College in New Hampshire. All rooms are individually decorated and all have private baths. Open year-round.

The Inn at Norwich
325 Main St.
(802) 649-1143
norwichinn.com
Moderate
A vintage village inn updated and with a good, reasonably priced dining room. Great packages available.

PUTNEY

The Putney Inn
57 Putney Landing Rd.
(802) 387-5517
putneyinn.com
Moderate
Large, well-decorated rooms, each with its own outside entrance. A creative chef prepares favorite New England dishes with artistic flair.

WOODSTOCK

Woodstock Inn and Resort
14 The Green
(802) 457-1100 or (800) 338-2745
woodstockinn.com
Expensive
With a pool, alpine and Nordic skiing, golf course, and indoor sports facilities, the inn is a complete resort in the center of the village.

Blue Horse Inn
3 Church St.
(802) 457-7159
thebluehorseinn.com
Expensive
Ten individually decorated rooms with private baths. Breakfast is included in the rates, as is the use of the wood-fired cedar soaking tub, bicycles, snowshoes, and outdoor heated pool.

Places to Eat in the Connecticut River Valley

BRADFORD

North Woods Cafe
530 Waits River Rd.
(802) 222-9294
Inexpensive
Don't be fooled by the location—the pancakes are delicious! Open daily at 5:30 a.m., to 8 p.m. Mon through Thurs and Sun, to 9 p.m. Fri and Sat.

CHESTER

Heritage Deli and Bakery
642 Rte. 103
(802) 875-3550
heritagedeliandbakery
.com
Inexpensive
A small, locally owned cafe that serves up more than just deli, although you can certainly get a delicious sandwich. Open daily 7 a.m. to 5 p.m.

TO LEARN MORE IN THE CONNECTICUT RIVER VALLEY

Building A Better Brattleboro (BABB)
157 Main St.
Brattleboro
(802) 257-4886
brattleboro.com

Brattleboro Chamber of Commerce
180 Main St.
Brattleboro
(802) 254-4565 or (877) 254-4565
brattleborochamber.org

Hartford Area Chamber of Commerce
5966 Quechee Rd.
PO Box 823
Quechee 05059
(802) 295-7900
hartfordvtchamber.com

Springfield Regional Chamber of Commerce
56 Main St., Suite 2
Springfield
springfieldvt.com

Woodstock Area Chamber of Commerce
4 Mechanic St.
PO Box 486
Woodstock 05091
(802) 457-3555 or (888) 496-6378
woodstockvt.com

FAIRLEE

Whistlestop Cafe
176 Rte. 5
(802) 331-1000
Inexpensive
Open Mon, Tues, and Thurs through Sat 6 a.m. to 8 p.m., Sun 8 a.m. to 3 p.m. for breakfast, lunch, and dinner. Service in this little cafe is friendly. We're partial to the mint chocolate chip pancakes.

THETFORD

Wicked Awesome BBQ
2930 Rte. 5
(603) 729-6213
wickedawesomebbqco.com
Moderate
The name pretty much says it all. Food is slow cooked and smothered with house sauce that tingles the senses. Open Thurs through Fri 11 a.m. to 6 p.m. and Sat and Sun 11 a.m. to 5 p.m.

QUECHEE

Shepard's Pie Restaurant by the Gorge
Route 4
(802) 281-4585
shepards-pie.com
Moderate
Open daily 11 a.m. to 9 p.m. for lunch and dinner. A great place to grab something to go enjoy outside, this restaurant is located close to many sights, including the VINS Nature Center, Killington Mountain, and Quechee Gorge.

SOUTHWEST VERMONT →

The southwestern corner of Vermont seems at times cut off from the rest of the state, largely because no interstate highway is within 40 miles of the far reaches of the area. The Green Mountains separate it from eastern Vermont, and Pownal, a town that is as far away from Montpelier, the state capital, as you can get, seems to have more in common with the bordering states of New York and Massachusetts than it does with the rest of its own state.

The landscape here is one of rolling hills and mountains, alternating with wide, flat, fertile valleys. The region is also historically rich, since it served as an early gateway to settlement in the rest of Vermont.

Although at one time or another all of Vermont has fallen to some kind of border dispute with neighboring states—and one foreign country—the southwest corner seems to have seen more than its share of fights over where Vermont ends and Massachusetts and New York begin—and even where New Hampshire ends.

The remote *tri-state boundary marker* that marks the exact spot where Vermont, New York, and Massachusetts converge is buried deep in the woods at the southwest

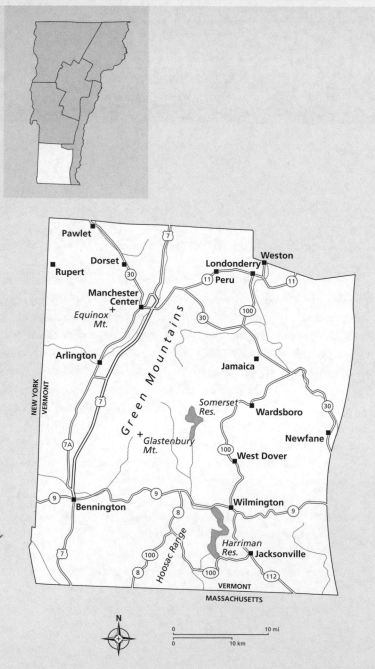

corner of Pownal, almost 2 miles from the end of the nearest dead-end road. The granite marker is 8 feet tall and 14 inches square and has four sides, three of them marked with the initials of the state they face. The final boundary was settled in 1812, but the marker wasn't erected until 1896. To find the marker, take Route 142 south to West Northfield Road. There is then a sharp left (north) turn onto a private gravel road. The marker is about 50 feet to the east into the woods. You should be able to see it from the road depending on foliage cover.

Bennington

Bennington is where it all began. It was the first town west of the Connecticut River to be chartered by New Hampshire royal governor Benning Wentworth. The charter was drawn up in 1749, when New York and New Hampshire both claimed the land.

During the American Revolution, the Battle of Bennington was fought in 1777 in lands from Cambridge, New York, to a point about 5 miles west of Bennington in Vermont. This single battle turned the tide against the British and caused British leader John Burgoyne to rethink his strategy in the war. Colonial militia, under the command of General John Stark, discovering General Burgoyne's plans, fought and destroyed British and Hessian forward elements of his army, leading to Burgoyne's retreat. The battle ended British plans to defeat the colonies by splitting them in half, and made the final American victory possible.

After the battle—which is immortalized by the 306-foot-high *Bennington Battle Monument* (15 Monument Circle; 802-447-0550), visible from most parts of town—Burgoyne wrote a letter describing Vermonters as "the most active and rebellious race on the continent."

The monument was built over the course of four years and dedicated in 1891 by President Benjamin Harrison. When an elevator was

vermonttrivia

The late fiction writer Shirley Jackson, author of *The Haunting of Hill House* and the famous short story "The Lottery," was a resident of Bennington. Jackson's husband taught at Bennington College, and she, formerly from upstate New York, incorporated into her fiction many of her feelings about small-town life in Bennington.

BEST ATTRACTIONS IN SOUTHWEST VERMONT

Equinox Skyline Drive	Green Mountain National Forest
Canoeing the Batten Kill	Bromley Ski Area and Alpine Slide
Magic Mountain Ski Area	Robert Todd Lincoln's Hildene

installed, a few Vermonters scoffed, believing that if the Green Mountain Boys could prove their valor by fighting the British, then it should be a small task by comparison to walk up the 412 stairs that make up the climb to the top. To visit the site of the actual battle, you'll have to travel into New York, following Route 67A (Northside Drive) to North Bennington, then Route 67 across the state line to the battlefield, about 5 miles from the center of North Bennington.

easycome, easygo?

The most illustrious native of Pownal was born in North Pownal in 1834. "Jubilee" Jim Fisk has been variously described as a railroad magnate, a Wall Street genius, and a playboy. Fisk took over the Erie Railroad and gambled in the gold market against another notorious New Yorker of the time, Jay Gould. Fisk's other accomplishments included purchasing an opera house, spending his fortune as quickly as he made it, and being murdered in a love triangle in what was then the Broadway Central Hotel in 1872.

Bennington is home to the second largest of the state's five fish hatcheries, the **Bennington Fish Culture Station** (South Stream Road; 802-447-2844). This is a fascinating place, especially for kids, who will be intrigued by the sight of thousands of brown, brook, and rainbow trout massing in the tanks. The hatchery is open daily from 8 a.m. to 3:30 p.m.

On one of Bennington's back streets is the **Bennington Potters Yard Factory Store** (324 County St.; 802-447-7531; benningtonpotters .com/potters-yard), which features high-priced pottery dinnerware at bargain prices. Here you'll find a full range of dinnerware and accessories, along with the seconds at lower prices. Open 9:30 a.m. to 6 p.m. Mon through Sat and 10 a.m. to 5 p.m. Sun.

On Route 7, 1 mile north of the junction with Route 9, is the ***Blue Benn Diner*** (314 North St.; 802-442-5140), a local institution offering everything from burgers and lasagna to tofu. The tabletop jukeboxes are equally eclectic, and the clientele ranges from Bennington College students to construction workers.

The lines and colors inside are sharp, with neon reflecting off the smooth chrome surfaces of the display cases and milk machine. Despite its 1950s diner look and atmosphere, the Blue Benn serves an updated version of comfort foods, with several Mexican favorites along with the meat loaf.

The Blue Benn is open Mon and Tues 6 a.m. to 4:30 p.m., Wed through Fri 6 a.m. to 7 p.m., Sat and Sun 6 a.m. to 4 p.m. We're risking upsetting the locals here, who seem to be in on the secret, but the wait is much, much

How Vermont Began

Colonial boundaries were determined by royal grants made in London and bore little relationship to land surveys or geographical landmarks. These vague boundaries led to inevitable disputes between colonies, particularly Massachusetts, which claimed areas around Brattleboro, as well as in New York and New Hampshire, which contested all of the area covered by Vermont. To royal governors, the granting of townships was an important source of income, and the governors of both New Hampshire and New York granted townships that often overlay one another, causing violent disputes over title.

The Allen brothers, Ira and Ethan, both highly independent landowners under New Hampshire grants, became ardent champions in defense of the New Hampshire grants, and against the attempts of New York to enforce its grants. Neither state was able to enforce its authority, however, and the residents finally established the Republic of Vermont. During the Revolution, this new republic even flirted with seeking a separate peace with the British.

After the war, New Hampshire and New York continued their tug-of-war over the Green Mountains, and Congress repeatedly failed to accept the Vermonters' application to join the union. It wasn't until Vermont paid New York $30,000 to give up all claims that Vermont was admitted to the union as the 14th state in 1791.

The Molly Stark Trail

It's ironic that Route 9, the only year-round route across the southern part of Vermont, should be named for a New Hampshire woman. Even more ironic, perhaps, is that it is named not for the heroic leader of the Battle of Bennington, but for the wife he rode home to after the battle. On a simple stone in the cemetery behind the white church in West Bennington, you'll find the carved inscription of General Stark's famous words, which he uttered before the decisive battle: "Boys, yonder are the redcoats, and they are ours, or this night Molly Stark sleeps a widow."

shorter if you head here for dinner rather than breakfast. But either way, the food is delish.

If you have a car enthusiast in your travel group, you won't want to miss a stop at *Hemmings Motor News Car Lover's Store* (216 Main St.; 802-447-9580; hemmings.com), located in a fully operating Sunoco filling station. *Hemmings Motor News,* in case you're not a fancier of old cars, advertises everything from the Volkswagen Thing to Model A Fords, from parts to entire cars and even fan clubs. Their store sells books on every kind of old car there is, back issues, *Hemmings* sweatshirts, 15-year subscription pins, toys, tools, models, every sort of automobilia—it's all here. Open daily 7 a.m. to 8 p.m. May through Oct. Until 7 p.m. Nov through Apr. Closed major holidays.

Vintage vehicles are also on display and open to the public daily from June through Oct, 10 a.m. to 3 p.m., weekends only in May. From Nov through Apr, it's by appointment only by calling the store. Here you will see at least 25 vintage cars, ranging from a 1929 Cretors Ford AA popcorn truck (very cool) to a 1969 Chevelle 396 SS big-block convertible (our favorite).

If you don't get your fill, cruise nights are hosted throughout the warmer months. *Hemmings Cruise-Ins* (216 Main St.; 800-227-4373; hemmings .com/events/cruiseins) take place in the parking lot behind the filling station from 5:30 to 8 p.m. on select Thursdays and some Fridays May through Aug. (Dates are listed on their website.) Inclement weather cancels these events, so check the site or call before heading out.

Off Route 9 west of Bennington is the *Bennington Center for the Arts* (44 Gypsy Ln.; 802-442-7158; thebennington.org). The permanent collection includes Native American pottery, nature art, kachinas, and Navajo rugs. Four galleries host permanent and touring exhibits, including a covered-bridge museum. The center is open Wed through Mon, 10 a.m. to 5 p.m. Admission is charged.

The nearby **Bennington Museum** (75 Main St.; 802-447-1571; bennington museum.org) has long been a favorite for admirers of Grandma Moses, one of the state's best-known primitive folk artists. The museum's extensive collection of her work, memorabilia, and schoolhouse studio are part of a new Grandma Moses Family Heritage Gallery. An addition added more space for displaying the museum's collections of fine art, Bennington pottery, furniture, toys, and colonial and Civil War–period artifacts. The outstanding collections of American glassware and early-to-Victorian quilts have a bit more elbow room now. Even if you saw this museum a few years ago, it is definitely worth another stop. It is open Feb through June and Nov through Dec, Thurs through Tues, 10 a.m. to 5 p.m., daily July through Oct. Closed Jan and major holidays. Admission is charged for those 18 and older.

Green Mountains South

Not long out of Bennington, Route 9 East begins to climb, then enters the **Green Mountain National Forest** (231 N. Main St.; 802-747-6700; fs .usda.gov/greenmountain). The forest's western border begins just outside Bennington and stretches eastward to the town of Wilmington, a good 20 miles away. This part of the forest is one of the largest, most uninterrupted tracts in the state, and its untamed look proves it. The forest spans more than 400,000 acres in southwestern and central Vermont. There are about 900 miles of multi-use trails throughout the forest, including parts of the Appalachian and Long Trails. A complete list of trails and directions to their trailheads is on the website.

On the right is **Greenwood Lodge** (311 Greenwood Dr.; 802-442-2547), an American Youth Hostel facility and campground that is rustic yet homey and welcoming. Many people stay here for its remoteness and for its access to Prospect Mountain and the Long Trail; the location provides opportunities for short hikes and walks as well as serving as a jumping-off point for hiking the entire Long Trail end to end. Swimming, fishing, boating, and biking are available.

Greenwood Lodge consists of 2 dormitories and 5 private rooms, sleeping a total of 50 people; 40 wooded campsites are also scattered throughout the hostel's 120 acres. The lodge is open mid-May through late Oct.

After its steep ascent, Route 9 drops into Wilmington, with an array of shops, eateries, and lodgings. From here, Route 100 swings west, paralleling (if a line so wiggly could be said to parallel anything) the Massachusetts border through Whitingham and Readsboro, before swinging north to join Route 8, which leads back to Route 9, a few miles west of Wilmington. It's a rolling, scenic loop.

vermonttrivia

Woodford, Vermont, has an elevation of 2,215 feet, making it the highest town in the state. But with just 314 people, it ranks among towns having the smallest populations.

On Route 8 you have a dramatic view of 11 huge white windmills of the *Searsburg Wind Power Facility.* These 550-kilowatt wind turbines stand in a row along the mountain ridge, and interpretive signs at a roadside pullout explain how they work. One of the largest wind-power facilities in the eastern US, this one was completed in 1997 as a research project, and its turbines generate enough power to run 1,600 average homes. While they look smaller from the road below, each blade is 64 feet long and made of black fiberglass to prevent ice buildup in the winter. It takes only a 10-mile-an-hour wind to turn the blades, and at their elevation of 2,800 feet, the wind blows so steadily that the turbines can operate 95 percent of the time.

Although Lake Champlain is probably the best-known body of water in the state, locals and visitors know that one of the most dramatic is the

South Central MOOver

If you see what looks like a Holstein with wheels rolling down a road, you're not seeing things. Well, it's not exactly a Holstein, but it's painted to look like one. The *Deerfield Valley Transit Association* (802-464-8487; mover.com) has about 24 buses that service eight communities, including Wardsboro, Readsboro, Dover, Whitingham, and Wilmington. The buses are all painted with a cow motif designed by local artist Skip Morrow in 1996. If you want a break from driving while in the area, visit DVTA's website for a complete list of schedules and routes.

Harriman Reservoir (also known as Lake Whitingham), west of Wilmington. Created as a hydroelectric lake by the Harriman Dam's restraint of Deerfield River, this beautiful body of water holds a hidden piece of history. When the river was dammed in 1923 to provide a power source to nearby towns, a former logging village called Mountain Mills was sacrificed. The waters flooded with the dam and covered the entire area. Today when the reservoir levels are low enough, watch for a glimpse of this doomed village. While significant erosion has obviously taken place since the village was flooded, occasionally a tree stump, a piece of foundation, outlines, and pieces from the Hoosac Tunnel & Wilmington Railroad trestle will appear. It's fascinating to see. It is also said that in some places, when the water is clear, the mill and other buildings can be seen. We've not witnessed this and are not sure of the statement's validity.

Heading north from busy Wilmington, Route 100 quickly becomes a rural byway again, winding along a valley bordered by rolling hills, its meadows dotted with farmhouses. Although most are no longer the hub of a working farm, one family has kept its farming traditions alive. Wilmington's *Adams Farm* (15 Higley Hill Rd.; 802-464-3762; adamsfamilyfarm.com) is a sixth-generation family farm that loves to share experiences with the public. Activities change, following the rhythms of the seasons, with winter sleigh rides, Halloween hayrides, tractor rides, feeding farm animals, and watching maple sap boil into syrup. The accent is on family activities, and young children will always find plenty to do here. Fresh vegetables are for sale in the summer, pumpkins in the fall, and locally made quilts, knitwear, and hand weaving all year. They also produce farm-fresh eggs, and offer natural and sustainable local meat products.

Just off Route 100, heading north out of Wilmington, in West Dover is the *Inn at Sawmill Farm* (7 Cross Town Rd.; 802-464-8131; theinnat sawmillfarm.com), a gracious and sophisticated country inn situated on 20 acres. A vintage barn has been skillfully transformed into sitting rooms, with a balcony room overlooking from the former hay loft. Despite the elegant furnishings, fine art, and soaring ceilings, the inn's atmosphere is invitingly warm and informal. The 21 guest rooms are divided between the inn itself and a dozen in adjoining outside buildings, some of which are separate cottages, and all of which have private baths. All of these outside rooms have working wood-burning fireplaces. Guests leave the outside world behind

JANUARY

Bennington Winter Festival

various venues
Bennington
(802) 447-3311
bennington.com/winterfest
A host of activities throughout the area in late Jan, including ice-carving competitions, a penguin plunge, cooking contests, wagon rides, pet fashion show, a carnival, children's activities, and more.

MARCH

Reggae Festival

Mount Snow Ski Area
39 Mount Snow Rd.
West Dover
(800) 245-SNOW
At this festivcal, held late in Mar, you can experience "pond skimming" (skiing down the hill and across the pond) and a Duct Tape Derby (cardboard sled race pitting guests against employees), all accompanied by live reggae music. Tickets available online.

AUGUST

Southern Vermont Art & Craft Festival

Camelot Village
60 West Rd.
Bennington
(802) 425-3399
craftproducers.com/festivals
Held in the beginning of Aug, this festival features the work of 150 of Vermont's most talented craftspeople, live music daily, and food vendors.

Admission charged for those 12 and older.

Bondville Fair

30 Old Rte. 30
Bondville
(802) 297-9810
bondvillefair.org
Held in late Aug, this is the oldest continuously held fair in Vermont. Has all the implements of a country fair.

OCTOBER

Manchester Fall Art & Craft Festival

The practice tee at Riley Rink
410 Hunter Park Rd.
Manchester
(802) 425-3399
craftproducers.com/festivals
Formerly the Hildene Fall Arts Festival, now held in early Oct in Manchester and featuring 150 juried artisan exhibits as well as a huge assortment of specialty food products. Spend the day browsing booths where local crafters display their wares. Admission for those 12 and older (join the mailing list and they send you a coupon).

DECEMBER

Torchlight parade and fireworks display

Mount Snow
39 Mount Snow Rd.
(800) 245-SNOW
mountsnow.com/event-calendar
Held one evening between Christmas and New Year's; also Thanksgiving, Martin Luther King's birthday, and Presidents' Day.

here, as the inn has no in-room telephones or television. In the summer two trout ponds on the property are well stocked. If you really want to go all out, arrange for spa services in the privacy of your room. Swedish, deep-tissue, and reflexology massages are all available with prior arrangements. Rates include breakfast. Dinner is served to nonguests by prior reservation.

The inn's an on-site restaurant, **Nonna's,** offers dinner from 5:30 to 9:30 p.m. The bar opens at 5 p.m. During the summer months (June through Aug), Nonna's serves dinner poolside. Tiki torches, floating candles, music, and a glowing fire in the fire pit all set the mood for the 4- or 5-course meal featuring hand-selected local wines. Seating is limited to 24 people, so be sure to make reservations by calling the inn.

About a half-hour drive east, you'll come to South Newfane, a tiny village greatly overshadowed by the grand buildings of better-known New-fane. But it's here you'll find **Olallie Day Lily Gardens** (129 Augur Hole Rd.; 802-348-6614; daylilygarden.com), a place well known to gardeners. This third-generation garden is entering its third decade of collecting and cultivating daylilies. What started with USDA geneticist Dr. George M. Dar-row's collection in Maryland, expanded to son Dan Darrow's family's Ver-mont farm in 1979. Today Dan's son Christopher carries on his grandfa-ther's tradition of carefully cultivating hardy daylilies. Christopher, with his own children and Ellen, his mother, organically grow more than 2,500 varieties.

lilytrivia

In 1993 Dr. George M. Darrow was inducted into the American Society for Horticultural Science Hall of Fame for his work in plant science.

The 6 acres of display plantings show an amazing variety of lilies in a riot of shades, with the peak sea-son being mid-July through mid-August. The Darrows invite you to stroll through their gardens, bring your own picnic lunch, pick your own blue-berries from their patch, and spend the afternoon. There's also a shop with books, gifts, and tools for the gardener. Open 10 a.m. to 5 p.m. Wed through Mon, Memorial Day through mid-Sept.

Although most people know about **Mount Snow** (39 Mount Snow Rd., West Dover; 802-464-4040; mountsnow.com) and its ski slopes, a less crowded time to visit is in summer. Many ski areas in Vermont open up their lifts for scenic gondola rides in the warm weather, but Mount Snow goes one better: They take you up, teach you how to ride a mountain bike, and then send you back down on one. You can go alone or with a group of friends, which is cheaper, and your fee includes the bike rental, necessary helmet and body armor, lift and one-hour trail pass, and an hour and a half of instruction with a guide. Reservations are required.

The town of Stratton, which is not to be confused with Stratton Mountain the ski area, is to the west of Route 100. You can reach Stratton the town by making a left in the town of West Wardsboro and driving about 4 miles into a tiny village. Stratton Mountain ski area is accessed by continuing north on Route 100, then heading west on Route 30 into the village of Bondville.

As you drive through the town of Stratton from West Wardsboro, continue on for 3 more miles to reach the ***Grout Pond Recreation Area*** (802-747-6700), a splendid, almost-unknown, 1,600-acre reserve within the Green Mountain National Forest. There is year-round camping available in the forest, and seasonal boating and swimming available on the 79-acre Grout Pond. You will also find more than 10 miles of hiking trails that connect with nearby trail systems to give you more options. It's a peaceful, unspoiled area that contrasts sharply with the developed ski area in the northeast corner of the town.

In Wardsboro, as Route 100 curves through the village center and crosses the river, be sure to notice the roof of the ***Wardsboro Country Store*** (23 Main St.; 802-896-6411), where the shingles form a giant American flag. Inside you'll find the usual assortment of baked goods, Vermont products, and beverages.

buttheydidn't buildcondos

Wardsboro, north of Stratton, holds the distinction of being the last town in Vermont that New Hampshire governor Benning Wentworth chartered, in 1764. The Vermont government officially granted the town's charter in 1780, when Vermont was its own republic, to a resident of nearby Newfane, Vermont—William Ward—along with 62 others. Although few chose to live and settle on their land grants, many people throughout southern New England wanted their own piece of Vermont even back then.

Just before Route 100 merges with Route 30 in Jamaica, it crosses West River on an old-fashioned green metal bridge so narrow that it has a traffic light to signal one-way traffic.

At *Jamaica Coffee House* (3863 Rte. 30; 802-874-4643), you might think you've stepped back into the 1960s, when Vermont had more back-to-the-landers than SUVs. From the mismatched chairs and tables to the long front porch, this is a piece of another era. The soups are homemade, the tea is organic, and the coffee is fair trade. The PB&J sandwiches are slathered with locally made strawberry jam, but why stop there when you can get black bean and cheese quesadillas; a bowl of piping hot, just-made chili; vegan Moroccan stew served over couscous; or a curried chicken salad? While you're waiting for your order, browse their consignment shop loaded with local and sustainable products. If you long for the days before Vermont's general stores sold latte and wraps, mellow out here. If you're lucky, you'll be there when musicians are jamming out the live music on the porch or inside, depending on the weather. It's also been rumored that the coffee house was recently used for a few shots in an upcoming movie. Keep your eyes peeled. Open from 7 a.m. to 5 p.m., Wed through Sun, to noon on Tues.

Green Mountains North

Route 100 weaves back and forth among the mountains as it makes its way north. As we mentioned before, if you now head west on Route 30 into the village of Bondville, you will come to *Stratton Mountain Ski Resort* (5 Village Lodge Rd.; Stratton; 802-297-4000; stratton.com). Since Stratton is about as on the beaten path as you can be, we'll let you do your own exploring here.

However, in addition to the famed skiing, there are warmer-weather, maybe lesser known outdoor activities near Stratton Mountain. For instance, *Zoar Outdoor* (7 Main St.; 800-532-7483; zoaroutdoor.com), based in nearby Charlemont, Massachusetts, runs a whitewater rafting

vermonttrivia

Route 100 connects so many of Vermont's ski areas—from Mount Snow to Stowe and even Jay Peak—that it's known as the Skiers' Highway.

OTHER ATTRACTIONS WORTH SEEING IN SOUTHWEST VERMONT

Bennington Potters
324 County St.
Bennington
(800) 205-8033 or (802) 447-7531
benningtonpotters.com
Huge selection of this famous pottery.

Kimberly Farms & Trail Rides
1214 Cross Hill Rd.
North Bennington
(802) 442-5454
kimberlyfarms.org
Offers trail rides on their 60-acre farm, which includes the state's oldest marble quarry and a wildlife preserve. All experience levels welcome.

Manchester Designer Outlets
97 Depot St.
Manchester Center
(800) 955-SHOP
manchesterdesigneroutlets.com
A large collection of designer outlet stores, enough to spend the entire day shopping.

Park-McCullough House and Gardens
1 Park St.
North Bennington
(802) 442-5441
A 35-room Victorian mansion built in 1864 by Trenor Park. Visit and learn about the three generations of Parks who lived here. Walk the beautiful grounds to imagine life way back when.

Weston Playhouse
703 Main St.
Weston
Box office: (802) 824-5288
Offices: (802) 824-8167
westonplayhouse.org
Vermont's oldest professional theater. Christopher Lloyd and John Lee Beatty got their starts here. Shows run through the summer into early fall. A complete schedule is available on the website.

trip on the Class III and IV rapids of the West River for rafters 12 years old or older. The trip is based out of Stratton Mountain Ski Area and starts with a strenuous walk down a rockbound trail to the river, just below the Ball Mountain Dam, and goes all the way south to the takeout at Townsend Dam. Along the way there is a picnic and swim opportunity along the river, and the trip finishes with a chicken barbecue. There are only a few trip dates each year, usually in April and September, so arrangements should be made early.

Once you're done in the Stratton Mountain area, head to **Weston,** a town that lies in a little valley, gathered around a large village green, and is home to the **Vermont Country Store** (657 Main St.; 802-824-3184 or

800-547-7849; vermontcountrystore.com), a step-back-in-time general store that offers goods in cracker barrels and penny candy amid the aura of an antique, wood-burning potbellied stove. Although you'll find a lot of moose T-shirts and cow-spotted socks designed for tourists, the overriding mission here is to provide those useful things you might have thought weren't made anymore. You'll also find good warm, sensible clothing and quality kitchen utensils. A sister store flourishes on Route 103 in Rockingham (1292 Rockingham Rd; 802-463-2224). The Vermont Country Stores are open 7 days year-round (except Thanksgiving and Christmas) 8:30 a.m. to 6 p.m.

The *Farrar-Mansur House* (802-824-5294; vermonthistory.org), a colonial tavern and home facing the attractive village green, is one of Weston's historical museums, showing furnishings, clothing, household implements, and firearms from the town's past. What distinguishes this from other historic-house museums in the state is its large collection of 18th-century household items brought to Vermont by a pioneer family (remember, this area was out west in the 1700s). The later generations who lived in the house added items from their own eras, making the museum a reflection of more than two centuries of Weston life.

Next door, and part of the same complex, is the *Old Mill Museum,* in a 1785 sawmill building that was later converted to a gristmill, and the *Band Wagon Museum.* Today they house collections of early trade tools, farm implements, and a Concord coach. You'll also find a tin shop and a water-powered woodworking shop.

The museums are located on the green and are open July through Aug, 1 to 4 p.m. Wed and Sun; 10 a.m. to 4 p.m. on Sat; or by appointment.

talkabout
unorganized!

Also in the vicinity of the Bennington Triangle, Glastenbury was once a thriving township with a population peak of 50 in 1834. The charcoal kilns in the town were located near the Bennington and Glastenbury Railroad, which was built after the Civil War ended. A hotel, houses, and a trolley line soon followed, but the bust came as quickly as the boom. Today you can find cellar holes that run along the Appalachian Trail in an area that has become a ghost town. The town was officially unorganized back in 1937 after one member of the only family remaining served in every town office, from supervisor and fire warden to town representative in the state legislature.

Weston is hardly undiscovered, but even in "tourist season" it maintains its rural village air and is a very pleasant base for exploring this part of Vermont. Right in the village, within an easy walk of everything, is the *Inn at Weston* (630 Main St.; 802-824-6789; innweston.com), with 13 guest rooms divided between 3 well-restored mid-1800s buildings. You can choose to stay in the Main Inn, the Carriage House, or the Coleman House. Each room is different in decor and furnishings. Those in the main house have charming antiques and handmade quilts; some have sitting areas, whirlpool tubs, and fireplaces, while the neighboring Colman House has comfortable rooms at somewhat lower rates. The Carriage House is attached to the Main Inn but has its own entrance. There are two rooms here that are the kings of the inn. No, really, they have king beds, fireplaces, sitting areas, HD flat-screen TVs, double-size whirlpool tubs, steam showers, and decks. Whichever room you choose (visit the websites for pictures of each one), you are invited to explore the grounds, visit the large library of books, curl up in a comfortable chair indoors in front of the wood-burning fireplace, or find a bench in the gardens. Rates include a full country breakfast prepared by the New England Culinary Institute–graduated chef, and a full afternoon tea.

Owner/innkeeper Bob Aldrich developed an interest in orchids when he took biology in college, and one of the first things he did upon buying the inn was build a 670-square-foot *orchid greenhouse* for his collection, which now numbers 375 species and hybrids. Bob is happy to show guests and visitors his collection, and a tour with him is a short course on these fascinating plants. You will learn, for example, that their highly specialized roots are coated with a spongy layer that absorbs and holds rainwater, and that some orchids have bulbous bases that act as water tanks during dry spells. The blooms, which range from tiny white blossoms to giant, showy, bright-purple flowers, are beautiful and the atmosphere—a humid rainforest environment of 80 degrees—is a welcome respite on a cold winter day. As you might expect, the inn's outdoor gardens are beautiful the rest of the year as well.

As you head north out of the town of Weston, where Route 100 and Route 155 meet, is a beautiful place called the *Weston Priory* (58 Priory Hill Rd.; 802-824-5409; westonpriory.org). This monastery of Benedictine monks welcomes the public to its daily services. The gift shop carries books and crafts, many of which are made overseas and in northern New England.

A variety of nativity scenes are on display from September through Christmas. One scene, from Spain, is made from terra cotta and lacquered cloth; another is made of hand-carved wood from a Mexican monastery; still another has soapstone sheep from Kenya. Colorful hand-painted and -carved wooden ornaments and Christmas decorations from El Salvador cover a wall of the shop, which is a serene place, in keeping with the overall tone of the priory's grounds.

The Weston monks are well known for their liturgical choral music, recordings of which are available at the shop and online. The art gallery downstairs displays the work of both Weston monks and brothers from around the world. Prayer services are open to the public four times a day in one of two chapels, depending on the season. Walking paths invite strolling throughout the grounds.

Just south of Weston, where Route 100 crosses Route 11, is **Londonderry.** Almost hidden in a little shopping center is a restaurant opened not long ago by the former chef at the Inn at Weston, Max Turner. At the **New American Grill** (5700 Rte. 100; 802-824-9844; newamericangrill.com), comfort food meets New American in a happy marriage of two culinary worlds. Dinner entrees might include seared sushi-grade ahi tuna with a tamarind-soy glaze, wasabi, and pickled ginger, on the menu next to turkey potpie or a homey lamb stew. Open for 3 meals a day, New American Grill can start your day with buttermilk biscuits and sausage gravy or a breakfast burrito—or a bowl of granola or old-fashioned grits. There's a kids' menu of 6 selections, and the entire menu is at family-friendly prices. The grill is open weekdays 11 a.m. to 9 p.m., and Sat and Sun 7 a.m. to 9 p.m.

If you're in the area in late September, be sure to visit the **Peru Fair** (Bromley Lodge Road; perufair.org), a wonderful example of a traditional country fair held during the peak of foliage season. Many residents plan all year for the event, much to the benefit of locals and visitors. The weekend-long fair has music, lots of food, arts and crafts, games, and an old-fashioned pig roast.

Before the mega-resorts hit the Green Mountains, **Magic Mountain** (Route 11; 802-824-5645; magicmtn.com) was known as a skier's mountain, one of those special places where people kept returning because of the variety and challenge of the runs. Then, in 1991, the last ticket was sold and trees began to grow on the slopes. No one expected to ski its trails again, but astute skiers who tired of long lines and snow bunnies helped the resort come back to life.

The 50 trails have been cleared, and a good portion of the mountain has snowmaking coverage. Vertical drop at Magic is 1,700 feet, and the longest run is Wizard, an intermediate-to-expert slope (read that high-intermediate, with sections of heart-stopping expert), a bit over 1.5 miles long. In fact, every trail, from beginner to expert, has at least one section that will challenge the skills of that level skier. Some of the double diamonds verge on extreme. Magic tends to be less crowded than other places, and during the week you could practically have it to yourself. The terrain here is fun, and it is a great family mountain; it has none of the high-pressure glitz of the bigger name brands, but all the services you need.

atownby anyname

Peru wasn't always named Peru. Back in 1761, the town was called Bromley, but in 1804 residents changed the name to Peru because they felt it was more affluent-sounding. Apparently the name Bromley conveyed the attitude of a slumlord and thus slowed economic growth. After the name was changed to Peru, the fortunes of the town began to look up—a situation that continues today in this quiet town of about 400 people. That wasn't the only time the town experienced a name change, however. In the late 1980s, welcome to peru signs were changed to welcome to hadleyville, but this was only temporary and due to the fact that a movie (*Baby Boom,* 1987) was being filmed here. Hadleyville was the name of the fictional town. Peru is still Peru.

If you'd like to stay in the area, the **Blue Gentian Lodge** (289 Magic Mountain Rd; 802-824-5908; bluegentian.com) may be the answer. Offering Ski & Stay packages to a variety of ski areas, the Blue Gentian has been hosting skiers since 1962. Owners have changed and updates have been completed since then, and the Blue Gentian continues to flourish.

The Blue Gentian is close to many ski areas, including the **Viking Nordic Center** (615 Little Pond Rd.; 802-824-3933; vikingnordic.com), which has been around since 1970— long enough to learn how to take care of the trails so that they are skiable even when the snow levels are low. Nordic's almost 25 miles of trails are all machine-groomed and tracked, on terrain that ranges from gently rolling to treks through forests.

Instructions and rentals are available, and they have night skiing. There are 2 trails designated for snowshoers. In summer the trails are used for hiking and bicycling.

Another great place for cross-country skiing is *Wild Wings Ski Touring Center* (246 Styles Ln.; 802-824-6793; wildwingsski.com) in Peru, off Route 11. Their 25 kilometers of trails, through woods and along brooks, are groomed with a Sno-Cat for track skiing with no skate skiing. Open from mid-Dec to as far into Mar as they can get, 9 a.m. to 4 p.m. (unless you purchase a season pass, then your hours can be extended). If you need a break from skiing, visit the warming room for hot chocolate and/or soup.

Another well-equipped but down-to-earth ski area is a few miles farther down Route 11 at *Bromley Mountain* (3984 Rte. 11; 802-824-5522; bromley .com), only 6 miles from Manchester. Bromley was one of the earliest Vermont ski areas, founded in the late 1930s by Fred Pabst, of brewery fame. This was always a pioneering area: In 1947 Pabst was the first to contour the slopes, and he pioneered grooming by being the first in the state to roll snow to keep it packed. Bromley was also one of the first to install snow-making machinery and its snowmaking covers nearly all its trails. Of the 46 trails, 32 percent are rated beginner, 37 percent intermediate, and the balance expert. For the skier of average to low expert ability, there is plenty of challenging terrain. Bromley is one of the few areas where trails of a given skill level tend to be located together. From the Alpine lift, beginners have mountain, not just base lodge, access to several novice trails. From the Sun lift, intermediate skiers have access to a number of intermediate trails. The vertical drop is 1,334 feet, and the longest trail, suitable for an advanced beginner or intermediate, is about 2.5 miles long. The variety of ability levels makes this a nice area for families.

Summers at Bromley also offer thrills on the mountain with the Mountain Adventure Park and its 2/3-mile alpine slide, one of the longest alpine rides in the world; the Aerial Adventure Park, with its ziplines and canopy tours; and the Sun Mountain Flyer, the 5-story, 0.5-mile long ZipRider. All these parks have so many attractions we couldn't possibly list them all. And since it's not *exactly* off the beaten path, we'll leave you to explore the details on your own.

As you travel south you come upon the towns known to be included in the *Bennington Triangle,* a name given to the area by paranormal author

Joseph A. Citro. It was in this area that between five and 10 people disappeared from 1920 to 1950. These disappearances have never been solved and only fan the fires of mystique in an area known for Bigfoot sightings, UFOs, and other unexplained sights and sounds. Were these people the victims of the Bennington Ripper? Did the Mad Murderer of the Long Trail claim them? Perhaps the Bennington Monster carried them away. Another, not-so-sinister theory is that these people discovered a magical stone on the mountain and were transported to another dimension. There are a few documentaries that have been made about this area and the mystery surrounding it. You can find them online. We may never know the fate of these unfortunate souls, but the mystery does lead us to pass along another story of death and mayhem—this one happening on the northern end of the Triangle.

Hikers have long traveled the Long Trail over the peaks of southern Vermont's Green Mountains, where it then dips down and back up the steep gulf around Route 140 before descending into a wild and desolate area above Wallingford known as *Patch Hollow.*

Running in a north–south direction, Patch Hollow is a deep trench of land high in the Green Mountains, formed by the steep slope of Bear Mountain to the west, and the gentler Button Hill to the east. In the center of this densely wooded bowl is a large swamp, its green waters occasionally punctuated by the skeletons of dead trees that twist toward the Wallingford skies above. During Hurricane Irene in 2011, the beaver dam broke with such force that it sent a large wall of water plowing down the steep hillsides, carving a jagged gorge into the land and completely taking out a chunk of Route 140. The bafflingly large boulders that were transported down the hill still rest along the roadside today.

It's hard to imagine a town being anywhere near this isolated area, but one must understand that when Vermont towns were being settled and the first roads were being cleared, often they were built through the highlands and the mountains because the valleys were prone to flooding and washouts. This means that at one time, Patch Hollow was on the main road to Mount Holly, the town immediately east of Wallingford.

So what happened here? The story goes back to 1831. One of the settlements in the hollow was owned by Rolon Wheeler, a "man of violent passions and jealous disposition," according to an account written in

1911. Wheeler was reportedly guilty of sexual acts with his wife's sister—a situation that, when it was leaked, created a great deal of resentment from the community.

Some community members from Wallingford and nearby Shrewsbury were so resentful they decided to tar and feather the man. The threats were made so publicly that Wheeler was forewarned and took measures to defend himself. He fashioned a knife from a large file and barred his door.

On the night of May 11, parties from Shrewsbury and Wallingford set out for Patch Hollow equipped with jugs of rum, a bucket of tar, and a sack of feathers. The party from Shrewsbury never made it—getting lost in the woods instead. Their pride damaged, the group returned home.

The Wallingford group didn't share the same fate, and arrived at Wheeler's house, forcing their way in by prying a hole in the gable end of the roof. Three men leaped into the house and struggled with Wheeler in the dark. Wheeler stabbed one man in the side and another was slashed 14 times. The door to the cabin was unbarred and more people poured into the cabin. A man named Isaac Osborne was killed during the scuffle. Wheeler wrestled out of his clothes and the hands of his attackers, crawled under the bed, pried up some floorboards, and escaped beneath the house.

In all the confusion, those within the house grabbed hold of Osborne's body and drew it about the floor thinking it was Wheeler. When they noticed the man was dead, the mob panicked and fled the house. Later, Dr. John Fox of Wallingford would visit the scene, which he recounted as "the most terrible sight he could recall." By the light of a candle, Fox saw "the livid body of Osborne on the bed and cabin literally soaked in blood."

Wheeler spent the night naked in the woods. Before dawn he stole a shirt from a clothesline, walked to the Hartsboro section of town (another village lost to history), and hid in a barn. Needing clothes, he spent part of the day crudely weaving a dress from rye straw he found in the barn, and then retreating to his sister's home in Pawlet.

Wheeler was eventually caught, arrested, and put on trial in a makeshift court held at the Baptist church in Wallingford—the only building in town that could hold the crowds eager to watch the proceedings. In the end, he was found innocent under terms of self-defense. The mob that assaulted him didn't get off so easily. Two of his attackers were fined $60 each, while three others were fined $40.

After the court hearing, something strange happened to Patch Hollow—it was never the same. Eventually all the residents left and Patch Hollow was abandoned. Perhaps the tragic events of that chaotic night left a scar in the minds of everyone who partook, forever troubling the land. To this day, no one has tried to rebuild it.

Today's Patch Hollow is quieter; as the mountain forests reclaimed the land, the only visitors now are the countless hikers who loyally hike the Long Trail to get lost in the Vermont woods for a little while, letting the wilderness and the solitude quiet their thoughts.

The Batten Kill Valley

As you travel up the Batten Kill Valley, you'll see the Taconic Mountains on the west and the Green Mountains on the east, divided by a valley that grows wider and flatter as you head north. These are fertile farmlands with rich alluvial soil, and in the north you will see large farms along the valley floor. Route 7 is a limited-access highway in some places, but the quieter Routes 7A and 30 provide an alternative.

Along Route 7A you will come to the town of *Arlington,* which is best known for its famous citizen Norman Rockwell, who painted things as he saw them right here. The *Norman Rockwell Exhibit* at the Battenkill Gallery (Route 7A and Sugar Shack; 802-375-6747; normanrockwellexhibit.com) focuses on Rockwell's Arlington years (1939–1953). Rockwell didn't travel far for his subjects; he painted more than 200 local residents and captured life as it was being lived. Visit the gallery and see these amazing works of art any day May through Dec. A small admission is charged to those 18 and older.

One of Rockwell's subjects, Arlington resident Dr. George A. Russell, was a much-loved local doctor and an avid collector of all things Vermont, but in particular items pertaining to the areas of Arlington, Sunderland, and Sandgate. He collected books about Vermont, books by Vermont authors, photos, historic memorabilia, and anything else he could get his hands on. The collection he amassed over his lifetime is considered to be one of the largest anywhere devoted to Vermont history and ephemera. When Dr. Russell passed away in 1968 at the age of 89, he willed the collection to the town of Arlington and today it is showcased at the Martha Canfield Library

Friends Forever

In 1946, when an 11-year-old classmate died of cancer, a group of Burlington girls raised $48 to buy a painting from Norman Rockwell to hang in the school as a memorial to her. Rockwell donated the painting *The Babysitter,* and the girls spent the money on a brass plaque to put on it. Class after class graduated, and the painting was, at some point, removed and stored in the boiler room. When the painting was found recently and appraised at $300,000, the school board decided to sell it and put the money toward the school budget.

But old friendships die hard in Vermont, and the classmates once again assembled and vowed to raise the money to buy the painting back from the school. They then donated it to the art gallery at the University of Vermont, this time as a permanent memorial.

(528 East Arlington Rd.; 802-375-6153; marthacanfieldlibrary.org and russell collection.blogspot.com). The ***Russell Vermontiana Collection*** can be viewed only in person on Tues from 9 a.m. to 5 p.m. or by appointment. The library has recently digitized the collection, to preserve the fragile photos and documents for future generations to enjoy.

One of the best ways to see the Batten Kill Valley is from the river itself. The river rises on the west side of the Green Mountains and flows down through Arlington before leaving Vermont, finally emptying into the Hudson River in New York. It offers some of the nicest, most scenic water travel experiences in the state. The stream is nonthreatening and passes through fields and forests, under covered bridges, and through tiny settlements. ***Battenkill Canoe, Ltd.*** (6328 Rte. 7A; 800-421-5268 or 802-362-2800; battenkill .com) has been running river trips for a quarter of a century. They offer a variety of services, from equipment rentals to packages that provide all the essentials, including drop-off and pickup. Packages are varied and interesting and range anywhere from overnight to 11 nights. There's even one so adventurous that they fly you in and canoe you out.

Norman Rockwell fans will relish the opportunity to reserve a room in his former home. The ***Inn on Covered Bridge Green*** (3587 River Rd.; 802-375-9489; coveredbridgegreen.com) sits on 5.5 acres along the Battenkill River. It offers 8 rooms and guest cottages. You can even stay in Rockwell's former studio. Rooms in the main house are nicely decorated, all with gas fireplaces, private baths, and air conditioning. Some overlook the village green and church. A full breakfast is included in your rates.

Readers of a certain age may recall, with a bit of nostalgia, the cheese stores that appeared along New England's most traveled highways during the 1960s and 1970s. They were yellow and shaped liked huge wheels of cheese with a chunk taken out. Often swiss-cheese holes were painted on the exteriors. After a while the fad faded and many of the franchises closed. But not so in Arlington, where *The Cheese House* (5187 Rte. 7A; 802-375-9033; thevermontcheesehouse.com) still stands. This is the first and original (albeit updated and renovated) cheese house built and operated by the Russell family in 1968. Twenty years later, The Cheese House gained a souvenir shop in addition to its cheese shop, and 10 years after that it gained new owners. Today Rick and Jody Serraro are the proprietors of this cheesy stop. In 2011 they grappled with damage from Hurricane Irene, which devastated the historic cheese room. But repairs and updates have been completed and the store boasts a new modern country look. Stop in to say hi and browse their array of Vermont-made products, including maple syrup, maple candy, jams, and jellies. But don't leave without sampling their cheese, especially their own Truck Driver Cheddar, which is a delicious Vermont white cheddar that is aged for four years. Open Wed through Mon, 10 a.m. to 5 p.m. year-round.

Mount Equinox, a long mountain that lies almost parallel to Route 7A, rises to more than 3,800 feet. It is the highest peak in the Taconic Range, which admittedly is not known for its high elevations. But Equinox has some splendid views from the top, which you can reach by car via *Mount Equinox Skyline Drive* (1A Saint Bruno Dr.; 802-362-1114; equinoxmountain.com). This toll road was completed in 1947 and is the longest privately owned paved toll road in the country. It takes you from Route 7A in Sunderland at 800 feet to the also privately owned summit of Mount Equinox at 3,848 feet. The 5.2-mile drive promises beauty and serenity as you climb and absorb the views, which during foliage season are breathtaking—even native Vermonters make the trip this time of year. Your car will thank you for keeping an even speed of about 25 miles per hour on the ascent. Even with automatic transmission, you should descend in low gear. Check their website for a coupon off the toll charge.

The town of **Manchester** has two distinct parts: Manchester Village and Manchester Center. The former is a gracious village with marble sidewalks and beautifully maintained homes—many of which are more like mansions—lining the main square. Just a short drive north, Manchester Center is a series of factory-outlet malls—albeit in nicely designed buildings, for the most part—where you can buy everything from designer clothes to kitchenware.

In the former, you'll find **Hildene** (1005 Hildene Rd.; 802-362-1788; hildene.org), the country mansion of Robert Todd Lincoln, son of the president and himself president of the Pullman railcar company. Built in the opening years of the 20th century, this sumptuous building is a fine example of a period country home of a wealthy business magnate. Many of the furnishings came from Mrs. Lincoln's family, and there are personal items of the president, such as his famous stovepipe hat. On the landing of the grand staircase, a thousand-pipe 1908 Aeolian organ works again after a 1980 restoration. The elegant Queen Anne–furnished dining room and the wood-paneled parlor face each other across a broad carpeted hallway. Outside, stunning formal gardens overlooking the valley have been restored, re-creating many of the original plantings, including the kitchen gardens. More than 8 miles of hiking trails take you through the grounds, with interpretive signs to guide you. There is also a more recently added solar-powered barn, which is home to a herd of goats that are responsible for some delicious goat cheese. The barn can be explored and the cheese-making process viewed.

In the winter Hildene's grounds are traversed by 21 groomed cross-country trails, with facilities for all levels, a warming hut, a ski rental shop, and refreshments in a carriage barn. Annually after Christmas the house has Candlelight Tours with horse-drawn wagons or sleighs to bring guests through the snow to the front door. The house aglow in the snow-covered landscape is a magical sight. The schedule of events is worth checking at any time of year, since there are many treats, from pops concerts to garden parties, antiques shows to fairs. Open daily 9:30 a.m. to 4:30 p.m. year-round.

Manchester has long been a tourist destination. Although the town was chartered in 1761, the town didn't earn its bustling, upper-crust reputation until the mid-1800s, when it was promoted as a mineral springs vacation destination. The geology of Vermont consists of bedrock made up of granite and sedimentary rocks such as limestone, shale, and sandstone. This means that the groundwater contains a higher level of minerals than water where the rock is less porous.

During the second half of the 19th century, many urbanites were drawn to small Vermont towns for the original "spa vacations"—back then the phrase had a meaning very different from today's version. Somewhere along the line in the mid-19th century, physicians and other health promoters claimed that regular partaking of this water would restore health to pasty-faced city people and even prolong life. Germany was then in the forefront of this "taking of the waters," and the practice spread to the US.

Thus tourism in Vermont was born. Some Vermonters—most of whom never drank this mineral water, which was usually full of sulfuric deposits and smelled like rotten eggs—began to push the waters to out-of-staters. The popular belief was that the worse it smelled and tasted, the better it was for you. Some enterprising Vermonters even bottled the water and shipped it to Boston and New York for sale. Of course, proximity to a railroad line—rails were also being aggressively laid at the time—didn't hurt sales.

This influx of wealthy summer visitors inspired the expansion of the **Marsh Tavern** (3567 Main St.; 802-362-4700; equinoxresort.com), which had stood in the middle of town since 1769, into a hotel, where guests could, for an extra fee, improve their health with Equinox Sparkling Water. Today the tavern is part of the sprawling Equinox Resort and still offers hearty New England fare. Lunch (think roasted corn chowder with applewood-smoked bacon, roasted pork loin smothered with maple-mustard barbecue sauce, or Tavern Meatloaf with whipped potatoes, braised short ribs, sautéed mushrooms, and brown ale sauce) is served from 11:30 a.m. to 2:30 p.m. when pub fare (think maplewood-smoked chicken wings, cheeseburgers, and local charcuterie boards) takes over until dinner (think maple plank–roasted wild salmon, seared swordfish, or a bouillabaisse with lobster, scallops, shrimp, and mussels in a lobster-saffron broth served over angel hair pasta) at 5 p.m. Can't decide? Stay at one of the resort's inns and make time to sample all three.

One of your choices of accommodations is the **Charles Orvis Inn** (3567 Rte. 7A; 800-362-4747; equinoxresort.com), which offers 14 rooms and suites. The inn is situated in the 19th-century home of Charles Orvis, founder of the fly-fishing business, who bought the "cottage" in 1883. He opened C.F. Orvis Company in the brick bank building next door, where he manufactured split-bamboo fishing rods and artificial flies. Today his former home still stands facing the classic white-spired church in the village. Orvis's legacy of fly fishing lives on in the inn's restrained fisherman's-club decor. Old photographs of fishing camps share wall space in the public and guest rooms with beautifully framed fishing lures. The suites in this very upscale lodging include full-size kitchens, gas fireplaces, phones, televisions, and a blend of custom-built furniture and antiques. Guests enjoy all the services of the Equinox Resort, plus their own concierge, a continental breakfast, and a complimentary bar adjoining the billiards room downstairs.

Next door to the Orvis Inn, devotees of fishing can complete their pil-grimage by visiting the *American Museum of Fly Fishing* (4104 Main St.; 802-362-3300; amff.com). Open Mon through Fri from 10 a.m. until 4 p.m., this small but interesting museum offers informative displays on the history of fly fishing, with special emphasis on women. They also have a gift shop stocked with an array of quality items.

Back at the Equinox is the *British School of Falconry* (1550 River Rd.; 802-362-4780; equinoxresort.com/thingstodo/falconry), a sport unique in New England (and rare in the US). While you may have seen raptors and read about them at the Raptor Center in Woodstock, here you get to see them up close and actually work with them, under the close observation of a falconry expert, of course. The school is the first of its kind in the US and was started in 1995 by Steve and Emma Ford, Scots who started teaching falconry in 1982.

While a lesson here will not make you into a certified falconer, you will learn about raptors and how they hunt. You also get a chance to see an African tawny eagle, a Lanner hawk, and Harris hawks, all used for hunting. All equipment, including warm jackets and boots, if necessary, is provided, and participants in the short lesson learn how to hold a falcon on their gauntleted hand, how to "cast" or release the bird into flight, and how to signal for the bird's return. It is a great thrill to see these magnificent birds in flight, but to see them do so at close quarters and to have them alight on your hand is a rare experience.

The school has a number of programs available. The introductory lesson lasts about one hour and 45 minutes, there are also Hawk Walks, during which you get the full lesson and also have the pleasure of seeing a free-flying hawk following behind you, landing in the branches of trees, and coming when you call. This program is also an hour and 45 minutes long, and you must participate in the introductory lesson before you're allowed to do this one, but don't worry, there are packages. Visit the website for complete details and pricing.

Mount Equinox rises steeply behind the Equinox Resort, and the land along this western slope is part of the **Equinox Preservation Trust** (802-366-1400; equinoxpreservationtrust.org), which works with a consortium of other conservation and environmental organizations to protect and preserve more than 900 acres of the fragile lands on the mountain. While preserving the land, they also operate and maintain a large series of trails used for hiking, skiing, and horseback riding. Trails lead to ponds and the upper slopes of the mountain.

The terrain of the mountain is quite varied and contains many rare species of plants. Among these is the very rare yellow lady's slipper, a member of the orchid family. The rare protected environments of Table Rock and Deer Knoll are accessible only on tours led by naturalists from the **Vermont Institute of Natural Science** (6565 E. Woodstock Rd., Quechee; 802-296-7373), which also maintains an office at the Equinox Resort in Manchester. Their programs focus on learning about the mountain's rare habitats.

There are two trailheads giving access to several trails, most of which are short. Although individual trails can be as short as a half mile, they do link together to create longer hiking opportunities. The Pond Road trailhead is at the end of Pond Road, the street south of the Equinox Resort. From here, a nice, easy trail rounds Equinox Pond to Bower Spring and the Mountain Bluff Trail (0.8 mile). To get to the Red Gate trailhead, take Seminary Road on the north side of the Equinox Resort to West Union Street, following it to the trailhead. The longest trail is the Blue Trail (2.8 miles), which starts at the Red Gate and climbs upward along an old roadway, leading to a narrow, steep trail to the summit and lookout rock. From this ledge are sweeping views of New York, New Hampshire, and Vermont.

Look for a map of the preserve and its trails in a brochure titled "Equinox Preservation Trust," which you will find at the Tourist Information Office, at the Equinox Resort, in brochure racks in most of the businesses in Manchester Village and Manchester Center, and on the website.

You can also access these trails from the **Southern Vermont Arts Center** (930 Southern Vermont Arts Center Dr.; 802-362-1405; svac.org), which sponsors exhibits and performances throughout the year. The art starts from the second you enter the grounds and continues all the way up the beautiful, gradually ascending drive to the main estate, the Yester House. The grounds at the top of the hill are nicely landscaped and highlighted by more sculptures. The 0.75-mile **Boswell Botany Trail** leads from the 1917 mansion into the woods, where you will find more than 100 varieties of native wildflowers and ferns. Many of these are rare species. The woodland flowers are at their best bloom in the spring.

vermonttrivia

Southern Vermont Arts Center displays the largest collection in the world of Luigi Lucioni's works.

Inside space is used for constantly changing exhibits of art and for performances that may include chamber music, dance, or vocal music. Admission is charged to the galleries, but the grounds are free. The center is open year-round Tues through Sat 10 a.m. to 5 p.m. and on Sun from noon to 5 p.m.

Manchester Depot is a tiny corner of Manchester Center, only a block off a short stretch of highway shared by Routes 11 and 30, but almost completely hidden. Locals know it for its charming architecture and for a clutch of shops that face Elm Street. At the intersection of Elm Street and Highland Avenue is a collection of wonderful old 19th-century storefronts that have not been defiled by modernization and are well worth the visit, including **Al Ducci's Italian Pantry** (133 Elm St.; 802-362-4449; alduccis.com), which in itself is worth the side trip. Once inside, it's like being transported to Boston's North End, with the same tangy smells, friendly service with a touch of wise guy, and products you didn't think could be found this far from a city. In the cold cases you'll find a nice selection of salads, links of their own premises-made sausages, and chunks of their own mozzarella, made daily. They have really good made-to-order sandwiches such as a veggie combo (roasted eggplant, roasted peppers, fresh mozzarella, tomato, basil), a prosciutto sandwich (with fresh mozzarella, roasted peppers, and basil), and chicken cutlet (with roasted peppers, fresh mozzarella, and basil). These are served on your choice of white Italian, French, semolina, focaccia, or

> # Free, But Valuable
>
> As you travel through the state, look for the *Vermont Country Sampler* (PO Box 197, North Clarendon, VT 05759; 802-772-7463; vermontcountrysampler.com), a small newspaper you can pick up free in tourist information centers, restaurants, and many other places. It features articles on historical subjects, along with features on local places you might not otherwise find. Seasonal activities and events are well covered, too, both in articles and in a calendar of events in each issue. Visit their website to find out how to receive a free copy.

multigrain breads. Get your sandwiches to go or to eat in the dining room next door, a bright little room with a molded tin ceiling and red checkered cloths on the tables.

Manchester has an abundance of places to eat, from bakeries, cafes, and pubs to elegant dining rooms. One that you'll find in a former tollhouse perched between the winding road and a rushing little brook in a ravine is *Mistral's at Toll Gate* (10 Toll Gate Rd.; 802-362-1779; mistralsattollgate .com), where classic French flavors and techniques are skillfully updated. For openers you can try the Frog's Legs Persillade. Their pâté *maison* is a triumph of flavor and texture, moist and lean with a tenderness that is almost crumbly, and a serving that is large enough to share. Entrees, which include bread, Salad Mistral (a mesclun of tender young greens), and vegetables, range from fish and seafood to chicken, duck, sweetbreads and beef, and specials. The signature dish of this chef-owned restaurant is the Norwegian salmon cannelloni, a pair of rolled salmon fillets, stuffed cannelloni style with a mixture of lobster and finely diced shallots and vegetables, in a light pink beurre blanc. The service is exceptional, always there when needed but almost invisible. Among their enticing desserts is the signature Coup Mistral: coffee ice cream rolled in toasted hazelnuts with hot fudge and Frangelico liqueur.

The restaurant takes full advantage of its setting, with more than half of the tables along the wall of windows overlooking the dancing brook. The ravine is flood-lit at night, and although it is lovely at any time of year, in winter, the brilliant white of snow and ice contrasts with the transparent darkness of rushing water and deep greens of the overhanging conifers.

Although they do virtually no advertising, Mistral is a top choice among knowledgeable locals, so a reservation is advisable even on weeknights. They are open Nov through June, Thurs through Mon for dinner from 6 p.m.

Anyone rushing along Route 7 north of Manchester will probably miss the small sign that points to **Danby,** a beautiful little town that once was the prosperous center of an active marble-quarrying industry. It sits on a hillside a quarter mile off the main road. Author Pearl S. Buck, who spent much of her life in China and wrote *The Good Earth,* spent her last years here, devoting much of her renowned energy trying to breathe life back into the town as the marble industry collapsed. Its 19th-century beauty has been saved, without the embellishments of more modern times, probably because no one had the money to modernize it.

Mountain View Ranch (502 Easy St.; 802-293-5837; mountainview ranch.biz) is run by horse-lovers Letitia and John Sisters, who with their experienced guides offer trail rides to those of all skill levels. There are plenty of options from which to choose, from 1-hour rides through woods and fields of this mountainous rural countryside to 2-hour rides up Dorset Peak. There are longer options too, including picnic rides, as well as rodeos. There are also donkey and pony rides for those less experienced or less tall. Reservations are necessary, so be sure to call ahead. In the autumn and spring, the ranch is open just about every day, but for winter riding the hours are 9 a.m. to 4 p.m. Mon through Thurs.

The Mettawee Valley

If you choose to drive north out of Manchester on Route 30, you'll soon come into the town of **Dorset.** So many artists, woodworkers, quilters, and other craftsworkers have set up shops in their homes along Route 30 that you could spend an entire day visiting them all.

Like Manchester, Dorset is genteel country, and you pass fenced-off estates lining both sides of Route 30. Dorset's population numbers half that of Manchester, with many more summer residents. In fact, the first summer house in Dorset was built in 1868, setting the tone for the future.

Some of the houses in the village were rescued from Massachusetts when whole towns were flooded to create the Quabbin Reservoir. They were taken apart and brought to Dorset for reconstruction, a project financed by a local philanthropist not only to save the fine old homes but also to provide work for local men during the Depression.

Mount Aeolus, which rises directly behind the village, was the site of Vermont's first commercial marble quarry and provided the stone for the columns and facing of the New York Public Library. About 25 quarries once employed hundreds in extracting, cutting, and shipping the marble, and you can still see one of them beside Route 30, just north of its intersection with West Road.

The *Dorset Playhouse* (104 Cheney Rd.; 802-867-5777; dorsetplayers .org) features performances by professional actors-in-residence in the summer and showcases community theater the rest of the year. Visit their website to see what will be playing when you are in the area.

North of Dorset the towns of Rupert and Pawlet are on the Mettawee River, which follows Route 30. Follow Route 315 West off Route 30 once you cross over the border of Rupert from Dorset. Look for the historical marker that designates the site of *Harmon's Mint.* Back when Vermont was an independent republic, resident Reuben Harmon Jr. received government permission to operate the Green Mountain State's only mint, where he worked with copper coins and created the Harmon cent. Minting was abandoned in 1789 and Harmon's cents are rarely found outside museums today.

Continue on Route 315 West until you come upon the *Merck Forest and Farmland Center* (3270 Rupert Rd.; 802-394-7836; merckforest.org), a massive, 3,000-plus-acre land preserve where a family can spend the entire day outdoors enjoying nature and farm life. There are hiking trails ranging from an easy walk to some that are more strenuous. The Joy Green Visitor Center and a barn filled with horses, chickens, and other farm animals are also interesting learning experiences. You can watch and learn about a variety of farm chores, from boiling down maple syrup to breaking in horses. Camping is available in cabins that have woodstoves, bunks, and outhouses. Lean-to shelters and tent sites are also available. The center serves as an active community resource, with a summer day camp for children and a series of nature and farming workshops for adults. The center is open daily from dawn to dusk. There is no admission fee.

Back in Rupert, Route 153 heads north into West Pawlet. Contrary to current appearances, this town was a bustling outpost back in 1850; it was, in fact, considered one of the 10 most populous employment centers in the state. You will see why as you leave the village heading north and cross the slate quarry and its slag piles. That explains the slate roofs on so many of the town's buildings.

Pawlet, on Lilly Road, is home to the **Pawlet Potter** (746 Lily Hill; 802-325-3238; marionwaldomcchesney.com), aka Marion Waldo McChesney. McChesney has opened her working studio to the public and encourages people to come and visit. She favors frog and seascape subjects, with oceanic color schemes brought out in her gently shaped pots and vessels. Look at the aqua plate that has frogs molded onto it; they're swimming and chasing flies and look like they're about to leap off the plate. She calls this style "Road Kill Impressionism." She has fun with the style and doesn't take herself too seriously with it. The studio is open "by chance," so you'll want to call ahead and make an appointment.

While you're in the artsy mood, travel down the road to **Valley Woodworking** (Route 30; 802-325-3910; valleywoodworkingvt.com), run by Jim Boyd. Boyd moved to Vermont in the late 1980s from Rhode Island, specifically to Rupert because there are a lot of craftspeople in this part of the state, and he wanted support from his peers. Jim does a lot of custom work, as well as refinishing, repair, and reproductions. He says he's been doing this kind of work "forever." He graduated from the Rhode Island School of Design and has created a business on quality. Along with detailed reproductions, Jim builds custom kitchen cabinets and vanities, and will work with you to repurpose a piece you love. He welcomes visitors and spends most days working in the barn workshop, but does go out to installations, so it's always best to call ahead.

Places to Stay in Southwest Vermont

ARLINGTON

Arlington Inn
3904 Rte. 7A
(802) 375-6532
arlingtoninn.com
Moderate
An elegant Greek revival mansion with antiques and an excellent dining room.

DORSET

Barrows House
3156 Rte. 30
(802) 867-4455
barrowshouse.com
Moderate to expensive
Rooms in 9 buildings spread over its extensive property, making it a favorite for families.

Inn at West View Farm
2928 Rte. 30
(802) 867-5715
innatwestviewfarm.com
Expensive
Comfortable rooms in an 1870 farmhouse with a relaxed country atmosphere. All have air conditioning and private full baths. Delicious food here, too, at this chef-owned inn.

RUTLAND

The Hikers Hostel
23 Center St.
(802) 775-9800
Inexpensive
Conveniently located near the bus station and trails, this is a great place to lay your head for an evening.

WESTON

Colonial House Inn and Motel
287 Rte. 100
(802) 824-6286 or
(800) 639-5033
cohoinn.com
Inexpensive to moderate
Combines a homey B&B with motel units. Serves home-style meals.

WILMINGTON

Horizon Inn
861 Rte. 9
(802) 464-2131 or (800)
336-5513
horizoninn.com
Inexpensive
This family-owned, motel-like inn offers contemporary rooms, indoor pool, sauna, Wi-Fi, and in-room coffeemakers. Located not far from Hogback Mountain summit.

Nutmeg Inn
153 Rte. 9
(802) 464-3907
nutmeginn.com
Moderate to expensive
A cozy New England classic, with wood-burning fireplaces. A full country breakfast is offered. Convenient to nearby Harriman Reservoir.

Places to Eat in Southwest Vermont

BRANDON

Cattails
2146 Grove St.
(802) 247-9300
cattailsvt.com
Moderate
Serves generous portions of American home-cooked creations in a rustic setting daily from 11 a.m. to 9 p.m.; breakfast can be found on Sat and Sun from 7 a.m. to noon.

MANCHESTER CENTER

Gringo Jack's Southwestern Bar & Grill
5103 Main St.
(802) 362-0836
candeleros.net
Moderate

TO LEARN MORE IN SOUTHWEST VERMONT

Dorset Chamber of Commerce
PO Box 121
Dorset 05251
dorsetvt.com

Bennington Chamber of Commerce
100 Veterans Memorial Dr.
(802) 447-3311 or (800) 229-0252
bennington.com.

Manchester & the Mountains Region
39 Bonnet St.
Manchester Center
(802) 362-6313 or (800) 362-4144
visitmanchestervt.com.

Mount Snow Valley Chamber of Commerce
21 Main St.
Wilmington
(802) 464-8092 or (877) 887-6884
visitvermont.com

The most popular Tex-Mex restaurant in the region, with a good selection of Hispanic dishes and New England regional foods at lunch and dinner

PAWLET

Mach's Brick Oven Bakery
18 School St.
(877) YUM-PIZZA or (802) 325-6113
vtpizzapie.com
Moderate
Serves lunch, snacks, and pizza, and sells fresh-baked breads and pastries. Thurs through Sun 4:30 to 9 p.m.

RUTLAND

Clem's Cate
101–103 Merchants Row
(802) 747-3340
Inexpensive to moderate
Under recent new ownership, this is a great breakfast spot to hit before the trails or slopes.

Johnny Boy's
182 Rte. 4
(802) 855-8043
johnnyboyspancakehouse.com
Inexpensive
This pancake house serves up huge portions that will leave you stuffed. Open daily 7 a.m. to 2 p.m.

Roots the Restaurant
51 Walos St.
(802) 747-7414
rootsrutland.com
Moderate to expensive
Using local, fresh ingredients, Chef Donald Billings whips up some amazing (and affordable) meals. He is committed to using minimally processed foods, which is good news all around. Serving lunch and dinner indoors and out, Roots opens at 11 a.m. Tues through Sun, closing at 9 p.m. Tues through Thurs and Sun, at 10 p.m. Fri and Sat. They take a break on Mon.

Yellow Deli

23 Center St.
(802) 775-9800
yellowdeli.com
Inexpensive

A unique dining experience in downtown Rutland. If you get a chance, go online and read the history on this place; it's fascinating. Either way, stop by to enjoy their groovy menu of delicious sandwiches and salads. Grab yourself a smoothie, too, while you're at it. Open Mon through Thurs 10 a.m. to 9 p.m., Fri 10 a.m. to 3 p.m.; closed weekends.

WESTON

The Bryant House Restaurant

Rte. 100
(802) 824-6287
Moderate

Located on the grounds of the Vermont Country Store in an 1827 building that still has the original soda fountain and ballroom, this restaurant offers lunch daily from 11 a.m. to 3:30 p.m. and dinner Tues through Sun from 4 to 9 p.m. A Sunday brunch is also available. Look for old-fashioned, homemade goodness here, such as hearty soups, potpies, sandwiches, and salads.

Cafe at the Falls

Weston Playhouse
(802) 824-5288
Innweston.com/cafe-at-the-falls.html
Moderate

Seasonal restaurant located in the lower level of the Weston Playhouse and run by the folks at the Inn at Weston. Thoroughly redone after Hurricane Irene caused extensive flood damage, this space is bright and airy and offers great views of the falls on West River and Mill Museum.

MIDDLE WEST VERMONT →

Within an area that stretches from the northern segment of the Green Mountain National Forest to the lower Champlain Valley and the New York border is almost everything that's considered typically Vermont. Here are snow-covered ski trails, the Long Trail for hiking, wide flat valleys painted green by farmland and dotted with red barns, dirt roads winding through woods and over mountains, country inns, lakes, small, tidy brick downtowns, and white-clapboard villages set around the tall spires of their meetinghouses.

But there is more than the postcard image to this part of the state, and you don't even have to leave its main roads to find it. Although some of the state's best-known slopes bring skiers pouring in during the winter, and the year-round resorts that cluster at their bases are filled in the summer, much of this part of Vermont remains—or at least seems—largely untouched, the legacy of the national forest lands that form its eastern third.

To the west are the lower but often still rolling lands that stretch to Lake Champlain, as it narrows and finally seems more like a very wide river. Wetlands here provide migration and nesting grounds for a wide range of bird life,

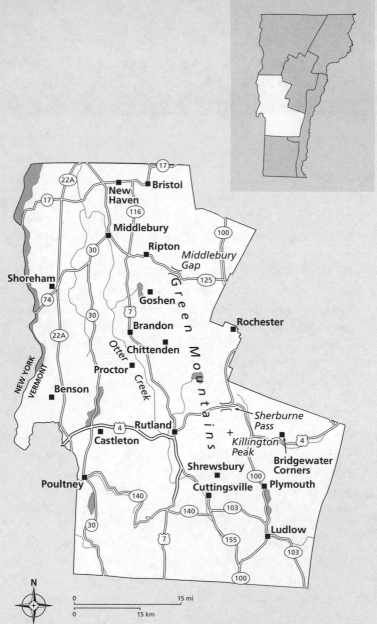

MIDDLE WEST VERMONT

Bristol
New Haven
22A
17
17
116
Middlebury
100
Ripton
30
Middlebury Gap
Shoreham
125
74
Goshen
30
7
Brandon
Rochester
22A
Chittenden
Otter Creek
Proctor
Benson
Green Mountains
Sherburne Pass
NEW YORK
VERMONT
Rutland
4
Castleton
Killington Peak
4
Shrewsbury
Bridgewater Corners
Poultney
100
Cuttingsville
Plymouth
140
140
103
30
155
Ludlow
7
103
100

N

0   15 mi
0   15 km

and smaller lakes provide swimming and boating, without being overrun by tourists.

Ludlow and Points North

Ludlow is a sizable town whose population doubles in winter. Ludlow is in Vermont's heavy snow zone—100 to 120 inches a year is not unusual. Standing tall behind the town, **Okemo Mountain** (77 Okemo Ridge Rd.; 802-228-4041; okemo.com) became a part of local economic life in 1955 when a group of local businessmen decided that the town should have a ski area. Starting small, it grew until it overcame a financial hurdle in the late 1970s. With new owners in 1982, rejuvenation began that has never ended. Since then it has become one of the top resorts in Vermont with keen client loyalty—and has become a year-round resort.

Today it boasts trails on 2 mountains and complete resort facilities, which make it popular with families year-round. At its highest point it has a vertical drop of 2,200 feet, and snowmaking covers more than 95 percent of its 119 trails. Nineteen lifts provide flexible access to trails with a good range of skiing for all skill levels. Okemo attracts boarders with 10 terrain parks, including the new Amp Energy Superpipe, which debuted in 2013. From its rebirth in 1982 the emphasis at Okemo has been service; on the slopes, this translates to some of the best snowmaking and grooming in the East. Conditions here are always good, and often great. An outstanding ski school, well-maintained rental equipment, and large, bright base lodges add to the package.

Service is also the keyword at the resort's lodgings, dining, and off-slope recreational facilities. Hotel and condo lodgings at the base and slopeside are in a number of price ranges (lodging: 800-78-OKEMO). Dining options range from casual snack bars and informal restaurants to romantic haute cuisine dinners in a wine cellar.

Ski and lodging as well as ski-only specials are numerous and varied at Okemo. Check in often to their website to take advantage of the latest deals being offered.

In the non–ski season the focus turns to the first-class golf facilities at two 18-hole courses nearby. **Okemo Valley Golf Club** (89 Fox Ln.; 802-228-1396; okemo.com/activities/golf/okemovalley.asp) is a 6,400-yard, par

BEST ATTRACTIONS IN MIDDLE WEST VERMONT

President Calvin Coolidge State
Historic Site

Texas Falls

Mount Independence

M/V *Carillon*

Chimney Point State Historic Site

70 course. It is a Heathland-style course with an 18-acre golf-learning center. The ***Tater Hill Golf Club*** (6802 Popple Dungeon Rd.; 802-875-2517; okemo.com/activities/golf/taterhill.asp), actually 22 miles away in North Windham, has another 18-hole course noted for its challenge and for its views. The ***Adventure Zone at Jackson Gore*** (802-228-1600; okemo.com/activities/adventurezone.asp) is Okemo's newest endeavor. It is a mammoth recreation facility that offers ziplining, minigolf, a climbing wall, a bungee trampoline, the Timber Ripper roller coaster, huge air bag, and more. Open weekends only until the summer season is in full swing. There's so much more to be explored at Okemo Mountain, but since it's not *exactly* off the beaten path, we'll leave you to explore the website for all the latest.

The ***Fletcher Farm School*** (611 Rte. 103 South; 802-228-8770; fletcher farm.org) near the Cavendish-Ludlow town line to the south comprises numerous outbuildings—barns, cabins, and motel rooms—that serve as accommodations for visitors and guests who want to spend two weeks painting, weaving, folk dancing, and engaging in other arts-and-crafts activities. The school is owned by the Society of Vermont Craftsmen, which also runs a small arts-and-crafts store on the premises during summer, selling items made by guests at the farm. A single reasonable price includes lodging, 3 family-style meals a day, lessons, and studio and practice space. The Fletcher Farm School offers classes from June through Oct.

From Route 103 in Ludlow, turn onto Buttermilk Falls Road at the VFW building and go to the end of the road to see ***Buttermilk Falls.*** The water rushes hard over the rocks even in a dry autumn, and it completely drowns out the sound of heavy traffic on nearby Route 103. A couple of big flat rocks in the river are perfect for sunning and picnicking. And along the road are other footpaths leading down to the river. There are two good spots, one at the very end of the road and the other a few tenths of a mile before the end. A path leads to the falls from Buttermilk Falls Road, about 1.3 miles from its intersection with Route 103 in town.

In the town of Ludlow, the **Black River Academy Historical Museum** (14 High St.; 802-228-5050; bramvt.org) sits in a stately old brick building perched above the main road on High Street. The first floor of this museum takes you down Main Street Ludlow, circa 1899. Built entirely by students, this exhibit features a barber shop, an ice cream parlor, a blacksmith's shop, and other places that show visitors what a Vermont town would have looked like in the late 19th century. There's even a complete reproduction of a typical 19th-century home (also built by students) that accurately displays period furnishings and decorations. Travel to the second floor to learn about the many barns that grace Ludlow as well as see an informative exhibit on the Finnish heritage of this area. But don't stop here. Keep going to the third floor, where you'll find a classroom restored to what it would have looked like at the turn of the 20th century. In fact, it looks very much like the classroom in which Calvin Coolidge, who graduated from the academy when it was a renowned private school in 1890, would have sat. There's also a doll collection on this floor that features Kewpie dolls wearing clothing hand-crocheted by Frances Kincade, an 1899 graduate of the academy.

The building itself was constructed in 1889 and today sits next to a former schoolhouse, the old District School No. 1, which now serves as Ludlow's senior center and community center.

The museum—a truly fascinating place—is open Tues through Sat, noon to 4 p.m., from Memorial Day to Labor Day; then weekends only through Columbus Day weekend; and then by appointment only during winter months. Admission by donation.

The **Crowley Cheese Factory** (14 Crowley Ln., Mount Holley; 802-259-2340; crowleycheese.com) is the antithesis of the mammoth Cabot Cheese Factory in Cabot. To find this little gem of a place, travel past the Crowley Cheese Store on Route 103 to Healdville Road. Take this left and travel 2 miles until you see the small, brown colonial house on your left. This is the factory, where several hundred pounds of cheese are made every day, by hand.

ANNUAL EVENTS IN MIDDLE WEST VERMONT

JULY

Independence Day Celebration
various venues
Brandon
(802) 247-6401
brandon.org/event/independence-day-celebration-2
Vermont's largest parade, along with music, food, and fireworks. On the Saturday nearest July 4.

Basin Bluegrass Festival
Wyman's Fields
Basin Road
Brandon
(802) 236-1096
basinbluegrassfestival.com
"Bluegrass pickin' and Vermont scenery." Held the weekend after the 4th. Tickets available at the gate, camping is available.

Summer Festival on the Green
Village Green
Middlebury
(802) 462-3555
festivalonthegreen.org
A week of performing arts early to mid-July. Admission is free and event is rain or shine. Donations are welcome.

SOAR Summerfest
Central Park
Brandon
(802) 247-6422, ext. 26
soarsummerfest.org
Music, food, children's activities, and more at the park. Begins with a pig roast and culminates with a jazz jubilee. All proceeds benefit summer programs.

SEPTEMBER

Vermont State Fair
Vermont State Fairgrounds
175 S. Main St.
Rutland
(802) 775-5200
vermontstatefair.net
Held in early Sept, this state fair is one of the biggest and brightest.

Plymouth Cheese & Harvest Festival
President Calvin Coolidge State Historic Site
3780 Rte. 100A
Plymouth
(802) 672-3773
This event in late Sept celebrates the harvest and one of the state's leading commodities—its cheese. Come for samples, guided tours, wagon rides, craft demonstrations, barbecue, contests, and more.

Built in 1882, this small building retains its original post-and-beam exterior. Inside, cheese makers start making the cheese by hand—a process that takes almost all day. You can stop in and see part of this process (depending on what time of day you arrive). Their product is all natural and uses whole, unpasteurized milk without additives or preservatives. There are samples available to help you decide what kind you'd like to take home. The factory is open 8 a.m. to 4 p.m. on weekdays. Sometimes they open on a Sunday, so take a chance and call. If you're in the area on a day the factory is closed, don't despair. Their cheese is available at many retail outlets.

As you head back to Route 103, you'll see that this is a good foliage road; Sawyer Rocks, a huge outcropping, is straight ahead, dotted with trees that in autumn are brilliant in their color.

As you travel Route 100, you'll notice lakes—lots of lakes. Running alongside the road you'll find Lake Rescue and Amherst Lake in Ludlow, and Echo Lake in Plymouth. In the summer these lakes are bustling communities of boaters, anglers, campers, hikers, and other warm-weather-loving folks. For those not looking to commune quite so much with Mother Nature, there's the inn named after one of the lakes.

Echo Lake Inn (2 Dublin Rd.; 802-228-8602 or 800-356-6844; echolake inn.com), an imposing structure with a long, rocker-studded porch, is one of only five inns in Vermont from the 1800s that were built as inns. It is said that Calvin Coolidge, Henry Ford, and Thomas Edison were guests at this 1840 inn at one time or another. The inn has been thoroughly modernized but has retained its character. It has probably retained more than most. In fact, a few former residents have been retained as well. Yes, we're talking spirits of the Casper variety. The ghost here at Echo Lake Inn favors Room 31 and seems to have a special affinity for the color yellow. Several episodes surrounded changing the wallpaper in that room from a sunny yellow to a dark blue. The ghost finally took measures to be sure the dark blue wallpaper was replaced and the new innkeepers decided to go with yellow. Nary a sound has been heard from the ghost since. Perhaps you'll book Room 31 and see if you have any encounters. We suggest you wear yellow.

The inn also has a fine dining room overseen by Chef Kevin Barnes, who has been with the inn since 1980. He gets creative with local ingredients and uses only the freshest, best choices for his dishes. *Vermont Magazine* calls dinner here "something of an event." Rates include a full breakfast for two, so how can you go wrong?

From Route 100A in Plymouth to Route 103 in Ludlow, Route 100 is known as the Calvin Coolidge Memorial Highway. Coolidge was one of two American presidents born in Vermont.

Coolidge was born in Plymouth Notch on July 4, 1872. His position as governor of Massachusetts led him to a spot on the ballot as running mate to Warren G. Harding in the 1920 presidential race. On August 3, 1923, while Coolidge was in Plymouth helping his father get in the hay, President Harding died in California. The presidential oath of office was administered to Calvin by lamplight over the family kitchen table at 2:47 a.m. When John Coolidge, the father of the new president, was later asked why he thought

OTHER ATTRACTIONS WORTH SEEING IN MIDDLE WEST VERMONT

UVM Morgan Horse Farm
74 Battell Dr. (Route 23)
Middlebury
(802) 388-2011
uvm.edu/morgan
Even those not horse crazy will enjoy this place. Learn about the history of the horses of the US Cavalry, take a guided tour of the facilities, and enjoy the beautiful old surroundings.

Lincoln Peak Vineyard
142 River Rd.
Middlebury
(802) 388-7368
lincolnpeakvineyard.com
Sample wines made entirely from grapes of this 12-acre vineyard. Live music on Fri evenings, the perfect complement.

New England Maple Museum
4578 Rte. 7
Pittsford
(802) 483-9414
maplemuseum.com
Learn all you ever wanted to know about the history of making maple syrup. Gift shop available, too.

McLaughlin Falls
Wheelerville Road
Killington
Gorgeous double waterfall but a bit tricky to get to. There is no path, but the sounds of the falls should lead you to them. Please obey any No Trespassing signs, as surrounding land is privately owned. Falls can be viewed from the bridge of Eddy Brook.

Bucklin Trail
Wheelerville Road
Mendon
A short distance from McLaughlin Falls, this 8-mile (round-trip) hike will take you to the top of Killington Mountain or to an intersection with Long Trail. There is limited roadside parking here. Trail can also be accessed off Route 4, where you may find more parking.

he was authorized to administer the presidential oath, his reply was characteristically Coolidge: "I didn't know I couldn't," he said.

Today Plymouth Notch is the **President Calvin Coolidge State Historic Site** (3780 Rte. 100A; 802-672-3773; historicsites.vermont.gov/directory/coolidge) with the village and homestead where he grew up furnished exactly as it was in 1923 (the president's son gave the house to the state). The cheese factory still produces cheese, and its original equipment is shown, along with other farm implements and horse-drawn vehicles, in the Wilder Barn. The Wilder House, once a tavern and the childhood home of Calvin's mother, Victoria, is now a small restaurant where you can have traditional dishes such as chowder and chicken potpie. After you are stuffed, walk off the calories on the walking trails that showcase flora, fauna, and cellar holes.

thesoundof silentcal

Stories, many of them fictional, abound illustrating the taciturn nature of the Vermonter known as Silent Cal. One of them involved a society matron who was introduced to President Coolidge at a particularly tedious garden party in Washington. "Oh, Mr. President," she said, "I have a bet with a friend that I can make you say more than two words!"

"You lose," he replied.

The site is open from 9:30 a.m. to 5 p.m. every day from Memorial Day through Columbus Day. Admission is charged to those 6 and older.

Past Lake Rescue and just before you reach Echo Lake as you're heading north on Route 100, take a right. About a mile up the steep, winding road is the **Plymouth Kingdom Cemetery,** where several Revolutionary War soldiers are buried. This cemetery was the first graveyard in town and today old slate markers stand in back of VFW markers and flags. The cemetery is surrounded by a split-rail fence, and stone steps lead up to the grave sites. Kingdom Brook rushes by on the other side of the road.

Back on this pastoral road is a pleasant drive, with rolling land, estates, and ponds. When you need a break from driving, consider a stay at **Hawk Inn & Mountain Resort** (75 Billings Rd.; 802-672-3811; hawkresort.com), right on Route 100 in the Black River Valley, where you can experience Vermont's out-of-doors without sacrificing luxury. The low-to-the-land buildings are contemporary, with large, comfortable rooms and public spaces built to please upscale young families. It is open all year and has a wealth of recreational facilities on its 1,200 acres, including an indoor pool, sauna, hiking trails, ice-skating, sledding, snowshoeing, and cross-country skiing. They also can arrange horseback riding or boating on Lake Amherst, and in the winter they offer sleigh rides. There's even an on-site spa.

The dining room, the *River Tavern Restaurant,* which is open to the public, is stylish and cozy, with views onto the well-landscaped grounds. The menu is New American, and dishes are well prepared; appetizers are often ample for an entree. As you might expect in a place catering to this clientele, the wine list is quite good. Reservations are wise, especially in ski season.

When you're back on the road, you can follow Route 4, which leaves Route 100 in West Bridgewater and heads through Bridgewater Corners and on east to Woodstock. A short distance from the intersection, on Route 4, you'll come to *Blanche and Bill's Pancake House* (586 Rte. 4; Bridgewater Corners; 802-422-3816; blancheandbills.com), which serves country-style, lumberjack-size breakfasts. The blueberry pancakes come heaped with blueberries, while the french toast arrives with cinnamon sugar liberally sprinkled over the fat slices of bread. Eggs and waffles are also on the breakfast menu, with burgers and grilled sandwiches the mainstay of lunch. Now run by Francia and Andrew Geller, who purchased the business (and learned all the secret recipes) from Blanche in 2009, Blanche and Bill's Pancake House is open Thurs through Mon 7 a.m. to 2 p.m., Tues 5:30 to 8:30 p.m. They are closed Wed.

If it's lunchtime, or if you've a mind to sample some Vermont brew, keep going until you reach the three grain silos that mark the *Long Trail Brewing Company* (5520 Rte. 4; 802-672-5011; longtrail.com). We like the philosophy of its founder and owner: Since beer is 95 percent water, it shouldn't have to be imported. Everything at the brewery is made in Vermont, from the brewing equipment to the woodstove and heavy wooden tables in the beer hall/pub. You can order a sampler of 6 different ales, and savor and compare them at the bar, at a table inside, or on a deck overlooking the river. Through a glass wall you can see the giant gleaming vats and the business part of the brewery. Good, sturdy, goes-great-with-beer food is served, too—bratwurst steamed in Long Trail Ale, chili, ale and cheddar soup, or soft pretzels, made on the premises with Long Trail beer. The pub and visitor center are open daily from 10 a.m. to 7 p.m., with food served from 11 a.m. to 6 p.m.

Just past the brewing company is the Bridgewater Mill, a large clapboard woolen mill that now houses an eclectic collection of shops and studios. Anchoring one end is the combined showroom of *Charles Shackleton Furniture* and *Miranda Thomas Pottery* (102 Mill Rd.; 802-672-5175; shackletonthomas.com). The furniture workshop is visible through glass windows, and Miranda's pottery studio is in a small building—where visitors are welcome—next door to the mill. The furniture is nothing short of spectacular—a Queen Anne–inspired sleigh bed, upholstered chairs that are at once Art Deco and classical, delicate candle stands. The pottery is a match for it, much of the work in a distinctive carved style that seems to turn damask into solid forms. The gallery is open Mon through Sat 10 a.m. to 5 p.m., Sun 11 a.m. to 4 p.m.

Several other crafts studios are in the mill, including a jeweler, an art gallery, a thrift shop, a potter, and a glass workshop.

You can take Route 100A here, then cut back southwest through Plymouth (passing the Coolidge homestead) and come out on Route 100, making a tidy little loop—a nice afternoon's excursion from the Echo Lake Inn.

As you're heading back to Route 100, *Killington Mountain* looms so large that at times it looks like you're going to drive right into it. Killington, the second-highest peak in the state, is where Vermont purportedly received its name. A minister from Connecticut was traveling on horseback through the area in 1763, and when he reached the top of Killington—all 4,241

Which Floor, Please?

Hurricane Irene devastated Bridgewater Mill in 2011 when she sent her floodwaters through the bottom floors of the building. When the waters began to recede, it could be seen flowing out under the doors of some of the stores there. Mill owner Jireh Billings was not to be beaten, though. He considered it an opportunity to clean out his basement to create more space—a job he had previously thought would take a few years. Many volunteers helped get the stores back up and running. There was, however, one unexpected visitor from the storm. A live brown trout was found in the elevator shaft. He now lives out his days on a nearby farm.

A Step Forward to the Past

Just in time for the 21st century, one Vermont town reclaimed the name it abandoned at the turn of the 19th century. In April 1999 the citizens of Sherburne, Vermont, voted to rename their town Killington once more. It had originally been chartered as such in 1761 but was renamed Sherburne in 1800 after Colonel Benjamin Sherburne, who owned land in the area. But since nearly everyone came to know the town as Killington, thanks to the mountain that dominates the area and the ski slopes and resorts that give it its fame, the residents decided it would just be easier to return to the original name.

feet of it—the Reverend Sam Peters was said to have called the land *verd mont,* French for "green mountain." (The French actually would have called it *mont verd.* Slavishly following this dictum, though, would have led to a decidedly less euphonious state name.)

From the many restaurants to the ski facilities and other activities around *Killington,* it's easy to get the feeling that the theme is indulgence. There is one place you can go in the area, though, where the focus is on fitness and self-preservation. *Jimmy LeSage's New Life Hiking Spa* (2617 Killington Rd.; 802-353-2954; newlifehikingspa.com) is located at the Inn of the Six Mountains, and although the participants at Jimmy's spa may be surrounded by people who are hell-bent on cramming as much as possible into their time at Killington, the New Lifers find it doesn't matter: They're having a great time anyway.

From mid-May through September Jimmy offers a variety of fitness weeks and weekends that combine just the right amount of healthfulness and pampering, from low-calorie meals that are nonetheless satisfying to a good dose of massages and leisurely walks, on which you can appreciate the activity for its sensual pleasures and not for the exact number of calories you've just burned. That's not Jimmy's focus. His goal is to have his guests gain a new philosophy on life—one aimed at healthful, peaceful living.

If the overwhelming size and masses of fashionably outfitted skiers at Killington Mountain Ski Area are too much for you, give *Pico Mountain Resort* (73 Alpine Dr.; Menden; 802-422-6200 or 866-667-7426 [PICO]; snow line, 802-422-1200; picomountain.com) a try. Although under the same ownership, Pico has retained its identity as a family-friendly, big-mountain venue for skiers.

The ski slopes run from the top of Pico Peak, which has an altitude of almost 4,000 feet, tumbling down over the side of the mountain and three of its shoulders almost 2,000 feet to the base lodge. Seven lifts from the base provide access to 53 trails covering 17 miles, with some nice long intermediate and expert trails from the top of Pico Mountain and a good choice of novice and intermediate runs. Boarders can enjoy the Triple Slope Terrain Park.

If you'd like to walk or ski to the slopes out your door, consider staying at the base of the mountain at the **Pico Resort Hotel & Condominiums** (866-667-7426; picomountain.com/winter/lodging_and_packages), where choices range from studios to 3-bedroom units. All have full kitchens, and some have fireplaces and washers and dryers. They also offer a free shuttle to Killington.

Pico Mountain generally opens mid-Dec and closes at the end of Mar. Hit the slopes Mon, Thurs, and Fri 9 a.m. to 4 p.m.; Sat and Sun (and select peak days) 8:30 a.m. to 4 p.m. The mountain is closed Tues and Wed.

For Nordic enthusiasts, **Mountain Meadows XC Ski Area** (2363 Rte. 4; 802 775 7077 [winter] or 802 775 0166 [summer]; xcskiing.net) offers 32 kilometers of machine-groomed and tracked trails on 500 acres. Trails are for all levels of experience—children are welcomed and encouraged, as is your dog (as long as you keep Fido on a leash around the ski center building). Ski instruction is also available. The trails, including 3 newer snowshoe-specific trails, wind through fields and hemlock and hardwood forests, and have views of Kent Lake from a trail around its perimeter. The owners were able to make some great updates after Hurricane Irene blew through the area and rearranged a few things. Plans are in the works, too, for some new events, including a skate clinic and women's ski days. Check their website for updates.

North of Stockbridge on Route 100, the town of **Rochester,** which abuts the Green Mountain National Forest, has always seen a lot of activity, although the businesses have changed their stripes over the years. The White River Valley Railroad once coursed through the town, logging and mining and dairy farming being the primary industries in former times.

Today Rochester has a tidy village green, a cafe, and several shops, including one that rents bicycles. It also has a working guest farm, **Liberty**

Hill Farm (511 Liberty Hill; 802-767-3926; libertyhillfarm.com), located just off Route 100. Make no mistake about it, this is a working farm. When you first step out of your car, you'll be greeted by the ubiquitous sign of a dairy farm: the smell of manure. When you step into the house, you'll find the welcoming aroma of fresh-baked something or other, and your stomach juices will gurgle in anticipation of what that night's dinner might be.

That "innkeeper" Beth Kennett prepares everything from scratch is indicative of the farm as a whole: Liberty Hill is a thriving, old-fashioned dairy farm, and this is your opportunity to step into an increasingly rare way of life for a few days. The *Liberty Hill Farm Inn* welcomes guests who can be as involved or not involved with the daily farm chores as they choose to be. Want to rise early and milk the cows? Be their guest. Want to sleep in and enjoy a leisurely breakfast on the porch? Be their guest. You are free to enjoy the farm's 125 acres as you choose—there's on-site or local skiing, fishing, hiking, and canoeing.

The inn is open year-round and offers 7 rooms (5 with queen beds, 1 with 2 singles, 1 with 5 singles) and 4 shared bathrooms. Rates include a full breakfast and a bountiful and family-style dinner in the evening. Sit back after a full day of work or maybe a full day of relaxing and let the sounds of the farm lull you to sleep.

Route 100 continues north into Granville, then the valley narrows suddenly and becomes *Granville Gulf,* which some say is the prettiest 9-mile stretch in the state, but don't let the others hear you. Vermont has several of these narrow passes where the road climbs alongside a stream through a ravine barely wide enough to accommodate both. They are beautiful at any time of the year, but please drive carefully, as moose and other wildlife do not obey road signs. Once you leave Granville, start looking for *Moss Glenn Falls* off to the left. Right past the falls is a small parking lot. Stop and drink in the serenity at this beautiful spot. There is a small wooden bridge you can cross to get even closer to the falls, which cascade over ledges.

In and around Middlebury

If you follow Route 125, it takes you over the Green Mountains, at Middlebury Gap, one of its few low spots (well, lower than most of the summits), with a road that's open all winter. As you begin to climb, look for a sign to *Texas Falls,* an easily accessed and lovely gorge, where the river compresses to rush through a narrow passage in the rocks, dropping through a steep chute before plummeting through the gorge and into a pool. After a June shower, it's a raging, swirling froth. The path leads down to a log bridge that spans the gorge and gives great views without ruining this woodland setting. It's one of the most accessible falls in the state, and one of the prettiest. The road sinews up (and up and up) until it reaches the height of land and begins to drop, more gently, onto the western side of the Green Mountains.

You know you're at a real "skier's mountain" when you find a can of Bag Balm on the ticket counter at a ski area. You'll also find smiles, families, college students, and laid-back skiers of all ages at *Middlebury Snow Bowl* (6886 Rte. 125, Hancock; 802-443-7669; middlebury.edu/about/facilities/snow_bowl), on uncrowded trails that work with the mountain's natural terrain. Gentle trails from the top are good for beginner and intermediate skiers, so you don't have to worry about getting on the wrong lift and finding yourself with nothing but black-diamond trails to the bottom. Experts will get a workout on several trails, too. Although the official number of trails is 17, Middlebury doesn't inflate the number by giving each segment of a trail a different name.

Grooming is good, lift operators know the trails and can give you reliable advice on their conditions and challenge, and the chili in the lunchroom (which closes at 2 p.m.) is rich and meaty. What more is there to a day's skiing? Rentals, which feature up-to-date equipment, are fast and easy; lift tickets are well below the glitzy places, and seniors and students ski for somewhat less.

The most unexpected feature is the library in the ski lodge, where you can seek quiet and a selection of books and magazines if you decide to leave the trails early or take a midday break. You'll find it well used during midterms, when Middlebury students hit the books and the slopes alternately.

Ripton is a tiny town that lies totally within the Green Mountain National Forest but is one of the largest towns area-wise in Vermont, at 32,704 acres. Its population, though, at last count was 556.

One such resident, albeit seasonal, was poet Robert Frost. Although he spent a good deal of his life in New Hampshire and Massachusetts, Frost spent many of his last summers writing in his cabin in Ripton, so Vermonters in this part of the state still like to think of him as one of their own. You can visit the **Robert Frost Cabin,** nestled in the heart of the Green Mountains on Frost's Homer Noble Farm. Frost lived in this little cabin while good friends lived in the main house and cared for Frost and his estate while he was grappling with the death of his beloved wife in 1938, a loss some say he never got over. But he must have found some solace in his writer's cabin. When you see the environs in which Frost worked, you'll better understand his intense creativity.

To get to the cabin, turn off at the Robert Frost Wayside picnic area; take the unmarked dirt road to the immediate right of the area. Drive 0.5 mile up the road, and you'll see the Homer Noble Farm, a white farmhouse. Park in the small lot and walk up the trail 100 yards beyond the house. There's an opening to the left. The cabin is unmarked from the main road because locals believe only those visitors who want to see it badly enough are worthy of receiving directions. Middlebury College owns the cabin and most of the land on both sides of Route 125 in this mountainous area. Although you can go only onto the porch and not in the cabin, the interior remains the same as when Frost lived there from 1939 until his death in 1963.

Across the street you'll find the **Robert Frost Interpretive Trail,** which meanders through woods and fields. This easy 1.2-mile loop is great for little feet and part of it is wheelchair accessible, as it travels along a wooden boardwalk. Open daily 6 a.m. to 10 p.m.

Lesson Learned?

Late in 2007 the Robert Frost cabin was vandalized by a group of young people, a source of dismay to nearby residents and distant Frost lovers alike. The group of more than two dozen youths were charged with trespassing or destruction of property and then handed an interesting "punishment." The group, ages 16 to 22, spent a period of time in class with Jay Parini, Frost biographer and literature professor at Middlebury College, who taught them about Frost and his work. He hoped to teach them how poetry is relevant and important. He chose Frost's "Out, Out," which is a violent and unsettling poem but is set in a location that these youngsters would recognize. He wanted to make an impression and leave them with a lesson they would remember. Perhaps they learned a little respect for the man. The cabin has since been repaired and is as viewable as before.

Robert Frost also enjoyed walking through the fields and woods and communing with nature. He was often joined by a friend, Reginald Cook, who had a hand in creating this trail. He chose the poems that are displayed on interpretive plaques along the path. If you'd like to learn more about Frost's friendship with Cook, visit frostfriends.org/ripton.html and click on the link to view an incredible photo essay.

A short distance from Homer Noble Farm is Bread Loaf campus of Middlebury College. Its maize-colored buildings are home to the annual *Bread Loaf Writers' Conference* (Middlebury College; 802-443-5286; middlebury .edu/blwc), the oldest writers' conference in the US. It all began with Robert Frost in 1926 and evolved into the thriving program it is today.

The land and buildings where the conference is held originally belonged to Joseph Battell, horse breeder and journalist from Ripton, who purchased the land, added to the original farmhouse, and built the surrounding cottages as guesthouses for friends and family. At Battel's death in 1915, Middlebury College inherited the property. When a program of studies on English and American literature was created at the college, it found its home in these buildings, which came to be known as the Bread Loaf campus. While the original idea to hold a writer's conference came from Frost, he had backers in Willa Cather, Katherine Lee Bates, and Louise Untermeyer, all teachers at the college. The program was created and organized by John Farrar and is today directed by Michael Collier, author of six published books of poetry, including *The Ledge* and *An Individual History*.

Maintained by Middlebury College, the 10-day conference is scheduled annually in mid-August, and writers travel from all over to meet with other writers, editors, agents, and the like to expand and hone their craft. Sitting on the front porch of the main building, known as Bread Loaf Inn, gazing out over the beautiful Vermont mountains, you can't help but be inspired.

Visit the area in the colder months and explore these surroundings on 50 kilometers of trails on skis or snowshoes at the *Carroll & Jane Rikert Ski Touring Center* (Route 125; 802-443-2744; middlebury.edu/about/facilities/ rikert). The trails accommodate all levels of experience, and rentals are available, as are equipment sales, repairs, and waxing rooms as well as a warm-up room where you can curl up next to a wood stove. Open 8:30 a.m. to 4:30 p.m., the facility now has snowmaking ability on 5 kilometers of their trails, which extends the season, much to skiers' delight.

Rates of Toll Ripton, VT

Route 125 through Vermont used to be known as Center Turnpike. It was chartered in 1800 and ran from Middlebury to Woodstock, but it wasn't free to use it. A sign at the Chipman Inn (see More Places to Stay section for this chapter) explains what it might cost you to travel it: man and horse, 8 cents; person on foot, 2 cents; and sleighs drawn by two oxen or horses, 12 cents, with each additional ox or horse costing 2 cents.

Sheep and swine could travel over the road for a half cent each if fewer than a dozen of them were traveling the road. More than 12 cost 3 cents a dozen. But no need to reach into your pocket; the road is now free, no matter how many sheep you have with you.

Middlebury College is a major draw to the area, and **Middlebury** proper serves as an extended college campus. It's a beautiful small village to explore on foot. Middlebury was chartered early in the state's history, in 1761, and received its name because it was located halfway between the adjacent towns of Salisbury and New Haven.

The **Vermont Folklife Center** (88 Main St.; 802-388-4964; vermont folklifecenter.org) is just off the green. The center encourages the promotion and development of Vermont folk traditions. It conducts special events in collaboration with its exhibits, which frequently involve children's art projects, from both Vermont and other places. The gallery at the center is open Tues through Sat 10 a.m. to 4 p.m. year-round. Admission is free. Check their website for upcoming events.

The **Henry Sheldon Museum** (1 Park St.; 802-388-2117; henrysheldonmuseum.org), in an 1829 marble-built merchant's home in the center of town, is the oldest community museum in the US. Like the Fairbanks Museum in St. Johnsbury, this museum was founded by a man who was a tireless collector, but Henry Sheldon's passion was for antiquities and local history. He sincerely wanted to share the items he had collected throughout his years, and wanted to create a sense of the past for future generations. In 1882 he opened the museum in the same location it occupies today, but on a much smaller scale.

Sheldon devoted the remainder of his life to the museum. But in 1907, at the age of 86, he died after a brief illness. While the museum had been his life, it had not provided much of a livelihood. Sheldon left his last $100 to the museum, but it was not enough to keep it open long. The collection and museum might have been lost had it not been for W. Storrs Lee and Arthur K. D. Healy, who in the 1930s inspected and appreciated the collection and all that it stood for. Funds were raised and the museum was once again up and running. Today 10 rooms showcase one of the state's best collections of early furniture, decorative arts, paintings, and implements of daily living. The museum is open 10 a.m. to 5 p.m. Tues through Sat year-round, and 1 to 5 p.m. Sun in summer and fall.

Outside of town, in the most unlikely of places, you will find three fascinating businesses to visit. Look for Exchange Street, which runs through the middle of an industrial park on the north end of town. From Route 7 North, turn west onto Elm Street, just north of the Methodist church. Exchange Street is the next street on the right.

You will come first to *Vermont Soapworks* (616 Exchange St.; 866-SOAP-4U2 or 802-388-4302; vermontsoap.com), makers of fine-grade handmade soaps and identified by a small sign at the roadside. (Look for the industrial building on the east side of the street.) Here are some of the mildest soaps made anywhere, the same ones you will find in the best gift and bath shops in Vermont (at much higher prices). The factory store has first-quality soaps for sale, as well as seconds—those bars that were slightly unshapely when cut for wrapping. Herbs and flowers create the wonderful natural scents in the soaps. Open weekdays 9 a.m. to 5 p.m.

A short distance from the soap factory, on the other side of the street, *Otter Creek Brewing* (793 Exchange St.; 802-388-0727; ottercreekbrewing .com) is one of the best small artisanal brewers in the state. Brews run from a light pale ale all the way to stouts, with many in between. They also produce Wolaver's, one of the few organic ales around. Organic hops, organic malt, Vermont water—how healthy can a brew be? Case specials are available; you never know what good deals they may have. The brewery is open daily 11 a.m. to 6 p.m. and they offer samples all day.

On the same side of the street, a few buildings farther along, is *Maple Landmark Woodcraft* (1297 Exchange St.; 802-388-0627 or 800-421-4223; maplelandmark.com), a real find if you have young kids in your life. This is a maker of high-quality small maple toys designed for toddlers. Little wooden engines with brightly colored cars run on grooved maple tracks that you can arrange into any configuration. Bright letters of the alphabet ride on flatcars, so you can personalize the train with the child's name. Other toys include wooden farm animals, wild animals, and old-fashioned cube-shaped blocks with deeply engraved alphabet letters. Look also for checkerboards, cribbage boards, domino sets, and other small cherry and maple gifts. Firsts and seconds are available, with seconds and discontinued items at half price. Open Mon through Fri 8 a.m. to 5 p.m., 9 a.m. to 4 p.m. on Sat.

A few miles north of Middlebury is the small town of New Haven, the *final resting spot of Dr. Timothy Clark Smith.* Dr. Smith died in 1893, but the stories surrounding his burial are alive and well. You see, in the 18th and 19th centuries, it was not unheard of for people to be mistakenly pronounced dead. Without modern medicine and medical knowledge, a person who had slipped into a deep coma, say, or someone who fainted and now registered a very low heart rate could be thought to have passed into the great beyond. Urban legends abound about people being buried with one end of a rope tied to their hands and another to a bell 6 feet above them on the surface. If they were unfortunate enough to wake and find themselves in the precarious position of being buried alive, they could simply pull on the rope, which would ring the bell, and hopefully bring help with shovels. Other horrific stories have been passed down (undoubtedly embellished) about loved ones being exhumed and corpses found with bloody fingernails and scratches lining the inside of their coffins.

Dr. Smith had most likely been well aware of these stories, and he had a healthy fear of being buried alive. When he died in Middlebury at the age of 72, he was buried in Evergreen Cemetery in nearby New Haven, but not in any old tomb. No, Dr. Smith's tomb was specially prepared to ease his fears. You will find his grave, which is visible from Town Hill Road, about midway between the cemetery's entrance and exit. You'll know it's his by the two flat stone markers, one on the top of a grassy mound and a larger one at the bottom. The bottom stone is said to cap a set of stairs that lead down into the two-room crypt (Dr. Smith's wife is buried with him). The smaller stone is said to lie directly above Dr. Smith's face, and it contains a glass window through which he could gaze should he awaken. It is also said that this window was to be used to gaze 6 feet down at Smith so his loved ones could be sure he was gone. Stories also circulate that there's a breathing tube attached that ends right above the doctor's face, that he had tools buried with him that, once upon a time, you could see laying next to him, and that he also had a bell with him to ring for help (although we're not sure how anyone would hear it). Today you can't see much due to the aging of the glass and condensation, but the story is an interesting one to contemplate. Evergreen Cemetery is located on Town Hill Road a couple miles outside the town proper if you want to pay your respects.

Upon leaving New Haven, you can take Route 17 east to the town of Bristol, a small but busy and attractive town. Route 116 will join Route 17 through town. Just shortly after the two separate again, you'll see a parking area for the **Bristol Memorial Forest Park.** One of Vermont's loveliest picnic sites, it has tables overlooking a gorge and paths along its brink with railings and bridges to give you the best and safest views of the entire gorge and its waterfalls.

If you follow Route 17, it will take you over the Appalachian Gap, with an elevation of 2,300 feet as it climbs over the sharp spine of the Green Mountains and drops into Waitsfield. An equally dramatic route over the mountains, on an unnumbered and less-used route, is across the **Lincoln Gap,** with a 2,400-foot elevation. Before Routes 116 and 17 diverge, take a road to the south marked lincoln, then follow signs to Warren. It is one of the state's most memorable drives, closed in winter because of the difficulties in keeping the road passable. When you see the pitch of the road, you'll know why the snowplows don't tackle it. The Long Trail crosses Lincoln Gap between Mount Grant and Mount Abraham.

As you leave Bristol, you can't miss seeing the **Lord's Prayer Rock,** a boulder on Route 17 on the eastern side of town that has the complete Lord's Prayer inscribed on it. There are two stories as to why Joseph C. Green, a doctor from Buffalo who grew up in Vermont, had the words inscribed here. One says that as a young boy, Green watched many loggers drag their loads and horses up this road, which back then was muddy most of the year. Since the trip was difficult, the language used by the men was often colorful, to say the least. The story goes that Green was offended by the laborers' language, so he paid a local stonecutter to chisel the complete Lord's Prayer into the rock. Hmm. The next story says that one of Green's jobs as a young man was to deliver logs to the Bristol sawmill along similarly difficult roads. When Green reached Route 17, it leveled out a bit and he always recited the Lord's Prayer in thanks for having made it through the worst part of the trip. This is why he later decided to have the prayer inscribed on the rock. Well. Which is true? You'll have to decide.

Bristol's short Main Street is a thoroughly charming place to shop or browse. Two facing rows of well-kept brick and wood mercantile buildings contain small shops, artisans' studios, cafes, and friendly people who take the time to chat. Park anywhere (no parking meters to worry about) and admire the architecture as you stroll. Admire, too, the signs, some of which are works of art, especially the metal one that announces the Bobcat Cafe.

The *Bobcat Cafe* (5 Main St.; 802-453-3311; bobcatcafe.com) is a small cafe and brewery that has been serving handcrafted brews and fresh, seasonal, simple food since 1993. While the draw might be more the beer than the food, the atmosphere is cozy and local. The bar opens daily at 4 p.m., with the cafe following at 5. Closing is at 9 p.m. Sun through Thurs and 9:30 p.m. Fri and Sat.

Almost next door is *Vermont HoneyLights* (9 Main St.; 800-322-2660 or 802-453-3952; vermonthoneylights.com), where chandlers Bonita Bedard and Shawna Sherwin work only in pure local beeswax. If you can tear yourself away from the beautiful candles and the antiques in which they are displayed, visit the workshop in the back to watch candles being poured and finished. You will learn a lot about candle making and about why you owe it to your lungs—and the ecosystem—to burn only those made of beeswax. The stylish candles made here are in solid colors—the amber and soft pearl of natural wax and warm earthy tones of sage, lavender, and mellow rose—and in shapes that reflect the season or imitate shapes of objects from artichokes to tassels. Square tapers of beeswax will burn for 24 hours, larger candles much longer. The antiques are for sale, although they were often chosen for the shop as decorative holders or companions for the candles. The shop is open weekdays 10 a.m. to 5 p.m., Sat to 4 p.m.

Down the street you'll find *Art on Main* (25 Main St.; 802-453-4032; artonmain.net), a cooperative gallery of fine crafts and art, much of it by local artists and artisans. Pottery, soaps, silver jewelry, handmade books, glass photography, original prints, paintings, and hand weaving are only some of the variety represented here. The gallery is open Jan through Apr, Tues through Thurs noon to 5 p.m., Fri noon to 6 p.m., and Sat 10 a.m. to 6 p.m.; May through Dec, Mon through Sat 10 a.m. to 6 p.m., Sun 11 a.m. to 3 p.m.

From mid-June to the Wednesday before Labor Day, Bristol's town band plays concerts in the bandstand at 7 p.m. on Wednesday evenings, just as they have since the Civil War. Bring your own chairs or blanket and enjoy a picnic dinner under the stars.

If you're up for another waterfall, head west on Route 116 to **Hell's Half Acre** (Lower Notch Road). The falls can be seen from Route 116, but if you take your first left onto South Street, this eventually becomes Lower Notch Road, portions of which are unpaved, and brings you closer. As you're gazing at the falls, look around the area and notice the pits and tunnels that pockmark the area. This is the result of more than 200 years of searching for a lost treasure. According to legend, a huge deposit of Spanish gold and silver coins was buried by renegade sailors from Boston. Many people have spent thousands of hours over the years trying to locate it, without luck. The story is a long one, involving foreign intrigue and revenge. Going to try your hand at locating it? Maybe you'll have more luck than the hordes before you.

Bird lovers and naturalists will not want to miss **Dead Creek Water- fowl Refuge** (Route 17, 1 mile west of Route 22A). This is birders' paradise, especially during spring and fall migrations, when thousands upon thousands of birds rest here during their journeys. Few sights in life can match that of a flock of snow geese filling the sky as they resume their trip. You can canoe here, except in the area south of Route 17 between the road and the dike, but be careful to stay well away from the shore between April and June, when birds are nesting.

At its southern end, Lake Champlain narrows to a small passage before broadening again even farther to the south. Originally settled by the French as a part of New France, the point became known as Chimney Point for the blackened chimneys rising from the cellar holes of homes burned by the settlers as they fled the advancing British during the French and Indian War. The narrows made this spot a popular ferry crossing, and, of course, where there was a ferry, there was a tavern to house and comfort travelers. **Chimney Point State Historic Site** (8149 Rte. 17; 802-759-2412), at the Champlain Bridge crossing of Routes 17 and 125, has its visitor center and museum in the 18th-century tavern on the banks of the lake. It has exhibits on the original native peoples and on the French settlers who were driven from this land. The site is open from Memorial Day through Columbus Day from 9:30 a.m. to 5 p.m. Wed through Sun, and Mon holidays.

The Brandon Area

A total of five routes, each with interconnecting side roads, lead from Middlebury to Brandon. The most direct is busy Route 7. More scenic are Route 30 to the west and Route 53 to the east around Lake Dunmore. Our favorites are the other two. Between Routes 30 and 7 is a sometimes-unpaved road through West Salisbury and Leicester Junction. And farthest to the east is the totally unpaved FR 32, which takes you through the thickly forested heart of **Moosalamoo National Recreation Area** (moosalamoo.org).

You won't find Moosalamoo on any map. It's an area defined by a unique partnership of landholders and groups with a passion for keeping the wild lands wild but accessible. Public Service, the Green Mountain National Forest, Branbury State Park, Middlebury College, the Green Mountain Club, the Audubon Society, the Vermont Institute for Natural Sciences, an association of snowmobilers, and a few inns are among the partners. Their purpose is to protect the unique natural environment, maintain trails for year-round use, and provide interpretive signs and materials for the people who use the area. Moosalamoo has a lot of raw wilderness, but it also has 3 numbered highways, homes, businesses, a boys' camp, and 2 ski areas. That's the point of it—a coexistence that is to everyone's benefit, including the moose. When planning a visit, starting at the website is a good

Take Your Pick

Wild berries are everywhere in Moosalamoo National Recreation Area. You'll find wild strawberries, currants, blackberries, and raspberries. The best places to pick these berries are usually closely guarded secrets, like the location of the best fishing holes. But there is one everybody knows about, since there are signs pointing it out and a parking lot for your car. The **Blueberry Management Area** is located on FR 32. You are welcome to go there with your pail and pick away—or to just wander in for a handful or two eaten on the spot. They ripen in midsummer. You can tell if they are ready by the number of cars in the lot; if it's empty, there are probably no berries. If you want a heads-up, "like" the Moosalamoo Association: Moosalamoo National Recreation Area on Facebook and watch the statuses. A recent one read: "Shhhhh! The blueberry crop at the management area in the Moosalamoo NRA is *amazing* this season. Get out and pick before the rest of the world finds out!"

idea. You can download a map and figure out how you'd like to explore the area—on foot, bike, ski, snowshoe, or snowmobile. If you don't want to go it alone, numerous establishments offer tours and packages to assist you.

In the middle of the Moosalamoo wilderness area, surrounded by national forest, is **Blueberry Hill Inn** (1307 Goshen-Ripton Rd., Goshen; 802-247-6735; blueberryhillinn.com), a handsome inn on a hilltop at an altitude of 1,600 feet. Some of the rooms are in the 19th-century farmhouse; others are in a carefully designed modern addition. This is the place for active outdoors lovers who want a pleasant place to relax at the end of the day.

The inn has beautiful gardens to explore, and 47 miles of trails lead through the nearby wilderness area, some connecting with the Catamount and Long Trails. The inn will provide shuttles for guests who want to walk segments of the Long Trail without doubling back. In winter it's a cross-country and snowshoe center, with equipment rentals and well-kept trails. As owner Tony describes it, "With 60 to 70 kilometers of different trail options available from the front door, there's no gerbil-cage skiing here."

After a hike, guests can grab a cookie (or two or three) from the jar in the large open kitchen and go out into the solarium to read a good book or just relax. The spacious and well-decorated guest rooms have private baths, and in each you will find a jar of the inn's own dreamy skin cream, made right here from extractions of calendula and chamomile petals and other herbs from the inn's gardens.

Rates include breakfast, and Blueberry Hill Inn also serves dinner, carefully prepared and presented—but you must reserve a space. The chef uses only the freshest local produce in season, much of which comes from the inn's own extensive organic gardens or from neighboring farms.

Route 73 leads east over Brandon Gap or west into the town of **Brandon.** This attractive town, filled with beautiful old homes, was first chartered in 1761 with the name Neshobe and is the birthplace of Stephen Douglas, Lincoln's adversary, and home to a whole slew of inventors, such as Quimby Backus, who invented one of the first electric heaters, and John Conant, who produced the first iron stoves in the state after bog iron was discovered in 1810.

This is only the beginning of Brandon's long and fascinating history, which includes its claim to a place in the Morgan-horse hall of fame, as well as the story of the early industry of Vermont and the Underground Railroad.

In town, in an elegant Arts and Crafts–period mansion, is the *Lilac Inn* (53 Park St.; 802-247-5463; lilacinn.com). Once the home of the Farr family, whose public and private benefactions are still appreciated by the people of Brandon, it was later owned by an architect, who made the house's transition from the home of a wealthy family to an inn so seamless that you wouldn't be surprised to find the formidable Mrs. Farr at the head of the breakfast table. Instead you'll find breakfast served in a sunny room overlooking the landscaped grounds, or outdoors, in the summer. Dinner is also a delicious affair in the inn's oak-paneled dining room, where a New American menu displays the skillful use of fresh ingredients.

On Fridays from late May through mid-October, the **Brandon Farmers' Market** (20 Park St.; 802-273-2655) is held in the town's Central Park. More than 50 local vendors sell local produce, flowers, and herbs, as well as maple syrup, baked goods, jams, and jellies.

East of Brandon are Orwell and Lake Champlain, composing an area that played a significant role in the American Revolution. On the way you will pass through Sudbury, through which the **Crown Point Military Road** was built. Its route here is marked by a monument, located a short distance west of Route 30, where it is joined by Route 73 from Brandon. A part of this original road is still passable to the north of the monument, but to the south it is little more than a trail. The road was built in 1759 by British general Jeffrey Amherst to connect Lake Champlain to the Connecticut River to supply Amherst's outpost at Crown Point during the French and Indian War. During the Revolution it was expanded as the need to protect Fort Ticonderoga and Mount Independence became imperative. Today modern roads have used the original route in some places.

As you travel through Vermont you may notice these granite markers that look like boundary markers or gravestones. Some of these have arrows at the top pointing in one direction or another. These markers are likely to be ones placed by Vermont chapters of the Daughters of the American Revolution (DAR) to mark the route of the Crown Point Military Road.

It has been an ongoing process to delineate the exact path of this military route. Historic maps are somewhat helpful, but a little sketchy on details. Historic records help but are up for interpretation. In the early 1900s, a few chapters of DAR attempted to solidify the route by placing these markers where they believed the road passed. During the same period of time, some towns added markers along the route in their area. Some of these markers display arrows to show the general direction of the road. The problem is, though, that some of these markers have been subsequently moved due to construction or other modern needs. So it's anybody's guess whether the arrows now point in the right direction.

It's also believed that sometimes the markers were placed based on people's recollections of where the road traveled. These recollections may not have been entirely correct (they would have been handed down through the generations, sort of like a long game of telephone). So, when you see one of these markers, don't take it for granted that it's in the right location, but do send up a silent thank-you to the ladies' efforts, because without them many sections of the road would have been lost and forgotten (they did get the majority of the locations correct).

The *Crown Point Road Association* (802-459-2837 or 802-773-6819; crownpointroad.org) is a group of dedicated enthusiasts whose purpose it is to research, locate, mark, and preserve the military road. From spring through fall, the group conducts hikes over the known sections of the road. You are invited to bring lunch (and mosquito repellent). They also offer a driving tour that takes you from monument to monument and imparts wonderful history along the way. They also publish a guide to these historical markers if you'd like to make the trip on your own. It's available on their website, as are the latest times and dates of their hikes and tours.

Mount Independence (497 Independence Rd., Orwell; 802-948-2000 [in season] or 802-759-2412 [off-season]; historicvermont.org) is one of our country's least disturbed and best preserved Revolutionary War sites. Its 300 acres have been largely untouched and its significant history well presented. In 1776 Mount Independence was an important sister fort to Fort Ticonderoga, across the lake in New York, and the two were connected by a floating bridge. Garrisoned by about 2,500 soldiers, it had extensive earthworks. In July 1777 it was attacked, and the defending continental troops finally abandoned it, retreating to Hubbardton, where they managed to beat back an attacking troop of British soldiers, blunting General Burgoyne's drive to the south. These two battles were precursors to the crucial Battle of Bennington. Mount Independence was briefly occupied by British and German troops before being abandoned in the fall of 1777. Its cannons, mortars, shells, and other cast iron were sold to make bar iron.

The land was poorly suited to farming, although a few tried through the 19th and early 20th centuries. In 1911 the land was fast being reclaimed by the forest when Stephen Pell of Fort Ticonderoga purchased 113 acres for preservation. The land sat largely forgotten until 1961, when the state recognized its importance as a historic site and began purchasing parcels of the land. It took 30 more years for the site to reach its current state, with 6 miles of trails to be explored and an interesting museum in which to learn more about the site's history. Special events and programs are conducted throughout the year, including the Retreat to Hubbardton Battlefield Reenactment on the weekend of July 4.

The well-marked trails at the site take visitors through fields and forest amid the ruins of batteries, barracks, and blockhouses. Stunning views of Lake Champlain can be seen as well. In winter the trails are available for cross-country skiing. All trails begin at the kiosk near the museum. Trail maps with historical notes and descriptions are usually available at either the trailhead or at the visitor center. The 1.6-mile Baldwin Trail is wheelchair accessible.

The park is open daily Memorial Day through Columbus Day, 9:30 a.m. to 5 p.m. Admission fee is charged for those 15 and older, and an admission pass is required to access the trails.

A great way to see Mount Independence and a lot of Lake Champlain is to take the **M/V Carillon** (4820 Rte. 74, Shoreham; 802-897-5331; carillon cruises.com), which leaves from Larrabee's Point, to the north in Shoreham. The 60-foot knife-bowed cruise boat was built in 1990 especially for this run. It is a replica of the sleek power yachts built for the wealthy from the 1920s through the 1950s, and, as was the custom, there's lots of shiny woodwork. The 1.5-hour cruise leaves at 1 p.m. Thurs through Sun in July and Aug and from mid-Sept through mid-Oct (foliage season). The boat does a figure eight between Larrabee's Point, Fort Ticonderoga, and Mount Independence. Be sure to check out their very cool sonar on board that allows passengers to see wrecks and artifacts on the lake bottom.

Off Route 22A south of Orwell, a small road is signposted to **Benson.** A half mile off Route 22A, the road intersects with Benson's main street. Up the hill to the right is one of the finest examples of what the Main Street of a small Vermont town once looked like. Along both sides of the street are beautiful 19th-century buildings, mostly big, well-spaced homes but also

Four Legs Good, Two Legs Bad?

The town of Orwell maintains two cemeteries, one on Chipman Point overlooking Lake Champlain and the other off Route 73 on the road to Shoreham. The maintenance of these two cemeteries created a bit of a town feud in 1991, when a flock of 17 sheep was placed in the cemeteries to graze and trim the grass.

Some townspeople thought it was a great idea; the town would save on gasoline and manpower. The sheep also ate everything from poison ivy to wild grapevines—things regular lawn mowers usually miss—and their owner, Jean Beck, transported them back and forth between the two cemeteries for one month before protests began from townspeople who didn't like the idea of sheep manure covering their loved ones' graves. Things even turned dicey when the sheep were threatened. A special town meeting had to be called to fire the sheep before any harm was done to them.

The controversy received so much attention that it even made the *New York Times*. Beck went as far as having T-shirts made that read "Let the Sheep Eat in Peace" to support her cause. A group of 10 residents volunteered to mow the cemeteries in place of the sheep, but selectboard chair Ronald Huntley warned that the volunteers would be closely monitored to make sure they were doing their jobs. "If they don't maintain the cemeteries, the sheep go back in," he said.

We know there must be some clever reference to George Orwell's *Animal Farm* here with this being in Orwell, Vermont, and all, but we can't quite put our finger on it. Please feel free to send us your ideas.

including the historic business fronts and the classic white United church. You could almost imagine that you had stepped back into a different world.

At the intersection at the foot of the hill is ***The Book Shed*** (733 Lake Rd.; 802-537-2190; thebookshed.com), a used-book store where you are likely to find local people sitting on the floor reading or browsing the racks of more than 15,000 books. It's a great place to get lost. Open Fri through Sun 11 a.m. to 5 p.m. Jan through Mar and Wed through Sun 10 a.m. to 6 p.m. Apr through Dec.

Beyond Benson, the road wanders through attractive countryside for 5.4 miles, over hills and around sharp corners until it reaches the narrow end of Lake Champlain. A boat launch provides the only place to put in canoes and kayaks for miles in either direction. It is also just a beautiful place to visit, with New York state a few hundred yards away across the water.

Rutland and Its Environs

Situated as it is on a bed of marble, and close to the western border of the Vermont–New York line, the city of *Rutland* has at various times been known as Marble City and Gateway City. Today it is a thriving city that serves as a business and social magnet for the surrounding towns.

It was named for Rutland, Massachusetts; John Murray, of the Massachusetts Rutland, was the first grantee of the town, which was chartered in 1761. The first settler of Rutland was James Mead, of Manchester, Vermont, who came to town in 1770 with his wife and 10 children. Mead built a log cabin and soon followed with a gristmill and a sawmill nearby, thereby cementing the active industry of Rutland that continues to this day.

Downtown Rutland is seeing an emergence of new and innovative businesses. *Same Sun Choice* (53 Merchants Row; 802-855-8664; samesun choice.com) is a new retail store that offers solar-powered goods from Vermont and around the country, including solar-produced maple syrup, salsa, wine, beer, and arts and crafts. If you have questions about solar power and how it can benefit you, these are the people to ask. Owners Marlene and Philip Allen have been studying and using solar power since 2007. When they saw how much it was benefitting their own family, they knew they had to share their knowledge. In 2011 they established Same Sun of Vermont to educate people and promote the use of this clean, simple, and effective power source. Their retail store is open weekdays 10 a.m. to 5 p.m. year-round.

A children's museum has also recently opened in Rutland. *Wonderfeet Kids' Museum* (17 Center St.; 802-774-8493; wonderfeetkidsmuseum.org) is the culmination of years of work by committee members and residents that showed how well received such a museum would be. They started by building and showcasing mobile exhibits at Friday Night Live venues and at the Saturday farmers' markets. The response was overwhelming. The use of space on Center Street allowed the museum to have a permanent home. Opened in August 2013, the museum offers hands-on exhibits to teach children to "appreciate their roles in local and global communities" and to "foster curiosity, inspire exploration, and engage the imagination through play." Sounds good to us! Fund-raising for the museum continues as they hope to expand and add exhibits. Hours are Fri and Sat 10 a.m. to

6 p.m. Space is also available for parties. Be sure to visit their website for updates as they continue to grow.Another newcomer to Rutland is *Griffin's Publick House* (42 Center St.; 802-772-7997; griffinspublickhouse .com). Housed in the former Downtown Tavern building, this English-style pub offers 16 beers on tap at the full bar. The food is fresh and local and features your basic pub fare (hot wings, fish and chips, burgers, pizza) but also some fun stuff such as gazpacho, panzanella salad, fish-market stew, duck-fat fries, white bean hummus, lamb "lollipops," and grilled local veggies. The pizzas are made in a huge brick oven and come with an amazing array of inventive topping choices. The cheese and charcuterie boards are beautifully presented as well. A children's menu offers macaroni and cheese, chicken tenders, grilled cheese, and cheeseburger sliders, all with fries or applesauce. If the interior is a little dark for your taste, take advantage of the outdoor dining on the deck. Fri and Sat evenings feature live entertainment.

Wilson Castle (2970 W. Proctor Rd.; 802-773-3284; wilsoncastle.com) may be the city's most unusual building. It is one of the few historic houses/ museums open to the public where you can walk on rugs, sit on chairs, feel the texture of the old draperies, and take flash pictures.

The castle was built in 1867 by Doctor and Lady Johnson at a cost of $1.3 million. It passed through several hands after that before being bought by Herbert Lee Wilson in 1939. Generations of Wilsons have lived in the castle since and his granddaughter, Denise Davine, is the current owner and operator.

The estate consists of 115 acres and 16 buildings. The castle was built in the mid-1800s, and its 32 rooms hold 84 stained-glass windows and 13 fireplaces. The rooms contain everything from a Louis XVI crown jewel case to a Tiffany chandelier. The castle also boasts a library, a music room, a drawing room, an art gallery, and a veranda.

Wilson's Castle is open daily from 9 a.m. to 6 p.m. from late May through mid-Oct. There is an admission fee, which includes a tour. The last tour begins at 5 p.m.

Also on the north side of town, on busy Route 7, is *Seward's Family Restaurant & Ice Cream* (244 N. Main St.; 802-773-2738), a local dairy and restaurant with window and table service and a gourmet food shop that sells freshly brewed Green Mountain Coffee in Thermoses that keep the coffee fresh and piping hot. Try the hazelnut cream coffee with a dollop of Seward's fresh milk—that is, if the Thermos isn't empty.

The dairy is out back behind the restaurant, and you'll find the milk in most local supermarkets and general stores. The restaurant offers food as fresh as at the dairy, along with sandwiches and soups, in a comfortable, homey atmosphere. Open daily from 6:30 a.m. to 10 p.m.

Just west of Rutland and Route 7 is Route 3, known as the Marble Valley Highway. This area is the heart of Vermont's marble industry. Each of the 50 states and some foreign countries have buildings made of Vermont marble. Two of the best known are the US Supreme Court and the Jefferson Memorial, both in Washington, DC. So versatile is this building stone that the Beinecke Rare Book and Manuscript Library at Yale University in New Haven, Connecticut, has even used thin luminescent slabs of this marble as "windows" to let in light.

The **Vermont Marble Museum** (52 Main St.; 800-427-1396 or 802-459-2300; vermont-marble.com), headquartered in Proctor, not far from Wilson Castle, explores this stone in a comprehensive exhibit. A visit starts with an 11-minute film about the company and about the immigrant workers who labored here. Displays include a miniature marble chapel with a carved Last Supper and the Hall of Presidents, which contains bas-relief busts of all US presidents. In the sculpting studio, visitors can watch the sculptor-in-residence at work.

The exhibit, displayed in 17 rooms with a total of 27,000 square feet of space, looks at how marble was formed, explaining the evolution of the earth and the titanic energy of its crust as the plates move, collide, and create new continents. "Raymond" is an actual cast re-creation of the only articulated triceratops ever found. Plan on several hours to explore all the corners of this fascinating place. Admission is charged. Open mid-May through Oct, 10 a.m. to 4:30 p.m. daily.

If the weather cooperates, plan a stroll from the museum to the **Sutherland Falls Quarry.** A recently completed scenic walkway takes you the short distance (0.25 mile) to the original Proctor quarry, which is a great place for a picnic. As you gaze out over the water and enjoy the beauty, imagine the lake bottom, a mere 150 feet below.

If you need one more place to stop to eat before leaving Rutland, try **Table 24** (24 Wales St.; 802-775-2424; table24.net), a chef-owned restaurant with a unique menu. Chef Stephen Sawyer creates wonderful concoctions on the wood-fired grill; everyone in your group will find something. Open Mon through Sat at 11:30 a.m. for lunch and 4 p.m. for dinner. Reservations can be made online.

A nice loop drive out of Rutland takes you into countryside far removed from the city's streets. Leave town on Route 4 East, which leads over the mountains toward Pico Peak and Killington. You will come to **Mendon** and a great place to stop for a bite to eat. Located in a rustic former sugar house, **Sugar & Spice** (45 Rte. 4; 802-773-7832; vtsugarandspice.com) is a family-owned restaurant where you are treated like family. They serve home-style comfort food using local ingredients when they can. They serve breakfast all day and their pancakes are a must-have, especially their Sugar & Spice stack of four baked with cinnamon and maple sugar. Be sure to order a cup of hot chocolate, which is actually a cup of whipped cream with the hot chocolate on the side. Yum! If lunch is more your style, you can choose from burgers, sandwiches, and salads—all delicious. Their on-site gift shop offers the usual assortment of Vermont products. Open daily 7 a.m. to 2 p.m.

After you are stuffed from eating, wander out to the far parking lot and look for a large rock in the woods. This is the **burial site of a Civil War hero**, and not many people know it's here. This isn't a hero of the human variety, however, it's the gravesite of the four-legged type. The inscription on the concave section of the rock reads: The grave of General Edward Ripley's Old John—gallant war horse of the great Civil War 1861–1865. You see the restaurant sits on a piece of General Ripley's former estate. During the Civil War, Ripley served as commander of Rutland's Light Guards, leading them astride his much loved Old John. The grave marker is part of only a few remnants of the former estate. You can also see an old sugar house, a small barn, and the older maple trees from the estate.

Just past this monument, a road goes north to East Pittsford and Chittenden, toward the Chittenden Reservoir. You will pass the **Fox Creek Inn** (49 Dam Rd.; 800-707-0017 or 802-483-6213; foxcreekinn.com), a quiet retreat on 7 wooded acres that is deceptively close to major attractions. The inn's 8 rooms vary in size and decor; some have gas fireplaces, most have Jacuzzi tubs, and all have private baths. The inn is elegant but comfortable, and breakfast is included in the rates. Children over the age of 12 are welcome.

soapand pittsford

Pittsford was the home of Samuel Hopkins, who received the first patent in the US, in 1790, signed by George Washington. It was for the making of pearl-ash, an ingredient for soap making, upon which was founded Vermont's first main economic base.

Since Dam Road dead-ends at the dam, you need to backtrack to the intersection and continue on to the settlement of Holden, where the road changes direction and follows Furnace Creek back to the south and into Pittsford. Here you pop into the **Pittsford Historical Society** (Main Street; 802-483-2040; pittsfordhistorical .com) to learn some interesting facts about the town. But they are open only on Tues, Apr through late fall, 9 a.m. to 4 p.m.

From here, follow signs left to Florence, on Kendall Hill Road, where you will soon see the **Hammond Covered Bridge** on your right. It is one of four in Pittsford, a 139-foot town lattice style built in 1842. In the infamous freshet of 1927, when much of Vermont was washed away, this bridge ended up in a field about a mile downstream from its abutments. The following winter they hauled it back to its original location, which is where you see it now. A new bridge has made it redundant, but you can still walk through.

Any of several left turns along here will take you south and back to Rutland. One goes through Proctor, where you can see the marble works, or you can follow signs to Whipple Hollow Road, for a real back-road drive past farms tucked into little hollows, meadows dotted with horses nibbling grass, and dairy farms where herds of Holsteins pasture with a backdrop of valley and mountain scenery.

At Route 4 you can turn west instead of going back into Rutland, and head for Castleton and Castleton Corners, home of Castleton State College, Vermont's first college, having been chartered in 1787. The **Christine Price Gallery** (45 Alumni Dr.; 802-468-1119) at Castleton State College is located in the foyer of the Fine Arts Center on campus. The display area is huge, and the exhibiting artists range from Castleton students who have created their own masks, to community residents who have combined the avant-garde and traditional Vermont themes in line drawings and paintings, as well as more traditional Vermont pastoral landscape scenes. A showcase contains works in progress in sketchbooks, and the smell of freshly dried oil paint permeates the room. The gallery also has international art in its permanent collection, from Africa, New Guinea, and India. The gallery and Fine Arts Center are open from 9 a.m. to 5 p.m. weekdays, year-round.

From Castleton Corners, the unnumbered East Hubbardton Road leads north about 7 miles to *Hubbardton Battlefield* (5696 Monument Hill Rd.; 802-273-2282). When American troops had to evacuate Mount Independence and Fort Ticonderoga on July 6, 1777, they withdrew to the east, planning to travel south again to join up with other colonists in Manchester. British advance troops, very sure of themselves and holding the ragtag local militia in contempt, caught up with them on July 7. At East Hubbardton the rear guard of the colonial troops turned and stood their ground on a broad hillside, firing from covered positions and showing a determination to stop the British and protect the retreat of the main force. To the chagrin of General Burgoyne, the royal troops were defeated and forced to withdraw back to Mount Independence. This victory saved the colonial army from destruction, freeing them for the Battle of Bennington and the ultimate defeat of the British northern army at Saratoga later that same year.

A 21-foot-tall marble monument was erected in 1859 and the dedication was attended by thousands of people, some of them descendants of those involved in the battle. The monument still stands today and is one of the oldest Revolutionary War battle monuments in the US. A visitor center museum is open 9:30 a.m. to 5 p.m. Thurs through Sun, Memorial Day through Columbus Day. If it's open when you visit, look at the fiber-optic map of the battle, then go out onto the battlefield to the walking trail that leads visitors to key points in the battle. Signs tell the importance of each stop along the way. The battlefield itself is open all year.

West of Castleton is Fair Haven, an unusual town with one large brick commercial block facing a broad common, with two fine mansions built of marble. On the southern edge of town, shortly before Route 22A crosses the border into New York, is *Maplewood Inn* (1108 S. Main St; 802-265-8039 or 800-253-7729; maplewoodinn.com), housed in a restored dairy farmhouse. The 1843 house is listed on the National Register of Historic Places and is furnished in antiques and reproductions, as well as the owners' collection of antique farm and household implements. The property was a working dairy farm until 1979 and was a private residence until 1986, when it was transformed into a bed-and-breakfast. In 2004 innkeepers Paul and Scott purchased the inn and run it today. All 6 rooms and suites offer private baths and are tastefully decorated. Hot drinks, with a good selection of teas, are available to guests at all times, along with complimentary cordials. The rate includes a hearty breakfast cooked to order.

South of Fair Haven and Castleton, and 3 miles south of Poultney, is the beautiful 117-acre *Lake St. Catherine State Park* (3034 Rte. 30, Poultney; 802-287-9158 in season), with trails, beaches, and a campground with boat access to the lake. Fifty campsites are spaced well, along the shore and in the woods, some with lean-to shelters. Flush toilets and paid hot showers are available. The park is open 10 a.m. to sunset, Memorial Day weekend until Labor Day weekend.

To the south, this region is bounded by Route 140, a very scenic drive through several interesting towns. Route 140 is not very long—only about 25 miles—but it's pretty any time of year, whether the maple forests that line it are hung with sap buckets and tubing or ablaze in fall color. The terrain seems never to rest, and the driver certainly can't, as the narrow road is constantly climbing, dropping, or turning.

Route 140 begins in Poultney, on the New York border, almost literally in the front lawn of Green Mountain College. After its short stretch as Poultney's main street, it climbs into the countryside before passing through East Poultney, a charming cluster of buildings around a common. These include an imposing schoolhouse and a classic general-store building.

The road follows the course of the Poultney River, which is visible much of the way to *Middletown Springs,* which may seem small, but when fed by a sudden spring melt-off or thunderstorms, can become quite a torrent. In July 1811 all but one of the mills along the river in Middletown were swept away, and the course of the river was changed. The one mill that survived became the factory for *Albert W. Gray,* a talented inventor who made New England farmers' lives much easier.

Gray began work in the mill beside the Poultney River at the age of 15. Six years later he was in business for himself; in 1844 he patented a treadmill operated by a horse.

The first treadmill operated a thresher, replacing a job that had consumed many hours of backbreaking labor. It revolutionized the family farm, and Gray's name became a household word on Vermont farms and as farmers began renting treadmills by the day from threshers who carried the machines from farm to farm, mounted on wagons. Large farms bought their own. Gray began to manufacture his treadmills at the same mill where he had worked as a boy, eventually keeping as many as 100 employees busy. Expanding on the theme, Gray designed treadmills to save labor in other farm chores, such as cutting silage and sawing wood.

Gray was a man of vision, and his next project changed the town's name and identity. Another flood once again altered the course of the river near his mill, and as he surveyed the damage, he noticed that a spring that had been covered up by the 1811 floods had appeared again. With his sons, he cleared the area and began bottling the water. By then—this was in the 1870s—taking the cure at mineral springs was the latest health fad, so Albert and his sons built a grand hotel, four and a half stories tall and the biggest in Vermont. The Montvert Hotel offered a number of treatments, including "Turkish showers" and massage, and its dining-room staff was imported from New York to cater to the exacting clientele.

Middletown changed its name to Middletown Springs, and its economy became very healthy indeed. But the fad faded and the wealthy clientele moved on to more fashionable watering holes. The hotel was torn down, and the 1927 floods again covered up the spring and washed away the spring house. In 1970 it was uncovered, and a replica of the spring house was built, which is now the centerpiece of a pleasant little riverside park on Burdock Avenue, close to a historic marker that tells about the treadmill factory. You can see an example of the treadmill in the free *Middletown Springs Historical Society Museum,* next to the church on the green, open Sun from 2 until 4 p.m. from late May through early Oct. The entire village center, which has several distinguished buildings, is a historic district listed on the National Register of Historic Places.

On a quiet section of Route 140, just west of Wallingford, in the threshold of a serpentine turn, sits *Bigfoot Rock,* a massive flat-topped rock. The giant boulder seems out of place, resting on a plot of land devoid of cliffs or other rock formations. Its level, flat, table-like surface does not appear to be man-made. However, the giant wooden chairs, made from cut timber logs from nearby, that surround this peculiar table definitely are.

There is something romantically archaic about this setup, accompanied by the sounds of chirping birds and the scent of wet grass. The roughly fastened chairs that encircle the rock are comically large, and would most likely only be comfortable for a giant, or perhaps, a family of Sasquatches. Which might be the reason some locals refer to this cool roadside oddity as "Bigfoot Rock." But does it have a story behind it? Not many people seem to really know. Some just think it's an eccentrically creative lawn ornament, and others just recognize it as a familiar way point as they pass by.

A brief e-mail with Gail from the Tinmouth town offices provided a little more information. This unique piece of craftsmanship was the work of local resident Marshall Squier. In fact, this is the second set of chairs, built after the originals rotted away. But Gail wasn't sure how the rock earned its fabled moniker, or the reason behind the chairs.

But perhaps "Bigfoot Rock" alludes to a peculiar happening in 1983, when a Vermont couple reported an extraordinary encounter while driving through nearby Tinmouth. As they came around a bend in the road, the husband noticed a giant human-like figure walking swiftly along a rocky ridge. He recalled how nimble this creature seemed to be, and his unusually swift pace as he clambered toward the ridgeline. When the creature stopped and turned to face them, the couple got a better look at whatever this was, and it wasn't human. Its arms were much longer than a normal man's and it was much larger and taller than any man they had ever seen. The sighting lasted for several minutes, as both startled parties waited for something to happen. Then the mysterious cryptid continued along the ridge and disappeared into the woods.

The man was so taken by what he saw that he wrote a letter to Castleton State College anthropologist Warren Cook. He first explained that he tried to rationalize what he saw, by suggesting that the strange creature was nothing more than a prankster in a suit, but the theory was ruled out after studying the creature's abnormal and swift movements, which were compared to those of a gymnast. With something that large and stalky, it just didn't seem to add up.

So did a couple passing through Tinmouth have an encounter with the infamous Bigfoot? After all, there have been plenty of other Bigfoot sightings reported in the woods of Vermont. Was it a hoax? Maybe a large animal was mistaken for something far more sinister. If this is the case, was this rock a witness?

Route 140 then climbs through maple woods and makes an abrupt left in the village of Tinmouth before climbing over more hills, doglegging through a valley farm, and climbing over another ridge to descend into the Otter Creek Valley. The vertical mountainside of White Rocks is straight ahead.

After crossing Route 7 in Wallingford, Route 140 climbs over the spine of the Green Mountains, through a narrow rocky defile that it shares with a rushing little brook. Before coming to the Long Trail, which crosses the brook on a wooden footbridge beside the road, you will come to the turn for ***White Rocks National Recreation Area*** (Sugar Hill Road, Wallingford; 802-747-6700). You can access these rocks on a strenuous hike of about 3 miles or you can admire them at a little more distance, from the picnic area below. If you do decide to make the hike, keep your eyes out for a disguised cave that is said to hold a fortune of silver, hidden here centuries ago by Spanish miners. Don't even think about digging for it, though; this is protected land and digging is strictly prohibited.

From the White Rocks, Route 140 twists its way through a deep gulf formed by the aptly named Roaring Brook before dipping into the village of Wallingford, where elegant Victorian houses climb down the hillside to the small downtown district. Here, at the only traffic light in town, sits another Wallingford curiosity.

It's made out of cast iron, colorfully painted, and depicts a young boy holding a boot that eternally drips water from a small hole into a circular

Ice Beds of White Mountain

Rising about 2,600 feet above the Valley of Vermont, White Rocks Mountain is an incredible sight. During the last ice age, glaciers scoured and exposed the quartzite cliffs that make up the framework of the mountain. Over time the slopes eroded to a point where the face of the mountain became weak, creating several massive rock slides that crumbled down the slopes to dales and glens below, sending gigantic quartzite boulders, some larger than an average house, down the mountain ripping up the evergreen forests as they made their visible scars. It is here amid this merciless landscape that an area known as the *Ice Beds* is found, where melting ice harbored deep within protected mountain caves feeds crystal-clear mountain streams that meander their way through the woodlands. The temperature drops a good 15 to 20 degrees here and is a welcome respite on hot summer days. Look for the Ice Beds Trail off Sugar Hill Road near the picnic area.—Reprinted with permission of Chad Abramovich, *Obscure Vermont* pool below—his faraway eyes forever depicting a state of reverie. This is Wallingford's *Boy with the Boot*.

At the base of the statue pool, there is a small plaque that reads: Erected to the memory of Arnold Young by his children, April 3, 1898. Arnold Young was the innkeeper of the Wallingford House hotel that sits directly behind the statue. It is said that Arnold's children thought that this statue would somehow be a fitting memorial and gift to their father. But it seems like a rather peculiar memorial that a well-respected innkeeper would choose. Would Mr. Young have chosen a different memorial, rather than a boy with a leaking boot? Or maybe there was some sort of comedy at work here—an inside joke perhaps, or something that the Wallingford of the late 19th century would have understood that has since been lost?

Around 1910 the Boy disappeared and was discovered 10 years later in the inn's attic. He was restored and has since stood in front of the hotel. The statue has become an icon of community pride, so much so that the Wallingford town website even features an animated Boy and the Boot.

But this isn't the only *Boy with the Boot* statue in the US. More peculiar perhaps is that there are 10 other statues across the country, all of them with mysterious origins and peculiar dedications. They appeared at one point or another around the late 19th century, but the creator of the statue and the idea behind it have all been lost to the annals of history.

Route 140 ends as abruptly as it began, in East Wallingford, where it meets Route 103 and Route 155, either of which connects to Route 100, the "Skiers' Highway."

Not far north of East Wallingford on Route 103 is Cuttingsville. In the village of Cuttingsville is **Vermont Industries** (Route 103; 802-492-3451; vermont industries.com), where they make hand-forged wrought-iron lighting fixtures and home accessories. The shop seems small when you first enter, but each room leads to another, taking you through a large building where you'll find candleholders, sconces, weathervanes, wall hangings, lamps, fireplace tools, garden furniture, hooks and racks, hinges, and decorative items. It's open daily 10 a.m. to 5:30 p.m. year-round.

If you choose to travel northwest on Route 103, make a detour in Shrewsbury, following signs up into the scenic hill towns to find one of the most comfortable, welcoming, and relaxing places in Vermont: **Maple Crest Farm Bed & Breakfast** (Lincoln Hill Road; 802-492-3367; smithmaplecrest farm.com). When it was built in 1808 by ancestors of the present owner, one side of the first floor was a coaching tavern and the other a general store and post office. Today these rooms are cozy places to curl up and read a book. Family antiques are used throughout the house, but you shouldn't get the idea that it's at all like a stuffy museum. Its comfy and casual atmosphere is popular with people hiking the nearby Long Trail. Rooms have shared or half baths. There are also 2 apartments, in which two couples on a getaway weekend could have separate bedrooms, a living room, and a full-size, well-equipped kitchen for very reasonable rates. Room rates include a full country breakfast (apartments are charged extra).

TO LEARN MORE IN MIDDLE WEST VERMONT

Addison County Chamber of Commerce
93 Court St.
Middlebury
(802) 388-7951 or (800) 733-8376
addisoncounty.com

Brandon Area Chamber of Commerce
PO Box 267
Brandon
(802) 247-6401
brandon.org

Killington Chamber of Commerce
2046 Rte. 4
Killington
(800) 337-1928
killingtonchamber.com

Okemo Valley Regional Chamber of Commerce
Okemo Marketplace
57 Pond St.
Ludlow
(802) 228-5830
yourplaceinvermont.com

Poultney Area Chamber of Commerce
The Stone Bridge, Route 30
Poultney
(802) 287-2010
poultneyvt.com

Rutland Region Chamber of Commerce
50 Merchants Row
Rutland
(800) 756-8880 or (802) 773-2747
rutlandvermont.com

Vermont Lakes Region Chamber of Commerce
PO Box 206
Fair Haven 05743
(802) 265-8600
vtlakesregionchamber.org

Places to Stay in Middle West Vermont

CHITTENDEN

Mountain Top Inn
195 Mountain Top Rd.
(802) 483-2311
mountaintopinn.com
Expensive
Located near Killington, this resort is situated on 350 acres of beauty. Also near the Green Mountain National Forest, there are endless opportunities for year-round fun. Pets are welcome as well.

MENDEN

The Vermont Inn
69 Rte. 4
(802) 775-0708
vermontinn.com
Inexpensive to moderate
A small inn located in a 19th-century home on 5 acres. Rooms are individually decorated and have private baths. Inn is near Killington Ski Resort.

MIDDLEBURY

Inn on the Green
71 S. Pleasant St.
(802) 388-7512 or (888) 244-7512
innonthegreen.com
Moderate to expensive
Elegant bed-and-breakfast inn located in the heart of Middlebury. This 19th-century home has been beautifully restored to offer 11 rooms and suites. Breakfast is included in the rates.

RIPTON

Chipman Inn
Route 125
(802) 388-2390 or (800) 890-2390
chipmaninn.com
Moderate to expensive
A bed-and-breakfast in a well-restored 1828 building with tastefully furnished guest rooms, some of which share a bathroom. Hearty breakfasts are included in the rates. Only 8 miles from Middlebury.

RUTLAND

The Paw House Inn
1376 Clarendon Ave.
(802) 558-2661
pawhouseinn.com
Moderate to expensive
A place that caters to pets and their owners. Fenced-in playground for the dogs, kennels, and welcome baskets that include treats for owners and their fur kids.

Places to Eat in Middle West Vermont

BRISTOL

Mary's at Baldwin Creek
1868 N. Rte. 116
(888) 424-2432 or (802) 453-2432
Moderate to expensive
Serves an innovative menu of dishes based on fresh local ingredients Wed through Sun from 5:30 p.m. Open Mon also in summer.

CASTLETON

Lake House Pub & Grille
3546 Rte. 30
(802) 273-3000
lakehousevt.com
Moderate to expensive
Located on the shores of Lake Bomoseen, this restaurant offers outdoor dining with terrific views. Open daily for lunch and dinner starting at 11 a.m. Live entertainment at their Tiki Bar on Sat nights in season.

FAIR HAVEN

Fair Haven Inn
5 Adams St.
(802) 265-4907
fairhaveninn.com
Moderate to expensive
Serves "finely prepared
Mediterranean food with
an American flair." Open
daily, year-round. Lunch is
served 11 a.m. to 2 p.m.,
dinner from 5 to 10 p.m.
Mon through Sat, from 11
a.m. to 9 p.m. Sun. Early-
bird specials are served
from 5 to 6 p.m. Mon
through Sat and 11 a.m.
to 4 p.m. Sun.

KILLINGTON

The Snow Angel Tavern
6105 Rte. 4
(802) 772-7163
thesnowangeltavern.com
Moderate to expensive
Chef-owned gastropub
where they serve a deli-
cious pork schnitzel with
fettuccine, baby spinach,
tomatoes, and lemon
caper butter. But that's
not all they do well;
everything on the menu
is carefully prepared and
wonderfully presented.
Open Tues through Sat
at 5 p.m. Closed Sun and
Mon.

Red Clover Inn & Restaurant
54 Red Clover Ln.
(802) 775-2290
redcloverinn.com
Moderate to expensive
A hidden gem that offers
amazing farm-to-table dining. Inspired by the sea-
sons, the menus change
often, but always offer the
freshest local ingredients.

Index